SCOTT, FORESMAN AND COMPANY

Problem Solving and Critical Thinking
Sourcebook

The Activities in this Sourcebook	Contents	Pages
One activity master, along with a Teacher Notes page, is provided for each lesson in the student text. There are four categories of thinking skills, each addressing a different area of mathematical reasoning. The four categories are Problem Solving, Critical Thinking, Visual Thinking, and Decision Making.	Professional Section with Correlation Chart of the activity masters to **Exploring Mathematics**, Grade 3	ii–viii
	Activity masters with Teacher Notes pages on reverse side	1–146

Correlation Chart

This correlation chart is an easy-to-use reference and index for the activity masters in this book. The objective numbers that are used for the activity masters are the same numbers that are used to identify the objectives in the Student Edition.

PROBLEM SOLVING

1 Write an Equation/ Number Sentence
2 Choose an Operation
3 Use a Formula
4 Make a Graph
5 Draw a Picture/ Draw a Diagram
6 Solve a Simpler Problem
7 Try and Check
8 Work Backward
9 Make a Table
10 Find a Pattern
11 Use Logical Reasoning

CRITICAL THINKING

1 Classifying and Sorting
2 Ordering and Sequencing
3 Using Logic
4 Drawing Conclusions
5 Using Number Sense
6 Finding/Extending/ Using Patterns
7 Making Generalizations
8 Reasoning with Graphs and Charts
9 Explaining Reasoning/ Justifying Answers
10 Developing Alternatives
11 Evaluating Evidence and Conclusions
12 Making and Testing Predictions

VISUAL THINKING

1 Spatial Perception
2 Visual Patterns

Indicates that these Activity Masters are available as overhead transparencies.

DECISION MAKING

1 Define the Problem
2 Identify the Options
3 Analyze the Options
4 Make Your Decision

Thinking Skills and Subskills

Activity/ Objective Number	Use with Pages	Problem Solving	Critical Thinking	Visual Thinking	Decision Making
1	4–5			1	
2	6–7		1		
3	8–9		3, 10, 12		
4	10–11			2	
5	12–15		1, 8		
6	18–19			1	
7	20–21		3, 6		
8	22–23				1–4
9	24–25	9, 10			
10	36–39			1	
11	40–41		1		
12	42–43			2	
13	44–45		2, 5		
14	46–47				1–4
15	48–49			1	
16	52–53	11			
17	54–57			1	
18	58–59		3, 11		
19	60–61			2	
20	62–63	11			
21	74–75	10, 11			
22	76–79			1	

Activity/ Objective Number	Use with Pages	Problem Solving	Critical Thinking	Visual Thinking	Decision Making
23	80–81		3		
24	82–83		4, 5		
25	84–85				1–4
26	88–89		3, 4		
27	90–91		1, 4		
28	92–93			2	
29	94–95	11			
30	110–113		1, 3		
31	114–117		5, 11		
32	118–119			1	
33	120–121		4, 5		
34	122–123			1	
35	124–125	11			
36	126–129				1–4
37	132–133		8		
38	134–135			2	
39	136–137		6		
40	138–139	11			
41	150–153	11			
42	154–155				1–4
43	156–157		10		
44	158–159			2	

Problem Solving and Critical Thinking Sourcebook

Purpose

Good problem solvers bring a wide variety of problem-solving strategies to bear upon a problem. After finding a solution or potential solution, they are able to look back and think critically about the solution. Successful problem solvers are resourceful and persistent in their search for a solution. The activities in this Sourcebook are designed to provide practice in problem solving and critical thinking. Students will be exposed to a wide range of problem-solving techniques. They will be given many opportunities to evaluate and criticize their solutions and decisions.

Many of these activities will help students recognize and understand the many mathematical and real-world problem-solving situations for which there may be more than one right answer. By focusing on the problem-solving process instead of "getting the right answer," the activities encourage alternate approaches to problem situations. As such, students will find these activities to be challenging, motivating, and interesting.

> Successful problem solvers are resourceful and persistent in their search for a solution.

How to Use This Sourcebook

You may assign pages of the Sourcebook to individual students, small groups, or the entire class. At your discretion, students may complete a page with little or no class discussion or teacher interaction. At other times you may want to teach the pages by leading a class discussion.

You may wish to introduce the activities to the class and then let students work individually or in small-group brainstorming units, which will yield a wider variety of possible approaches than students could possibly experience on their own. In some instances, you may want to use one or more activities as "Problem(s) of the Week" and give students several days to work on them individually before discussing them as a class.

Optional Overhead Transparencies are available for thirty of the Visual-Thinking activities. They can be used in a variety of ways:

- For presenting problems to the class
- For leading class discussions
- For considering possible solutions

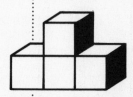

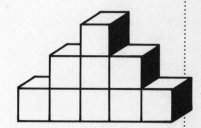

On the reverse side of each Activity Master is a Teacher-Notes page. A sample Teacher-Notes page is shown below, along with an explanation of its main features.

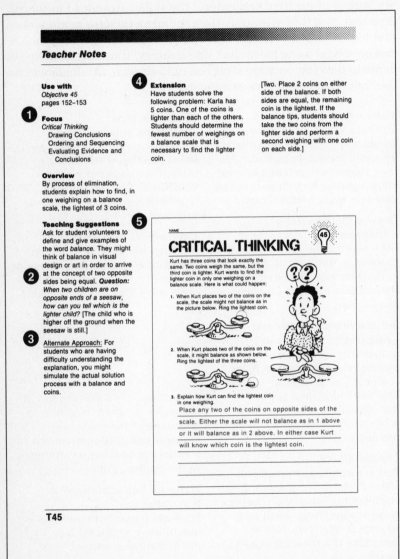

Teacher Notes

Use with
Objective 45
pages 152–153

 Focus
Critical Thinking
  Drawing Conclusions
  Ordering and Sequencing
  Evaluating Evidence and
  Conclusions

Overview
By process of elimination, students explain how to find, in one weighing on a balance scale, the lightest of 3 coins.

Teaching Suggestions
Ask for student volunteers to define and give examples of the word *balance*. They might think of balance in visual design or art in order to arrive at the concept of two opposite sides being equal. *Question: When two children are on opposite ends of a seesaw, how can you tell which is the lighter child?* [The child who is higher off the ground when the seesaw is still.]

 Alternate Approach: For students who are having difficulty understanding the explanation, you might simulate the actual solution process with a balance and coins.

 Extension
Have students solve the following problem: Karla has 5 coins. One of the coins is lighter than each of the others. Students should determine the fewest number of weighings on a balance scale that is necessary to find the lighter coin.

[Two. Place 2 coins on either side of the balance. If both sides are equal, the remaining coin is the lightest. If the balance tips, students should take the two coins from the lighter side and perform a second weighing with one coin on each side.]

NAME

CRITICAL THINKING (45)

Kurt has three coins that look exactly the same. Two coins weigh the same, but the third coin is lighter. Kurt wants to find the lighter coin in only one weighing on a balance scale. Here is what could happen:

1. When Kurt places two of the coins on the scale, the scale might not balance as in the picture below. Ring the lightest coin.

2. When Kurt places two of the coins on the scale, it might balance as shown below. Ring the lightest of the three coins.

3. Explain how Kurt can find the lightest coin in one weighing.
   Place any two of the coins on opposite sides of the scale. Either the scale will not balance as in 1 above or it will balance as in 2 above. In either case Kurt will know which coin is the lightest coin.

T45

A description of each of the four categories of thinking skills is provided on the following pages.

Focus
Identifies the category of thinking skills that the activity focuses on (Problem Solving, Critical Thinking, Visual Thinking, or Decision Making) as well as the subskills that are taught.

Question
Reveals and clarifies the substance of the activity, using leading or guiding questions. Students think through problems and are directed to a method of solution.

Alternate Approach
Offers suggestions and strategies for students to approach problems in a different way. These may be especially helpful for less-able students.

Extension
Provides opportunities for students to solve new problems that stem from the original problems.

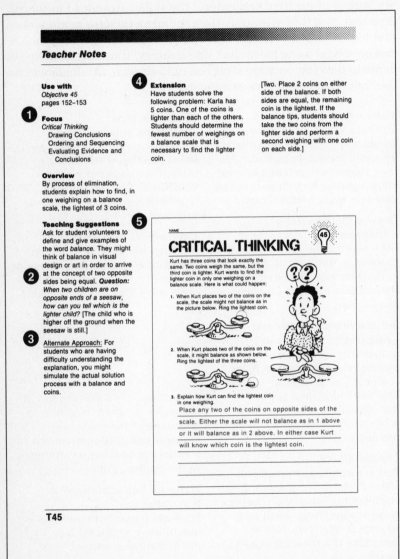

Pupil Page
The activity master is clearly reproduced, with the answers overprinted in red.

Problem Solving

These activities focus students' attention on solving nonroutine problems. The activities include real-world situations to stimulate interest, while highlighting nonroutine problem-solving strategies. Students will practice and extend the skills introduced in the student text, and they will apply the general method for mathematical problem solving that is developed in the text. Many of the problems can be solved using more than one strategy, thus encouraging students to develop creative methods of their own. Students will use the following nonroutine strategies:

Make a Graph
Making a graph, or in some way graphically depicting quantitative information, will help students read values between and beyond known points, as well as organize data into more useful forms.

Draw a Picture/Draw a Diagram
Representing the information in a problem in the form of a picture or diagram may help students see the conditions of the problem more clearly.

Solve a Simpler Problem
Using smaller numbers or temporarily ignoring some problem conditions often helps students find a solution method. This method is then applied to the original problem and may prove useful with more complex problems.

Try and Check
This is a systematic process of making reasonable guesses. It is often helpful when the number of possible solutions is small and when it is relatively easy to determine if a reasonable guess is correct.

Work Backward
Students examine, in counter-chronological order, the steps leading to a final result in order to discover initial conditions.

Make a Table
By making a table, students can organize large amounts of data and can often recognize hidden patterns that lead to general conjectures.

Find a Pattern
Identifying numerical and geometric patterns is often used in conjunction with making a table. Finding patterns allows students to find elegant solutions to otherwise difficult or tedious problems.

Use Logical Reasoning
Students use logic or deductive reasoning to determine reasonable processes and answers. This helps them solve a variety of problems.

In addition, the following routine strategies are used, largely at the beginning of the book, until students have been introduced to a variety of nonroutine strategies in the Student Edition.

Write an Equation/Number Sentence
Students translate real-world, quantitative situations into mathematical language.

Choose an Operation
Students decide which is the correct or best operation to use for a given problem. They may use this method with simple word problems as well as with multiple-step problems.

Use a Formula
Students use known formulas to solve mathematical problems. At upper grades, students may infer formulas to fit given data.

Critical Thinking

Critical Thinking activities challenge students to examine their own thinking about math and about related content areas. The problems and situations in these activities involve higher-order thinking skills such as analysis, synthesis, and evaluation. In becoming more aware, more critical, of their thinking, students become better problem solvers; they learn to examine and evaluate their own reasoning. Students will use the following strategies:

Classifying and Sorting
When classifying and sorting, students identify similarities and differences among objects and elements. Students also begin to group informational components according to specific characteristics.

Ordering and Sequencing
Students learn to recognize numerical and logical order and sequence.

Using Logic
Students identify logical fallacies, hidden assumptions, and illogical structures.

Drawing Conclusions
When drawing conclusions, students use deductive and inductive reasoning. They infer and draw logical, well-founded conclusions.

Using Number Sense
Students learn to judge relevance and completeness. They determine when there is too much or too little information, and they try to make well-founded estimates.

Finding/Extending/Using Patterns
While working on these problems, students interpolate and extrapolate number patterns and sequences. They may also infer mathematical properties.

Making Generalizations
Students build or propose a structure or they propose hypotheses. Students fit parts of a problem together to form a whole.

Reasoning with Graphs and Charts
Students learn to interpret numerical and graphical data. They interpolate and extrapolate needed information from graphs and charts.

Explaining Reasoning/Justifying Answers
Students begin to explain their reasoning process and to justify and defend their answers.

Developing Alternatives
Students begin to think more flexibly when they develop alternate ways to approach and solve problems. This in turn may promote divergent and creative thinking.

Evaluating Evidence and Conclusions
Students test generalizations and logical validity. They also determine probabilities and evaluate evidence and conclusions by referring to internal or external standards.

Making and Testing Predictions
Students make predictions based on incomplete or probabilistic information. They perform experiments or use deductive reasoning to test their predictions.

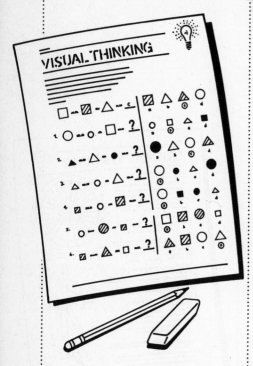

Visual Thinking

These activities exercise students' ability to perceive and mentally manipulate visual images. They also allow some students, who may not be proficient in other areas of mathematics, to excel. Additionally, students' capacity to visualize can be extremely useful to them in solving a variety of problems and in learning to think critically. Thirty of these activities are available as overhead transparencies (optional) that can be used to facilitate class discussion of the thought processes that lead to solutions. Students will use these strategies:

Spatial Perception

These activities encourage students to recognize hidden symbols or pictures and to recognize congruent or similar figures that have been slid, flipped, or turned. Students manipulate forms mentally and create mental images.

Visual Patterns

Students learn how to infer or extend visual patterns and sequences. They are also challenged by visual analogies.

Decision Making

These activities present real-world situations that require students to make a decision. In most cases, there are no clearly right or clearly wrong answers. This gives students the opportunity to carefully weigh alternate courses of action—as well as to consider their personal experiences and preferences. The following four steps of decision making will help students make and evaluate their own decisions:

(1) Define the Problem

Students should consider why a decision is needed, what goal they wish to meet, and what tools and techniques they can use to reach their decision.

(2) Identify the Options

Students identify information that will be relevant to the decision-making process. Such information might include cost, time, rules, preferences, or practicality. Based on this information, students then develop alternative courses of action.

(3) Analyze the Options

At this stage, students consider the advantages and disadvantages of each option, considering both the positive and the negative consequences.

(4) Make a Decision

Students decide which choice is best. Students may be called on to justify their decisions with specific references to advantages and disadvantages. Because different students will weigh each advantage and disadvantage differently, this concluding step can lead to useful, worthwhile class discussion.

NAME _____

VISUAL THINKING

Ring the letter of the figure in each row that
is different.

a.　　　　　　b.　　　　　　c.　　　　　　d.

a.　　　　　　b.　　　　　　c.　　　　　　d.

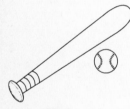 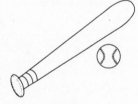 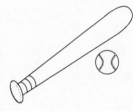 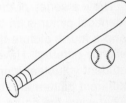

a.　　　　　　b.　　　　　　c.　　　　　　d.

a.　　　　　　b.　　　　　　c.　　　　　　d.

a.　　　　　　b.　　　　　　c.　　　　　　d.

Problem Solving and Critical Thinking/**EXPLORING MATHEMATICS** © Scott, Foresman and Company/3 　　　　Use after pages 4–5.

Teacher Notes

Use with
Objective 1
pages 4–5

Focus
Visual Thinking
Spatial Perception

Overview
Students compare figures to determine which one is different from the others.

Teaching Suggestions
Tell students that it is important to be a careful observer. Point out that although at first glance some objects look alike, there are often slight differences that can be identified when the objects are studied more closely.

Draw a series of three identical pictures on the board and a fourth picture that is slightly different. Have a student volunteer identify the different picture and tell in what ways the figure is not like the others. Repeat this activity, having a student draw the pictures. Have students offer suggestions for other ways of making the fourth figure different. That is, lead them to see that any of several tiny details can be changed to make a fourth figure differ from the other three.

Extension
Have students design a visual thinking activity using likes and differences. Encourage them to make their activities as difficult as possible. Then have students exchange their papers with a partner and solve each other's activities.

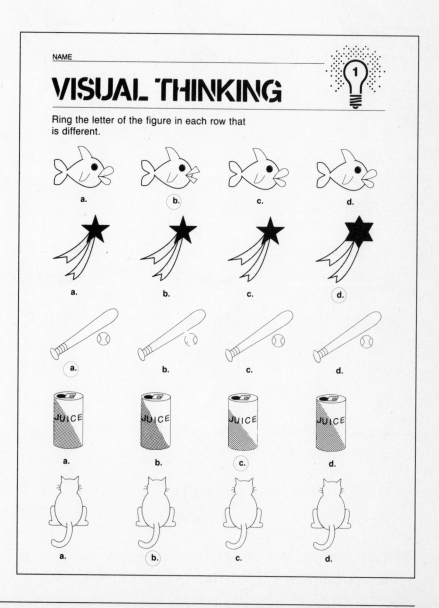

CRITICAL THINKING

Look at the picture of the animals. Finish filling in the table.

Animal	Legs	Wings	Tails
Kangaroo	2	0	1
Cow	4		
Horse			
Snake			
Chicken			
Bird			

1. Look at the table. Are there more wings or more tails? _____

2. Which of the animals have legs, wings, and tails? _____

3. Make a picture of your own animal. It should have 6 legs, 3 eyes, and 2 tails.

Use after pages 6–7.

Use with

Objective 2
pages 6–7

Focus

Critical Thinking
   Classifying and Sorting

Overview

Students use a table to *classify and sort* information gathered from pictures of animals.

Teaching Suggestions

Remind students that a table is a good way to *classify and sort* information. Have students brainstorm types of information or objects that might be sorted and classified. Elicit ideas such as food, toys, furniture, pets, cars, houses, and so on. Explain that these, and many other categories of information, can be broken down into and sorted by their component parts or attributes. Make the following table on the chalkboard:

Plant	Leaf	Needle	Flower
Maple	X		
Evergreen		X	
Cactus		X	X
Rose	X		X
Ivy	X		

Then ask student volunteers to fill in the chart by placing an X in the appropriate boxes.

Questions: *Are there more plants with leaves or with needles?* [Leaves] *How many plants have flowers?* [2] *Which plant has both leaves and flowers?* [Rose] *Which plant has only needles?* [Evergreen tree]

Have students add names of plants to the table and then complete the chart. Alternately, have them add other categories (fruit, seeds, thorns, and so on) and rework the table.

Extension

Tell students to make a list showing favorite foods of classmates. Instruct them to list the names of five classmates in the column on the left and the names of three or four favorite foods across the top. Then have them find out which of the foods each student likes best and fill in a table.

NAME _____

CRITICAL THINKING

Look at the picture of the animals. Finish filling in the table.

Animal	Legs	Wings	Tails
Kangaroo	2	0	1
Cow	4	0	1
Horse	4	0	1
Snake	0	0	1
Chicken	2	2	1
Bird	2	2	1

1. Look at the table. Are there more wings or more tails?

   More tails

2. Which of the animals have legs, wings, and tails?

   Chicken, bird

3. Make a picture of your own animal. It should have 6 legs, 3 eyes, and 2 tails.

CRITICAL THINKING

1. Find your way through the mazes without
breaking this rule: If the square you are
on is not white, then the square you enter
must be striped.

EXIT

EXIT

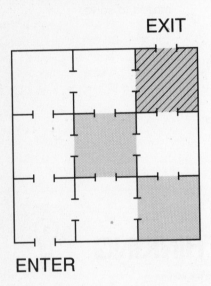

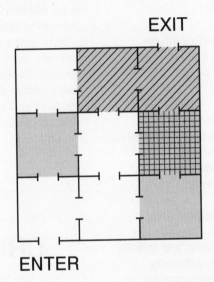

ENTER

ENTER

2. Find your way through the mazes without
breaking this rule: If the square you are
on is not white, then the square you enter
must not be striped.

EXIT

EXIT

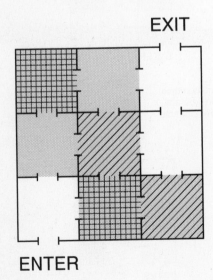

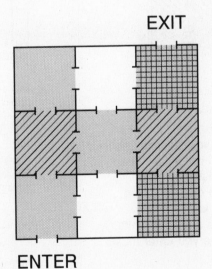

ENTER

ENTER

Use with
Objective 3
pages 8–9

Focus
Critical Thinking
   Using Logic
   Developing Alternatives
   Making and Testing
     Predictions

Overview
Students utilize *Critical Thinking* and reasoning skills to determine a workable path through a maze based on given stipulations.

Teaching Suggestions
Ask students to define *maze*. Find out if students are familiar with mazes. Give them an opportunity to describe any experiences they have had working mazes. Draw the following maze on the chalkboard.

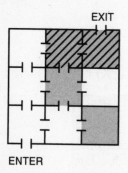

Ask a student volunteer to find a path through the maze. Then tell students that they must follow a rule to determine the path. The rule is this: If the square you are on is not white, then the square you enter must be striped.

Have another volunteer find a different path using the rule. Discuss the trial-and-error nature of the problem. Point out that certain squares need to be eliminated in order to determine the route.

Note that there is another possible path for the second maze in Problem 1. From the white center square, students can also go right into the checked square and then up to the exit.

Extension
Have students design similar mazes for classmates to solve. Encourage students to also bring to class other types of mazes to solve.

NAME

CRITICAL THINKING

1. Find your way through the mazes without breaking this rule: If the square you are on is not white, then the square you enter must be striped.

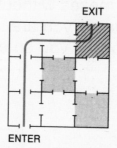

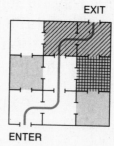

2. Find your way through the mazes without breaking this rule: If the square you are on is not white, then the square you enter must not be striped.

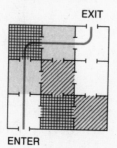

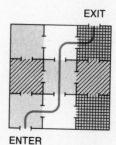

VISUAL THINKING

Find the pattern in each row. Draw the next figure in each row.

1.    _____

2. 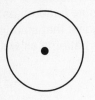   _____

3.   _____

4.    _____

5.   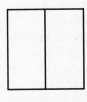 _____

6.    _____

7.   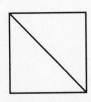 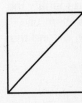 _____

Teacher Notes

Use with
Objective 4
pages 10–11

Focus
Visual Thinking
  Visual Patterns

Materials
Poster paper for the
  bulletin board
Wallpaper
Visual Thinking transparency
  (optional)

Overview
Students recognize the relationship among objects in a pattern and use this relationship to complete the pattern.

Teaching Suggestions
Remind students that there are patterns all around us. Show a piece of wallpaper with a repeating pattern and point out the repetition. Ask a student volunteer to identify a pattern visible in the classroom. [Possible answer: The formation of the desks; a pattern on the fabric of someone's clothes; the pattern of the floor covering] Choose four students to come forward and have them stand in a pattern. The pattern might be brown hair, blond hair, brown hair, blond hair; or boy, girl, boy, girl. *Question: What pattern do you see in this arrangement?* [Help students discover the pattern you established.] Have students study the order and identify the pattern. Then have them use other classmates to extend the pattern.

Repeat this activity, using more complex patterns, such as tennis shoes, buttons, freckles, eye color, or clothing.

Alternate Approach: If students are having difficulty, use the transparency and work through several of the problems as a class.

Extension
On a bulletin board, post a large sheet of paper with the heading "Patterns All Around Us." Encourage students to observe *visual patterns* at home, in nature, at school, or elsewhere, and write examples of such patterns under the heading. Urge students to list as many unusual patterns as possible. Suggest that students illustrate their patterns as well.

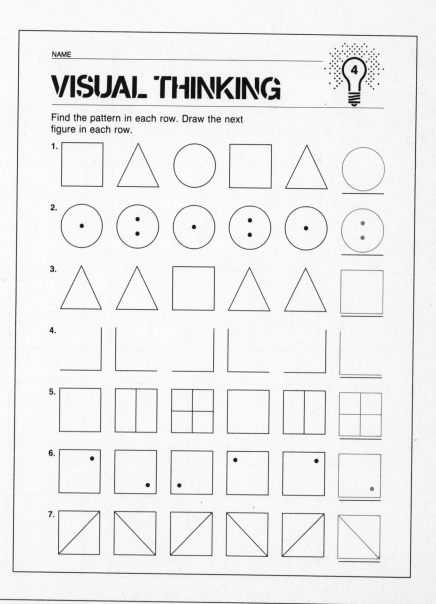

NAME _____

VISUAL THINKING

Find the pattern in each row. Draw the next figure in each row.

CRITICAL THINKING

Drawings can be used to show family relationships. The diagram below helps to organize relationships by using symbols.

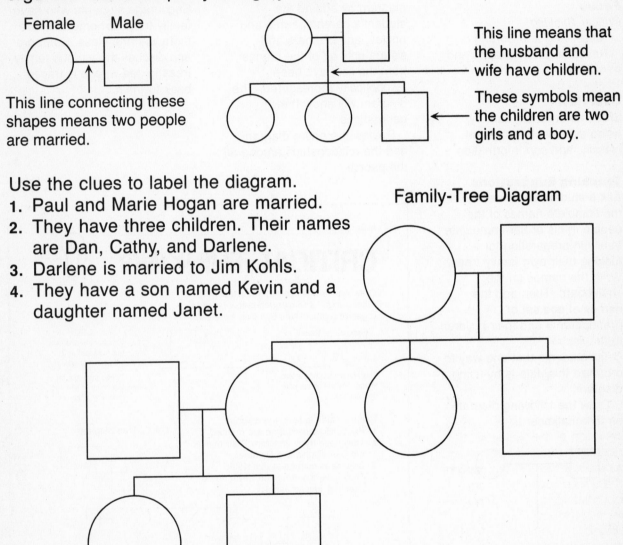

Female Male

This line connecting these shapes means two people are married.

This line means that the husband and wife have children.

These symbols mean the children are two girls and a boy.

Use the clues to label the diagram.

1. Paul and Marie Hogan are married.
2. They have three children. Their names are Dan, Cathy, and Darlene.
3. Darlene is married to Jim Kohls.
4. They have a son named Kevin and a daughter named Janet.

Family-Tree Diagram

1. What is the name of Kevin and Janet's grandmother?

_____

2. What is Cathy's last name?

_____

3. What is the name of Kevin and Janet's uncle?

_____

Use with
Objective 5
pages 12–15

Focus
Critical Thinking
Classifying and Sorting
Reasoning with Graphs and
Charts

Overview
Students organize data by
using symbols to represent,
classify, and *sort* information.

Teaching Suggestions
Ask a student volunteer to list
the complete names of the
people in his or her immediate
family in preparation for
making their own family trees.
Write the names on the
chalkboard. Then add the
names of one set of
grandparents and their children
to the list.

Tell students that one way to
organize this data is by using a
diagram.

Draw the following diagram
on the chalkboard:

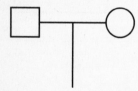

Explain that the square is a
symbol for male and the circle
is a symbol for female. Point
out that the horizontal line
connecting the two figures
indicates that these two people
are married, and the vertical
line means the husband and
wife have children.

Write the grandparents'
names inside the square and
circle that you have drawn on
the chalkboard. Continue the
diagram by adding the
student's parents, aunts and
uncles, and brothers and
sisters until all of the names
from the list have been
symbolically represented. The
diagram will show three
generations.

Review the entire diagram
and the relationships among all
the people.

Extension
Have each student draw a
family-tree diagram like the
one on the chalkboard.
Encourage students who have
family trees at home to share
them with the class. Compare
and discuss the various family
trees to see whose is traced
back furthest.

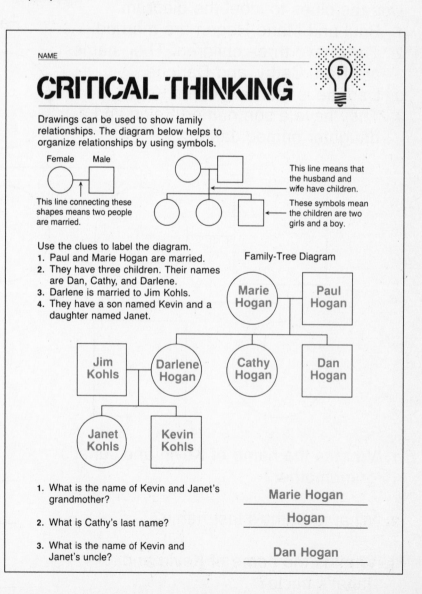

NAME

CRITICAL THINKING

5

Drawings can be used to show family
relationships. The diagram below helps to
organize relationships by using symbols.

Female   Male

This line connecting these
shapes means two people
are married.

This line means that
the husband and
wife have children.

These symbols mean
the children are two
girls and a boy.

Use the clues to label the diagram.
1. Paul and Marie Hogan are married.
2. They have three children. Their names
   are Dan, Cathy, and Darlene.
3. Darlene is married to Jim Kohls.
4. They have a son named Kevin and a
   daughter named Janet.

Family-Tree Diagram

Marie Hogan — Paul Hogan

Jim Kohls — Darlene Hogan   Cathy Hogan   Dan Hogan

Janet Kohls   Kevin Kohls

1. What is the name of Kevin and Janet's
   grandmother?   Marie Hogan

2. What is Cathy's last name?   Hogan

3. What is the name of Kevin and
   Janet's uncle?   Dan Hogan

NAME _____

VISUAL THINKING

This figure contains 5 triangles.

Figure

4 small triangles

1 large triangle that contains
the 4 small triangles

Study the figure below.

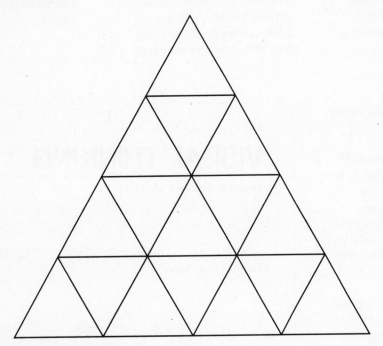

1. How many small triangles are there? _____

2. How many triangles containing 4 small
   triangles are there? The triangles
   can overlap. _____

3. How many triangles containing 9 small
   triangles are there? _____

4. How many triangles containing 16 small
   triangles are there? _____

5. How many triangles are in the design
   in all? _____

Use with

Objective 6
pages 18–19

Focus

Visual Thinking
   Spatial Perception

Materials

Paper squares that are
   divided into sixteen small
   squares; 4 × 4, as a grid
Visual Thinking transparency
   (optional)

Overview

Students visualize the
relationship among component
parts of a figure.

Teaching Suggestions

Pass out the paper squares to
each student and instruct
students to see how many
squares they can find inside
the large one. Tell students that
the squares can overlap and/or
be contained inside one
another.

   *Questions: How many small
squares are there?* [16] *How
many squares containing
4 small squares are there?* [9]
*How many squares containing
9 small squares do you see?*
[4] *How many squares
containing 16 small squares are
there?* [1] *How many squares
are in the design in all?* [30]

   Have students show on their
squares how they arrive at
each answer. Be sure that they
understand that they must add
the numbers of each size of
squares to discover how many
squares there are in all.

Alternate Approach: Students
should have no trouble
counting the small triangles
and the one large triangle. If
they have difficulty counting
the triangles containing 4 small
triangles or the triangles
containing 9 small triangles,
encourage them to use
different colors to outline these
triangles. If students continue
to have trouble, use the
transparency to show them
how to outline the triangles.

Extension

Give students another paper
square that is divided into
sixteen small squares and tell
them that they will make a
puzzle. Instruct students to
draw a picture on the large
square and then cut out the
individual small squares. Have
them exchange puzzles with a
partner and solve each other's
puzzle.

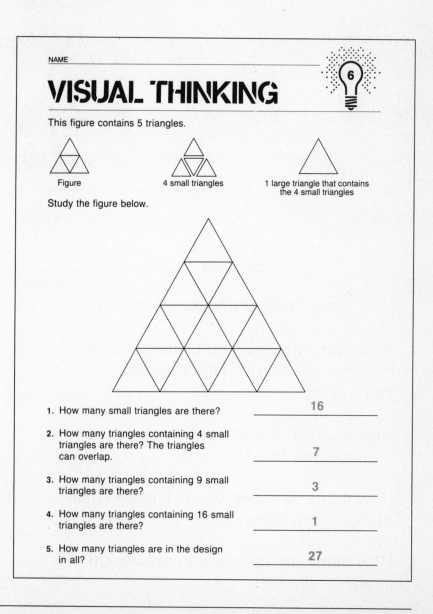

NAME

VISUAL THINKING

This figure contains 5 triangles.

Figure   4 small triangles   1 large triangle that contains
                                the 4 small triangles

Study the figure below.

1. How many small triangles are there? _____ 16

2. How many triangles containing 4 small
   triangles are there? The triangles
   can overlap. _____ 7

3. How many triangles containing 9 small
   triangles are there? _____ 3

4. How many triangles containing 16 small
   triangles are there? _____ 1

5. How many triangles are in the design
   in all? _____ 27

NAME _____

CRITICAL THINKING

Tom has a set of double-three dominoes that looks like this:

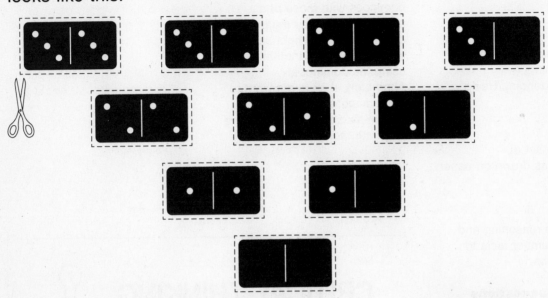

Tom said, "I arranged my dominoes in the following pattern. The number on each domino stands for the total number of spots on the domino. This number matches the addition fact for each. Look at the example."

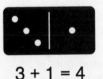

3 + 1 = 4

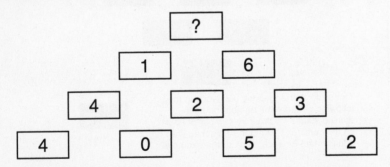

1. Cut out the set of double-three dominoes. Write the addition fact for each.

_____

_____

2. By matching your dominoes with Tom's pattern, find which domino is on the top.

_____

Use with

Objective 7
pages 20–21

Focus

Critical Thinking
Using Logic
Finding/Extending/Using
Patterns

Materials

Double-three set of
dominoes as drawn on paper
Scissors

Overview

Students use reasoning and
mastery of number facts to
solve problems.

Teaching Suggestions

Define what a set of
double-three dominoes is for
your students. [A set of
dominoes whose greatest
number of combined dots is
6 (double three) rather than 12
(double six)] Have students cut
out the set of double-three
dominoes and ask them to find
the "3-1" domino. **Question:**
*What is the addition fact for this
domino?* [3 + 1 = 4] Have
students look at the rest of the
dominoes. **Question: Which
domino can you match with the
domino in Tom's arrangement
that has a 5 on it?** [The 3-2
domino, since the addition fact
for that domino is 3 + 2 = 5]

Continue to have students
match the rest of the dominoes
with Tom's arrangement to find
which domino is on top.

Students should *use logical
reasoning* to see that there are
two possible dominoes that can
be matched with the unknown
dominoes.

Extension

Tell students to combine their
dominoes with those of a
partner and to play a game of
dominoes. They might also
wish to make up another game
using the dominoes.
Alternately, they might want to
make a more extensive
double-six set of dominoes and
play with those.

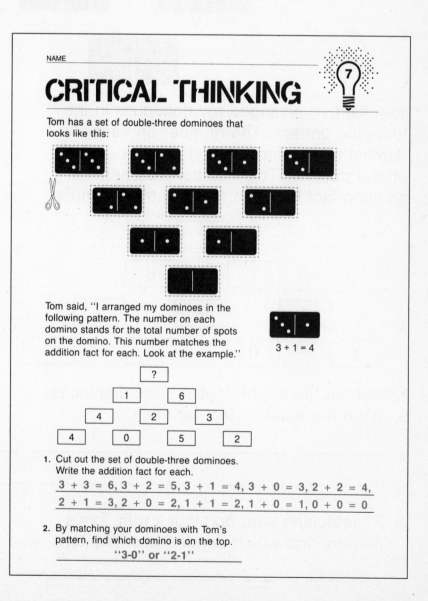

NAME _____

CRITICAL THINKING

Tom has a set of double-three dominoes that
looks like this:

Tom said, "I arranged my dominoes in the
following pattern. The number on each
domino stands for the total number of spots
on the domino. This number matches the
addition fact for each. Look at the example."

3 + 1 = 4

```
          [ ? ]
      [ 1 ]   [ 6 ]
   [ 4 ]   [ 2 ]   [ 3 ]
[ 4 ]   [ 0 ]   [ 5 ]   [ 2 ]
```

1. Cut out the set of double-three dominoes.
   Write the addition fact for each.

   3 + 3 = 6, 3 + 2 = 5, 3 + 1 = 4, 3 + 0 = 3, 2 + 2 = 4,
   2 + 1 = 3, 2 + 0 = 2, 1 + 1 = 2, 1 + 0 = 1, 0 + 0 = 0

2. By matching your dominoes with Tom's
   pattern, find which domino is on the top.

   "3-0" or "2-1"

DECISION MAKING

Rachel and Robin are planning a party. Help them decide in which order to do the following activities.

- Hang streamers
- Write invitations
- Hang balloons
- Choose party games
- Prepare food

1. In which order should they do the activities? Explain your answer.

_____

_____

_____

_____

Robin likes to help her mother cook. Rachel likes to write and decorate.

2. Which jobs should Robin do?

_____

_____

3. Which jobs should Rachel do?

_____

_____

Use with
Objective 8
pages 22–23

Focus
Decision Making

Overview
Students analyze data and organize information about, planning a party to make decisions among alternate courses of action and to accomplish a task in a logical manner.

Teaching Suggestions
Tell students that success is often a result of thorough planning and that to accomplish a task it is frequently important to do things in a certain order. Make a list on the chalkboard of activities that can be accomplished by following a certain sequence of steps. Answers might include: cooking a meal; building a model; getting ready for school; or planning a party.

Then have students select one of these activities and list the steps, on a separate sheet of paper, that might be involved in completing the activity.

Extension
Have students design a toy that needs to be assembled. Instruct them to draw a picture of the toy and to write the directions for assembling it. Emphasize that the directions must be clear and concise and written in a logical order. Combine the papers to make a book entitled "Our Toy Catalog."

NAME

DECISION MAKING

Rachel and Robin are planning a party. Help them decide in which order to do the following activities.

- Hang streamers
- Write invitations
- Hang balloons
- Choose party games
- Prepare food

1. In which order should they do the activities? Explain your answer.

Possible answer: Write invitations to give guests notice. Buy prizes after choosing games so they match. Hang streamers and balloons so house is not decorated too long. Prepare food last so it is hot.

Robin likes to help her mother cook. Rachel likes to write and decorate.

2. Which jobs should Robin do?

Possible answer: Prepare food, buy prizes, choose party games.

3. Which jobs should Rachel do?

Possible answer: Write invitations and hang balloons and streamers.

NAME _____

PROBLEM SOLVING

The 10 students in Ms. Paul's class each drew a picture of a vehicle in which they would like to ride to school. They would like to know the fewest number of thumbtacks they need to attach the pictures in a line around the room.

Each corner must have a tack in it. The corners may overlap.

1. How many thumbtacks are needed to attach two pictures separately?

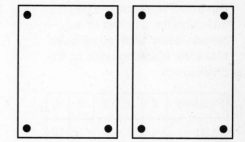

_____

2. How many tacks are needed to attach 2 pictures if the corners overlap?

_____

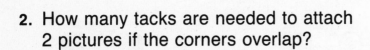

3. How many tacks are needed to attach 3 pictures if the corners overlap? 4 pictures?

_____

4. What is the fewest number of tacks needed to attach the 10 pictures in a line?

_____

Teacher Notes

Use with

Objective 9
pages 24–25

Focus

Problem Solving
  Make a Table
  Find a Pattern

Materials

Five 8″ × 10″ pictures, as
  described in the activity
Box of thumbtacks

Overview

Students solve problems by
making a table to *find a
pattern.*

Teaching Suggestions

Have students complete
Problems 1–3. Explain that
making a table is a good way
to organize information.
Illustrate Problems 1–3 by
attaching the pictures to a
bulletin board with thumbtacks.
Make the following table on the
chalkboard.

Pictures	1	2	3	4	5
Tacks	4	6	8	10	12

*Question: Can anyone find a
pattern?* [Yes, the bottom
number is 2 more than twice
the top number.] Point out that
students can use the pattern to
solve Problem 4 without
drawing a diagram of
10 pictures in a line.

Extension

Ask students how many tacks
would be needed if the
10 drawings were very large
and needed to be attached as
follows:

Encourage students to *make
a table* to solve the problem.
Discuss the pattern that occurs
in this problem. [The number
of tacks is 3 more than 3 times
the number of pictures.]

Pictures	1	2	3
Thumbtacks	6	9	12

NAME _____

PROBLEM SOLVING

The 10 students in Ms. Paul's class each
drew a picture of a vehicle in which they
would like to ride to school. They would like
to know the fewest number of thumbtacks
they need to attach the pictures in a line
around the room.

Each corner must have a tack in it. The
corners may overlap.

1. How many thumbtacks are needed to
attach two pictures separately?

         8 tacks

2. How many tacks are needed to attach
2 pictures if the corners overlap?

         6 tacks

3. How many tacks are needed to attach
3 pictures if the corners overlap?
4 pictures?

    8 tacks; 10 tacks

4. What is the fewest number of tacks
needed to attach the 10 pictures in
a line?

       22 tacks

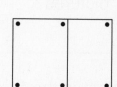

VISUAL THINKING

Each figure on the left was made by folding
a square sheet of paper in half

and then in half again.

Then a shape was cut out of each piece of
folded paper. Write the letter of the piece of
unfolded paper on the right that could be
made from the folded and cut paper on
the left.

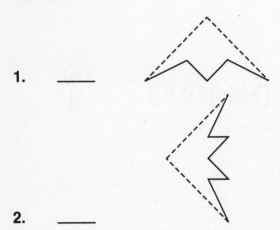

1. _____

2. _____

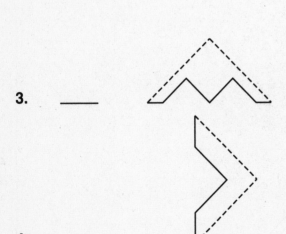

3. _____

4. _____

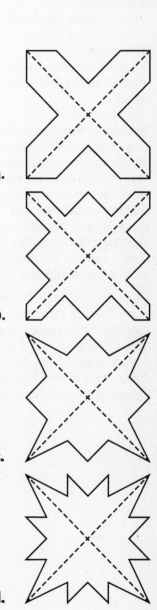

a.

b.

c.

d.

Use with
Objective 10
pages 36–39

Focus
Visual Thinking
  Spatial Perception

Materials
Construction paper
  and scissors (optional)

Overview
Students visualize the end
result of folding paper several
times.

Teaching Suggestions
This activity may be done in a
group, as some students may
have difficulty visualizing the
paper folds. Make sure
students understand the
example, and that dotted lines
illustrate folds. You may want
to demonstrate the example
using a piece of paper.

Alternate Approach: If the
students have difficulty,
suggest that they look at each
folded shape as 1/4 of the
original shape. They then can
match the folded shape to its
outline in the original shape.

Extension
Students may recognize the
shapes on this page as
"snowflake designs." Have
them make their own
snowflakes using paper folded
in fourths or eighths. Display
their designs in mobiles or on
the bulletin board.

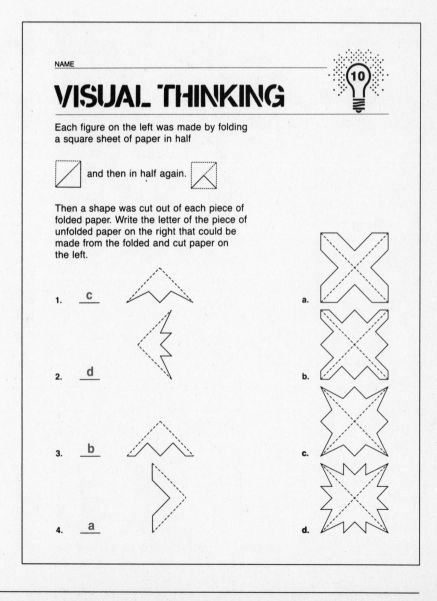

NAME _____

VISUAL THINKING

Each figure on the left was made by folding
a square sheet of paper in half

and then in half again.

Then a shape was cut out of each piece of
folded paper. Write the letter of the piece of
unfolded paper on the right that could be
made from the folded and cut paper on
the left.

1. __c__   a.

2. __d__   b.

3. __b__   c.

4. __a__   d.

CRITICAL THINKING

Sort this collection by writing the number for each figure in the correct box. Each of the figures can be classified more than one way. You will need to use each number more than once.

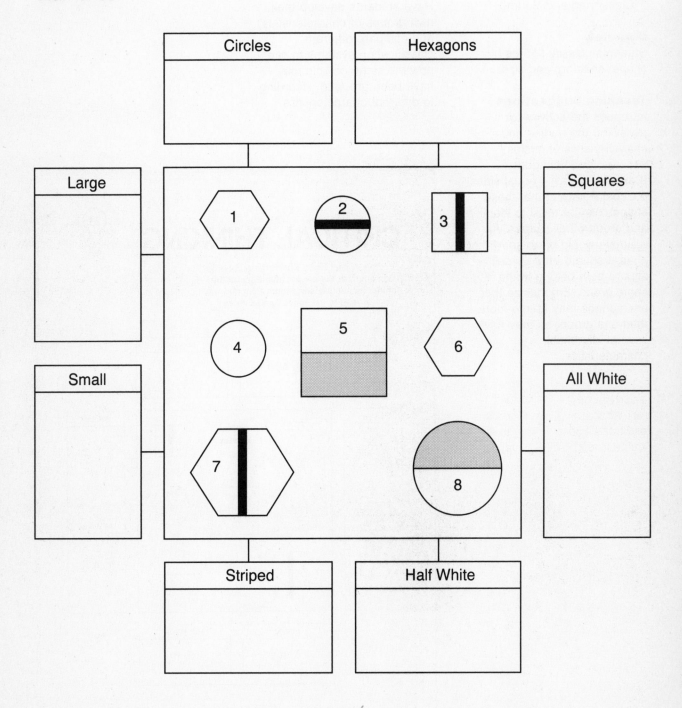

Teacher Notes

Use with
Objective 11
pages 40–41

Focus
Critical Thinking
  Classifying and Sorting

Overview
Students *classify* figures by shape, shading, and size.

Teaching Suggestions
Introduce the activity by reviewing the names and characteristics of circles, squares, and hexagons. [Perfectly round, 4 equal sides, 6 sides] Point out that these shapes can be used to identify and group other shapes. An example would be to show that a large square and a small square both belong in the same group. Emphasize that each shape may fit into more than one group, as they have several identifiable characteristics.

Extension
Have students work in small groups to classify other objects in the classroom, such as blocks, erasers, pencils, crayons, markers, and so on. Have students develop their own groups of characteristics, and compare different classification systems to see how the same objects may have been grouped according to different characteristics.

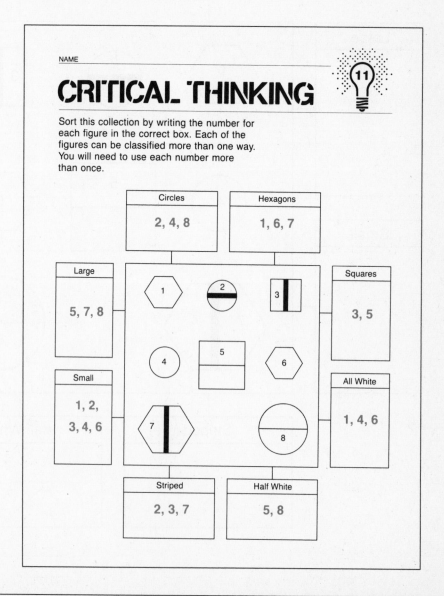

NAME _____

CRITICAL THINKING (11)

Sort this collection by writing the number for each figure in the correct box. Each of the figures can be classified more than one way. You will need to use each number more than once.

Circles	Hexagons
2, 4, 8	1, 6, 7

Large
5, 7, 8

Squares
3, 5

Small
1, 2, 3, 4, 6

All White
1, 4, 6

Striped	Half White
2, 3, 7	5, 8

VISUAL THINKING

Find the pattern in each row of figures. Then draw the fourth figure in each row.

1. 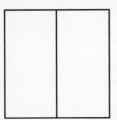 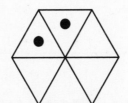 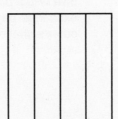 |

2. 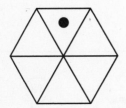 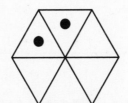 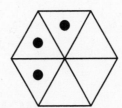 |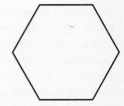

3. 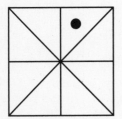 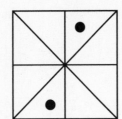 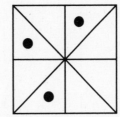 |

4. 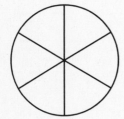  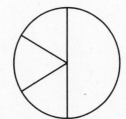 |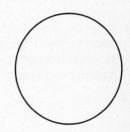

5. 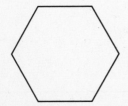 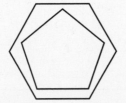 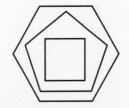 |

Use with
Objective 12
pages 42–43

Focus
Visual Thinking
   Visual Patterns

Overview
Students recognize the relationship in a *visual pattern* and use this same relationship to complete the pattern.

Teaching Suggestions
Make sure students recognize that a pattern can be a repeating characteristic in a sequence. For example, the counting numbers from 1–10 can be formed by adding 1 to each preceding number (1 + 1 = 2, 2 + 1 = 3, 3 + 1 = 4, and so on). If students have difficulty, you may do Problem 1 as an example. *Questions: What is the difference between the first square and the second square?* [One vertical line is added.] *Between the second square and the third square?* [Another vertical line is added.] *What would be the result of continuing this pattern to the fourth square?* [A square with 4 vertical lines inside] If necessary you can guide students through the other patterns in a similar way.

Extension
Have students design their own *visual patterns* and exchange papers to try each other's challenges.

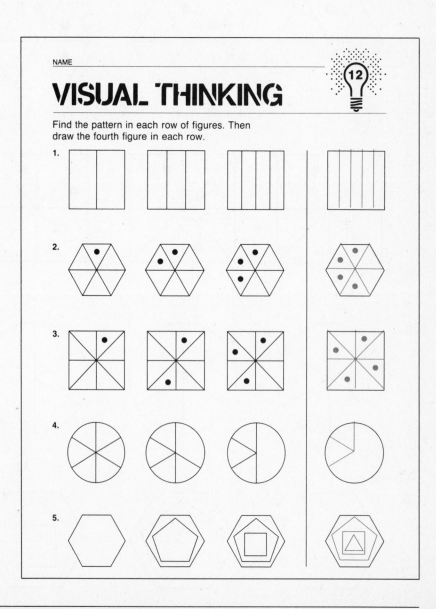

NAME

VISUAL THINKING

Find the pattern in each row of figures. Then draw the fourth figure in each row.

1.

2.

3.

4.

5.

CRITICAL THINKING

Ted's class arranged 3-digit numbers in the pattern below for a game at the school carnival. To win a prize, Ted must draw a line from Entrance A to Exit A so that each 3-digit number the line crosses is greater than the last. Then he must draw a line from Entrance B to Exit B so that each 3-digit number the line crosses is less than the last. He may go in any direction. Help Ted win a prize.

Entrance B   Exit A

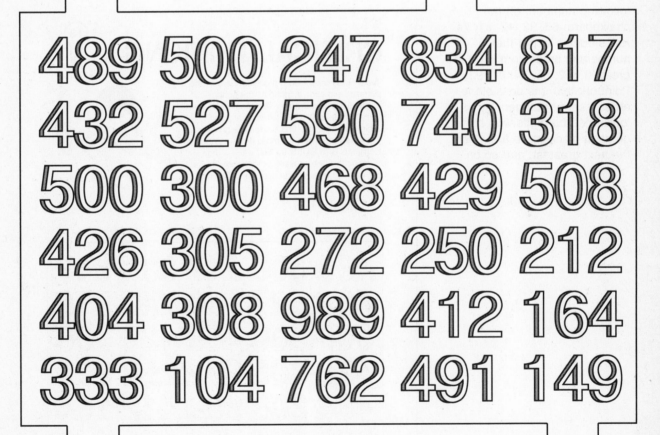

489	500	247	834	817
432	527	590	740	318
500	300	468	429	508
426	305	272	250	212
404	308	989	412	164
333	104	762	491	149

Entrance A   Exit B

Teacher Notes

Use with
Objective 13
pages 44–45

Focus
Critical Thinking
Ordering and Sequencing
Using Number Sense

Overview
Students determine a path
through an array of numbers
by determining which numbers
are greater or lesser.

Teaching Suggestions
Review greater and lesser
numbers by writing the
following numbers on the
chalkboard: 56, 92, 12, 81, 74.
Ask students to put the
numbers in order from least to
greatest. [12, 56, 74, 81, 92]
Point out that it is possible to
order a set of numbers by
looking at the digits with the
greatest place value first, then
the next greatest, and so on.

Extension
Have students create their own
similar patterns using 4- or
5-digit numbers. They can
exchange patterns and try to
get through each other's
arrays.

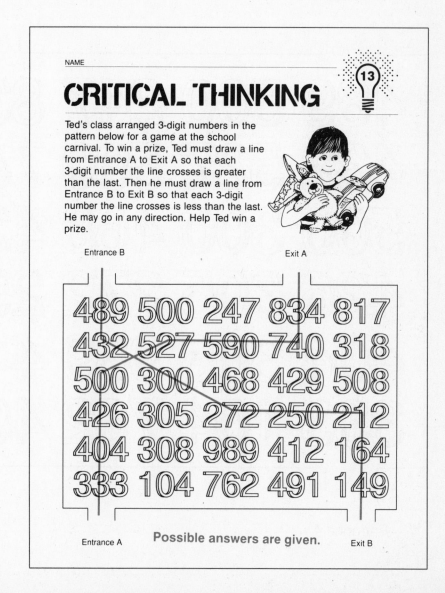

NAME

CRITICAL THINKING

13

Ted's class arranged 3-digit numbers in the
pattern below for a game at the school
carnival. To win a prize, Ted must draw a line
from Entrance A to Exit A so that each
3-digit number the line crosses is greater
than the last. Then he must draw a line from
Entrance B to Exit B so that each 3-digit
number the line crosses is less than the last.
He may go in any direction. Help Ted win a
prize.

Entrance B   Exit A

489 500 247 834 817
432 527 590 740 318
500 300 468 429 508
426 305 272 250 212
404 308 989 412 164
333 104 762 491 149

Entrance A   **Possible answers are given.**   Exit B

DECISION MAKING

14

Jonathan has a bicycle. It is 4 years old and needs a few repairs. He took it to a repairman, and he gave Jonathan a repair list.

> **Repair List**
> New brakes
> New tires
> Fix handlebars.
> Fix frame.
>
> Bill $53

Before getting his bicycle repaired, Jonathan thought he should look at a new bicycle. He saw one for $96. He can buy the bicycle only if his dad loans him the money and he pays it back.

1. The new bicycle would cost how much more than getting his old bike repaired? _____

2. Should Jonathan repair his old bicycle or buy a new one? Explain your answer.

_____

_____

_____

Use with
Objective 14
pages 46–47

Focus
Decision Making

Overview
Students decide whether to repair an old bicycle or borrow money to buy a new one.

Teaching Suggestions
After students complete Problem 1, guide them through the decision-making process. *Questions: What are Jonathan's choices?* [Repair old bicycle, buy new bicycle] *What are some advantages and disadvantages of repairing the old bicycle?* [Possible answers: Will not have to borrow money; will still have an old bicycle] *What are some advantages and disadvantages of buying the new bicycle?* [Possible answers: Will have a brand-new bicycle; will have to borrow money from his father] Then have students complete Problem 2. Ask several volunteers to tell what decisions they made, and explain why they made them.

Extension
Discuss other situations in which a decision between repairing an older item and buying a new one is required. Examples include cars, stereos, televisions, and houses.

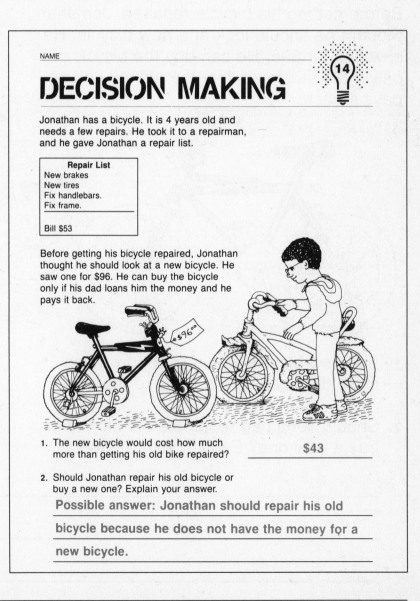

NAME

DECISION MAKING

Jonathan has a bicycle. It is 4 years old and needs a few repairs. He took it to a repairman, and he gave Jonathan a repair list.

Repair List
New brakes
New tires
Fix handlebars.
Fix frame.

Bill $53

Before getting his bicycle repaired, Jonathan thought he should look at a new bicycle. He saw one for $96. He can buy the bicycle only if his dad loans him the money and he pays it back.

1. The new bicycle would cost how much more than getting his old bike repaired? _____ **$43**

2. Should Jonathan repair his old bicycle or buy a new one? Explain your answer.

   Possible answer: Jonathan should repair his old

   bicycle because he does not have the money for a

   new bicycle.

VISUAL THINKING

Use toothpicks to help you answer the following questions.

1. Make the following figure using 12 toothpicks. Now take away 2 of the toothpicks so that you will have only 3 squares. Each toothpick is part of a square.

2. Using the same figure below, take away 2 toothpicks to make 2 squares. The squares do not need to be the same size.

3. Make the figure below using 17 toothpicks. Take away 6 toothpicks so that you will have only two squares.

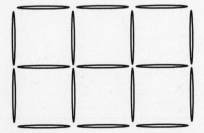

Use with
Objective 15
pages 48–49

Focus
Visual Thinking
   Spatial Perception

Materials
Toothpicks, straws, craft sticks,
   or strips of paper

Overview
Students visually arrange
toothpicks to create new
shapes.

Teaching Suggestions
If the students are having
difficulty, give the following
hints:
1. Squares do not have to be
   the same size.
2. Sometimes toothpicks are
   moved; sometimes they are
   taken away.
3. Squares can be inside or
   outside other squares.

Alternate Approach: If students
have difficulty visualizing the
changes necessary, have them
manipulate toothpicks (or other
sticks) to solve the problems.

Extension
Have students solve the
following triangle puzzle:

Take away four toothpicks so
that only four triangles remain.

NAME _____

VISUAL THINKING

Use toothpicks to help you answer the
following questions.

1. Make the following figure using
   12 toothpicks. Now take away 2
   of the toothpicks so that you will
   have only 3 squares. Each
   toothpick is part of a square.

2. Using the same figure below,
   take away 2 toothpicks to make
   2 squares. The squares do not
   need to be the same size.

3. Make the figure below using
   17 toothpicks. Take away
   6 toothpicks so that you will
   have only two squares.

PROBLEM SOLVING

Pierre would like to find out how many circles are common to the square and the triangle, but not to the octagon.

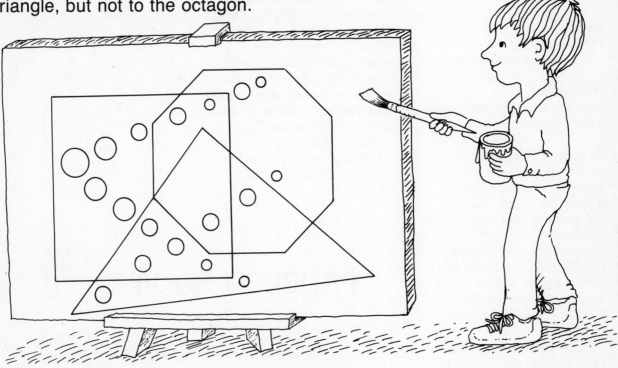

1. How many circles are inside the square? the triangle? the octagon?

_____ _____ _____

2. How many circles are *not* inside the square? the triangle? the octagon?

_____ _____ _____

3. How many circles are inside the square, but not inside the triangle or the octagon? _____

4. How many circles are common to all 3 shapes? _____

5. How many circles are common to the square and the triangle, but not to the octagon? _____

Use with
Objective 16
pages 52–53

Focus
Problem Solving
   Use Logical Reasoning

Overview
Students solve problems using a Venn diagram.

Teaching Suggestions
In order to solve this problem, students need to be able to identify the square, the triangle, and the octagon in the picture.

   If students have difficulty with Problem 1, they might draw a picture of each shape separately and count the number of circles inside each of them.

   For Problem 2, students need to count the number of circles outside each shape. It may be helpful for them to cover each shape with their hand or a piece of paper, and then count the circles outside the shape. For Problems 3, 4, and 5 students need to count the circles that are inside one, two, or all three shapes. It might be helpful to draw the figures on the chalkboard, point to individual circles, and have students name the shapes that the circles are inside of.

Extension
Have students make a diagram using these facts: Aaron (A) likes math and science, Betsy (B) likes math and reading, Clark (C) likes reading, science, and math, Doris (D) likes reading, Elliott (E) likes math and reading, and Fran (F) likes reading. Have them draw 3 intersecting circles, labeled "Math," "Science," and "Reading," and then put the letters in the appropriate section.

The completed diagram might look like this:

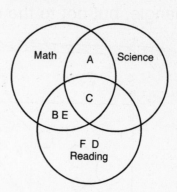

PROBLEM SOLVING

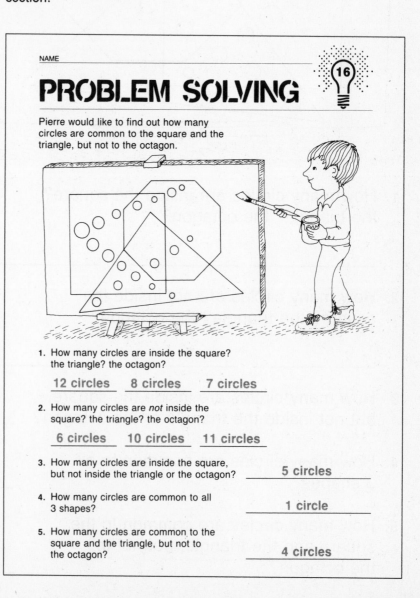

NAME

PROBLEM SOLVING 16

Pierre would like to find out how many circles are common to the square and the triangle, but not to the octagon.

1. How many circles are inside the square? the triangle? the octagon?

   12 circles   8 circles   7 circles

2. How many circles are *not* inside the square? the triangle? the octagon?

   6 circles   10 circles   11 circles

3. How many circles are inside the square, but not inside the triangle or the octagon?   5 circles

4. How many circles are common to all 3 shapes?   1 circle

5. How many circles are common to the square and the triangle, but not to the octagon?   4 circles

VISUAL THINKING

Ring the letters of the figures in each row
that are the same.

1.

     a.   b.   c.   d.   e.   f.

2.

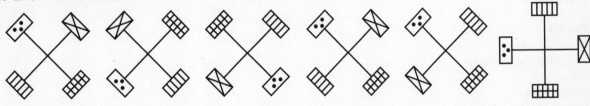

     a.   b.   c.   d.   e.   f.

3.

     a.   b.   c.   d.   e.   f.

4.

     a.   b.   c.   d.   e.   f.

5.

     a.   b.   c.   d.   e.   f.

6.

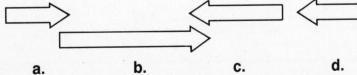 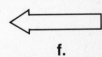

     a.   b.   c.   d.   e.   f.

Use with
Objective 17
pages 54–57

Focus
Visual Thinking
   Spatial Perception

Materials
Visual Thinking transparency
   (optional)

Overview
Students compare figures to
determine which two shapes
are the same.

Teaching Suggestions
Introduce the activity by
drawing the following pictures
on the chalkboard:

*Question: Which figures are
exactly the same?* [The two
triangles]

Have students complete
Problems 1–6. If they have
difficulty, ask them to describe
each figure in terms of its
distinguishing characteristics.
For example, in Problem 1, the
two congruent figures have
dots in the upper left box, an **x**
in the upper right box, lines in
the lower left box, and a grid in
the lower right box. By starting
with more obvious
characteristics, students can
systematically eliminate
possibilities and arrive at the
two congruent figures. Remind
students that any two of the
five figures may be the same,
as some will look for a figure to
match the first in each row.

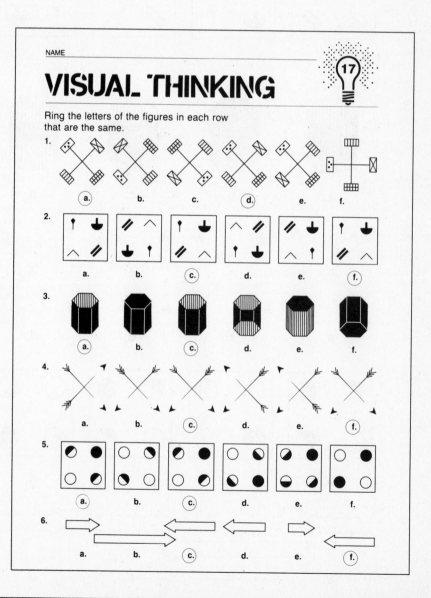

CRITICAL THINKING

Ant Matty said to Ant Gus, "Mr. Leff's class hopes to have a picnic today. If it does not rain, then Mr. Leff's class will have the picnic. If they have the picnic, then we ants will have a picnic, too!"

Suppose these statements are true:
    If it does not rain, then Mr. Leff's
        class will have the picnic.
    It does not rain.

You can conclude that Mr. Leff's class will have the picnic.

Each pair of statements below is true. Write the conclusion for each pair.

1. If the class has the picnic, then the ants have a picnic. The class has a picnic.

    Conclusion: _____

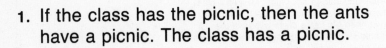

2. If Erin and Roy make the sandwiches, then they will taste good. Erin and Roy make the sandwiches.

    Conclusion: _____

3. If the picnic starts at 1:00, then the ants' picnic starts at 1:00. The picnic starts at 1:00.

    Conclusion: _____

4. If the crumbs are left on the ground, then the ants carry the crumbs home. Crumbs are left on the ground.

    Conclusion: _____

Use with
Objective 18
pages 58–59

Focus
Critical Thinking
   Evaluating Evidence and
      Conclusions
   Using Logic

Overview
Students use deductive reasoning to make valid conclusions based on given information.

Teaching Suggestions
Introduce this activity by discussing everyday statements that contain the words *if* and *then*. For example: "If you finish your work, then you may play a game." When the condition is met (the work is finished), the statement following *then* is carried out (you may play a game).

   Students use this concept to deduce conclusions in the activity. Stress that in order to make a conclusion from the *if . . . then* statement presented, the entire statement and the condition must be accepted as true.

   After students have completed Problem 4, challenge them to make a conclusion by assuming these statements are true:
- *If the picnic ends at 4 o'clock, then the ants will be happy.*
- *The picnic does not end at 4 o'clock.*

A common error is to negate the conclusion. For example, students may erroneously conclude that the ants will not be happy. Discuss the fact that since there is nothing that tells how the ants feel if the picnic does not end at 4 o'clock, no other assumptions may be made.

Extension
Challenge students to create their own *if . . . then* statements. Have them ask each other to provide a logical conclusion, if possible, for each.

NAME

CRITICAL THINKING 18

Ant Matty said to Ant Gus, "Mr. Leff's class hopes to have a picnic today. If it does not rain, then Mr. Leff's class will have the picnic. If they have the picnic, then we ants will have a picnic, too!"

Suppose these statements are true:
   If it does not rain, then Mr. Leff's class will have the picnic.
   It does not rain.

You can conclude that Mr. Leff's class will have the picnic.

Each pair of statements below is true. Write the conclusion for each pair.

1. If the class has the picnic, then the ants have a picnic. The class has a picnic.

   Conclusion: _____ The ants have a picnic.

2. If Erin and Roy make the sandwiches, then they will taste good. Erin and Roy make the sandwiches.

   Conclusion: _____ The sandwiches will taste good.

3. If the picnic starts at 1:00, then the ants' picnic starts at 1:00. The picnic starts at 1:00.

   Conclusion: _____ The ants' picnic starts at 1:00.

4. If the crumbs are left on the ground, then the ants carry the crumbs home. Crumbs are left on the ground.

   Conclusion: _____ The ants carry the crumbs home.

VISUAL THINKING

An analogy compares two pairs of objects as in the following example. Write the letter of the figure on the right that correctly completes the analogy on the left.

Example:

a large square | is to | a small square | as | a large circle | is to | a small circle

1. is to as is to **?** ____

a.

2. is to as is to **?** ____

b.

c.

d.

3. is to as is to **?** ____

e.

f.

4. is to as is to **?** ____

g.

5. is to as is to **?** ____

h.

Use after pages 60–61.

Use with
Objective 19
pages 60–61

Focus
Visual Thinking
   Visual Patterns

Materials
Visual Thinking transparency
   (optional)

Overview
Students apply *visual patterns*
to complete visual analogies.

Teaching Suggestions
Make sure students
understand the example. The
relationship of the first pair of
figures (large to small) is the
same as the relationship of the
second pair of figures (large to
small). Point out that the
relationships in each analogy
may involve the amount and
position of shading, and the
size of figures.

   Students should see that the
relationship in Problem 1 is a
flip, in Problem 2 is an
enlargement, in Problem 3 is a
flip, in Problem 4 is a change
of pattern, and in Problem 5 is
a turn.

Extension
Challenge students to make an
analogy that uses the
relationship of turning, flipping,
and enlarging.

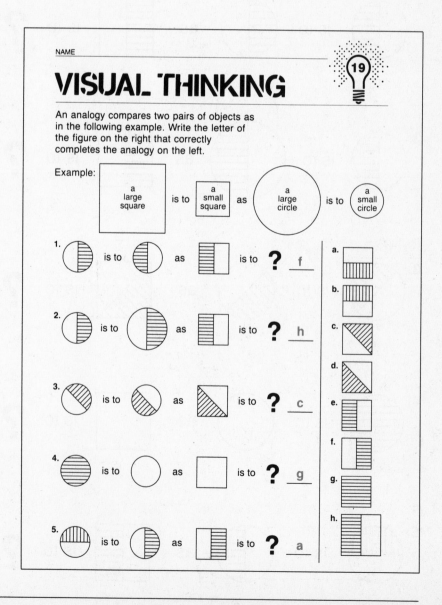

PROBLEM SOLVING

Coach Karen listed the wins and losses of 8 teams in a basketball tournament:

Round 1:   Eagles heat Dolphins. Lions won. Bears lost. Pelicans scored more points than Tigers.

Round 2:   The winner of Game 2 won Game 5. The winner of Game 4 lost Game 6.

Round 3:   The winner of Game 5 lost.

1. In the diagram below, fill in the teams which played in Round 2. Use the information about Round 1.

2. Which teams played in Game 7? Fill in the diagram.

ROUND 1   ROUND 2   ROUND 3

Dolphins
GAME 1
Eagles   Eagles
Hawks   GAME 5
GAME 2
Lions
Penguins   GAME 7
GAME 3
Bears   GAME 6   WINNER
Tigers
GAME 4
Pelicans

3. Which team won the tournament? Fill in the diagram?

_____

Use with

Objective 20
pages 62–63

Focus

Problem Solving
   Use Logical Reasoning

Overview

Students use logic to determine the winner of a tournament from given information.

Teaching Suggestions

In Problem 1, students use the information about Round 1 and the diagram that shows the teams which played in the first four games. *Questions: Who won Game 1?* [Eagles] *Game 2?* [Lions] *Game 3?* [Penguins] *Game 4?* [Pelicans]

   Before students fill in the diagram, make sure they understand that winners from one round advance to the next round. Point out that they are to record the winners from Round 1 in the column for Round 2.

   In Problem 2, students use the information about Round 2 to determine who played in Game 7. They have to look back at Round 1 and use information such as "the winner of Game 2 won Game 5." Since the Lions won Game 2, the Lions also won Game 5 and advanced to Round 3. Students should fill in the diagram showing that the Lions and the Penguins played in Round 3.

   For Problem 3, students use the information about Round 3 to complete the diagram and find that the Penguins won the tournament.

Extension

Have students use the facts below to draw a diagram and find the winner.

Round 1: Red beat White in Game 1. Blue lost to Green in Game 2. Brown beat Pink in Game 3. Gray scored more points than Yellow in Game 4.

Round 2: The winner of Game 2 lost Game 5. The winner of Game 3 won Game 6.

Round 3: The winner of Game 3 lost Game 7.

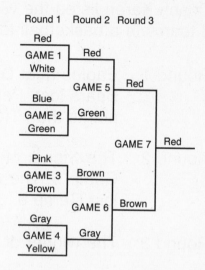

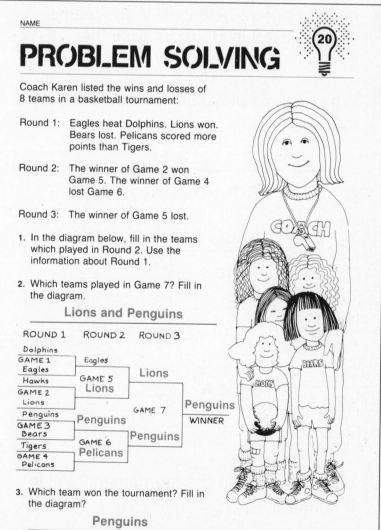

NAME _____

PROBLEM SOLVING (20)

Coach Karen listed the wins and losses of 8 teams in a basketball tournament:

Round 1:   Eagles beat Dolphins. Lions won. Bears lost. Pelicans scored more points than Tigers.

Round 2:   The winner of Game 2 won Game 5. The winner of Game 4 lost Game 6.

Round 3:   The winner of Game 5 lost.

1. In the diagram below, fill in the teams which played in Round 2. Use the information about Round 1.

2. Which teams played in Game 7? Fill in the diagram.

Lions and Penguins

3. Which team won the tournament? Fill in the diagram?

Penguins

PROBLEM SOLVING

Tom wants to have $1 using only pennies and dimes.

1. How can Tom use only pennies to make a dollar?

_____

2. How can Tom use only dimes to make a dollar?

_____

3. How can Tom use pennies and 1 dime to make a dollar?

_____

4. How can he use 10 pennies and 10 dimes to make a dollar?

_____

5. Complete the table at right to find all the other ways to combine pennies and dimes to make a dollar. How many ways can Tom have one dollar using only pennies and dimes?

_____

Number of Pennies	Number of Dimes
100	0
90	1

Use after pages 74–75.

Use with

Objective 21
pages 74–75

Focus

Problem Solving
    Use Logical Reasoning
    Find a Pattern

Materials

10 pennies, 11 dimes,
    1 dollar bill
Items or pictures of items
    that can be used to set up
    a store

Overview

Students find combinations of
pennies and dimes equal to
one dollar.

Teaching Suggestions

Put 10 pennies next to a dime,
and 10 dimes next to a dollar
bill. Use this arrangement to
illustrate the following.
*Questions: Which is worth
more, a penny or a dime?*
[Dime] *How many pennies does
it take to make a dime?* [10]
Ask students to find out how
many pennies are in 2 dimes,
3 dimes, and so forth until they
are comfortable with this
exchange. *Question: If it takes
10 pennies to make a dime,
how many pennies are in ten
dimes?* [100]
    Encourage students to look
for a pattern when completing
the table in Problem 5.

Alternate Approach: Have
students use play money or
colored plastic chips to
represent dimes and pennies.
Have them show one dollar
with 10 dimes. Tell them to
replace one dime with
10 pennies and record the
combination in a table. Help
them continue replacing each
dime with 10 pennies until they
show one dollar with
100 pennies.

Extension

Have students set up a school
supply store with items that
cost one dollar. Ask students to
use play money or plastic
chips for coins to pay for the
items in pennies, dimes, or
combinations of pennies and
dimes. Label each item with a
sign such as 3 dimes and ?
pennies. Have students use
their tables to find the missing
number of coins needed to
make one dollar.

NAME _____

PROBLEM SOLVING

Tom wants to have $1 using only pennies
and dimes.

1. How can Tom use only pennies to make
   a dollar?

   100 pennies

2. How can Tom use only dimes to make
   a dollar?

   10 dimes

3. How can Tom use pennies and 1 dime to
   make a dollar?

   90 pennies, 1 dime

4. How can he use 10 pennies and 10 dimes
   to make a dollar?

   9 dimes, 10 pennies

5. Complete the table at right to find all the
   other ways to combine pennies and dimes
   to make a dollar. How many ways can
   Tom have one dollar using only pennies
   and dimes?

   11 ways

Number of Pennies	Number of Dimes
100	0
90	1
80	2
70	3
60	4
50	5
40	6
30	7
20	8
10	9
0	10

VISUAL THINKING

Ring the letter of the figure in each row that is different.

1.

a.   b.   c.   d.

2.

a.   b.   c.   d.

3.

a.   b.   c.   d.

4.

a.   b.   c.   d.

5.

a.   b.   c.   d.

Use with
Objective 22
pages 76–79

Focus
Visual Thinking
  Spatial Perception

Materials
Stencils of shapes
Visual Thinking transparency
  (optional)

Overview
Students compare figures to
determine which one is
different from the others.

Teaching Suggestions
Make two columns on the
chalkboard with the headings
"Same" and "Different." Have
students study Problem 1 and
classify each part of the figures
under one column. For
example, "Eyes" would be
under the column marked
"Same." Guide students to find
the characteristic that is
different. Allow time for
students to complete the
remaining problems.

Alternate Approach: Have
students work in small groups
to discuss each problem and
decide which figure is different.
Have students say how the
figure is different. Ask a
volunteer from each group to
explain their decisions.

Extension
Using stencils, have students
make similar Problems. (They
may draw from 2 to 4 figures.)
Students should exchange the
drawings.

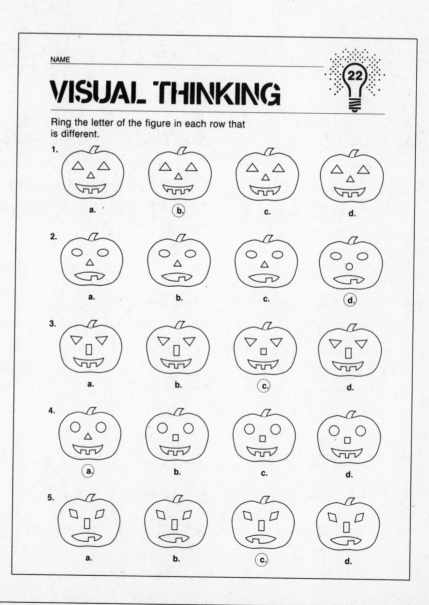

NAME _____

VISUAL THINKING

Ring the letter of the figure in each row that
is different.

CRITICAL THINKING

Georgia's birthday party is the day after tomorrow. The day before yesterday was Tuesday.

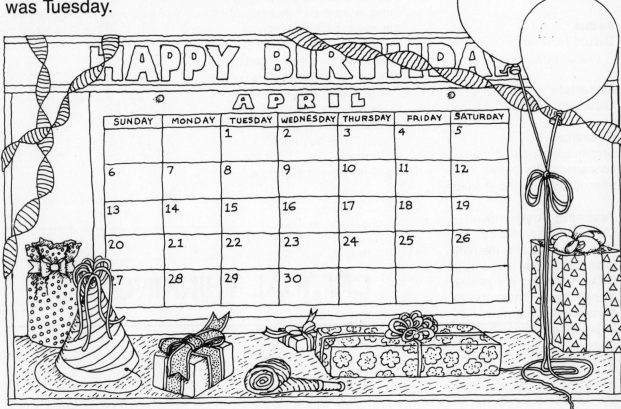

APRIL

SUNDAY	MONDAY	TUESDAY	WEDNESDAY	THURSDAY	FRIDAY	SATURDAY
		1	2	3	4	5
6	7	8	9	10	11	12
13	14	15	16	17	18	19
20	21	22	23	24	25	26
27	28	29	30			

1. What day of the week was the day before yesterday? _____

2. If the day before yesterday was Tuesday, what day is today? _____

3. What day is tomorrow? _____

4. What day is the day after tomorrow? _____

5. On what day is Georgia's birthday party? _____

6. If the day before yesterday was

_____,

what day is the day after tomorrow? _____

Use with
Objective 23
pages 80–81

Focus
Critical Thinking
   Using Logic

Materials
Classroom calendar

Overview
Students think about the concepts of day before, day after, tomorrow, and yesterday.

Teaching Suggestions
Display a classroom calendar.
Questions: What is the date today? What day of the week is today? What day of the week was yesterday? What day of the week is tomorrow?
[Answers will vary.]

Alternate Approach: Ask a student volunteer to point out and name the dates of all the Mondays on the calendar, all the Tuesdays, and so on. Then have a volunteer point out the present day and tell what day of the week it is. Have a volunteer do the same for yesterday and tomorrow.

Extension
Extend Problem 6 with such questions as the following. If today is April 10, what day of the week is it? What day is tomorrow? What day is the day after tomorrow? Have students pick school days from the current calendar and make signs with that date and day, "The day before yesterday was ____," "The day after tomorrow is ____." Put the signs up around the room.

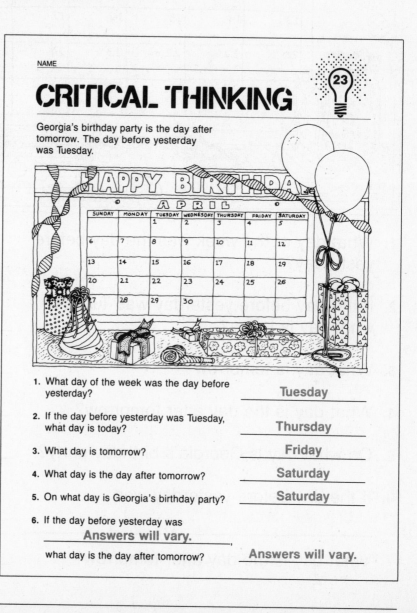

NAME _____

CRITICAL THINKING (23)

Georgia's birthday party is the day after tomorrow. The day before yesterday was Tuesday.

1. What day of the week was the day before yesterday? **Tuesday**

2. If the day before yesterday was Tuesday, what day is today? **Thursday**

3. What day is tomorrow? **Friday**

4. What day is the day after tomorrow? **Saturday**

5. On what day is Georgia's birthday party? **Saturday**

6. If the day before yesterday was
_____ **Answers will vary.** _____,
what day is the day after tomorrow? **Answers will vary.**

CRITICAL THINKING

At the Fall Fun Fair, Becky hit the target with 5 darts.

1. What is her largest possible score? _____

2. What is her smallest possible score? _____

3. If only 2 darts hit the center section, what is the largest possible score? _____

4. If only 2 darts hit the outside section, what is the smallest possible score? _____

5. What is the score if each dart hits a different section? _____

Teacher Notes

Use with
Objective 24
pages 82–83

Focus
Critical Thinking
   Using Number Sense
   Drawing Conclusions

Overview
Students *draw conclusions* about possible scores on a dart board.

Teaching Suggestions
Explain to the class how the game of darts is played and scored. Inform them that an official dart board may be used or a dart board may be made with its own point values. *Questions: If Becky hit the center section with 5 darts, what would her score be?* [45] *If Becky hit the outside section with all 5 darts, what would her score be?* [15] Have students find Becky's score for given throws; for example, 1 dart in the 3 section, 1 dart in the 5 section, 2 darts in 7 section, and 1 dart in the 9 section. [31]

Alternate Approach: Have students work in cooperative groups to complete the activity. Then ask a volunteer from each group to explain the reasoning for their answers.

Extension
Ask students to work in small groups and write one number sentence for each possible score, 15 through 45, using 5 darts.

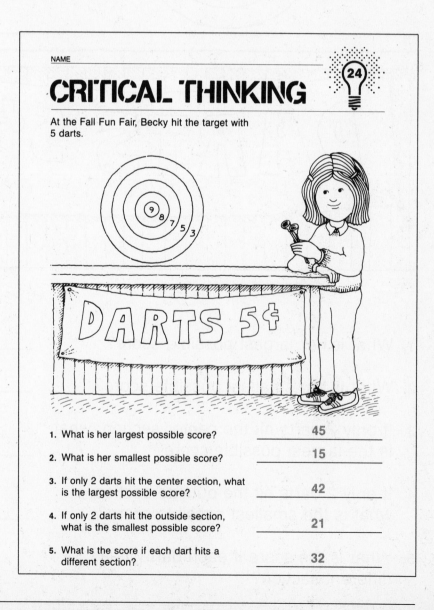

NAME

CRITICAL THINKING 24

At the Fall Fun Fair, Becky hit the target with 5 darts.

1. What is her largest possible score? ___45___

2. What is her smallest possible score? ___15___

3. If only 2 darts hit the center section, what is the largest possible score? ___42___

4. If only 2 darts hit the outside section, what is the smallest possible score? ___21___

5. What is the score if each dart hits a different section? ___32___

DECISION MAKING

Use the picture and the story to help you
make a decision.

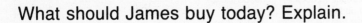

James has 10 dollars. He needs some
art supplies.
He has lost his scissors.
His sketch pad is nearly used up.
He needs a new red marker.
He loaned his colored pencils to his brother.
Construction paper is on sale for 2 for the
price of 1, and he will need construction
paper for a scout project next week.

What should James buy today? Explain.

Use with
Objective 25
pages 84–85

Focus
Decision Making

Overview
Students analyze given information and use it to decide which art supplies to buy.

Teaching Suggestions
Have students write a shopping list for James using the information in the story. Ask a student volunteer to write the shopping list on the board. [Shopping list: scissors, sketch pad, red marker, colored pencils, construction paper] *Questions: What is the cost of each item that James needs?* [Scissors, $2; sketch pad, $4; marker, $1; colored pencils, $4; construction paper, $3] *What is the cost of all the supplies James needs?* [$14] *Does James have enough money?* [No] Based on this information, students should develop alternatives for buying the items on the shopping list.

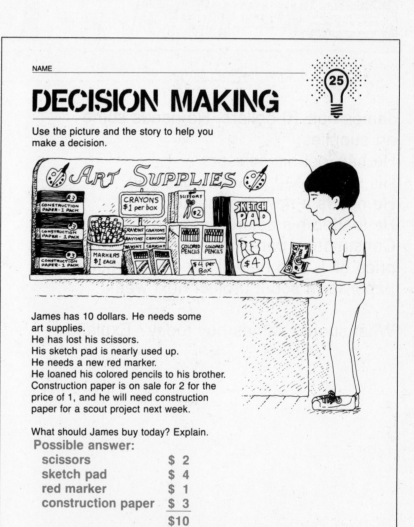

NAME

DECISION MAKING
25

Use the picture and the story to help you make a decision.

James has 10 dollars. He needs some art supplies.
He has lost his scissors.
His sketch pad is nearly used up.
He needs a new red marker.
He loaned his colored pencils to his brother.
Construction paper is on sale for 2 for the price of 1, and he will need construction paper for a scout project next week.

What should James buy today? Explain.
Possible answer:

scissors	$ 2
sketch pad	$ 4
red marker	$ 1
construction paper	$ 3
	$10

He can get the colored pencils from his brother and buy the paper he needs while it is on sale.

CRITICAL THINKING

Use the picture to help you answer the questions.

Robert, Mary, and William are trying to find their presents. Study the pictures above to answer the following questions.

1. Robert's present has plain paper. There is ribbon around the box. It has a bow. Which present is Robert's? _____

2. Mary's present is not the smallest. It has ribbon around it. There is no bow. Which present is Mary's? _____

3. William's present has paper with a design. There is no bow. It is not the smallest. Which present is William's? _____

Use with
Objective 26
pages 88–89

Focus
Critical Thinking
   Using Logic
   Drawing Conclusions

Overview
Students use a picture and read a story to *draw conclusions* about the ownership of presents.

Teaching Suggestions
To help students organize the characteristics of each package, have them complete the following table.

	A	B	C	D
Size of box	Medium			
Bow		Yes		
Kind of paper				Plain
Ribbon				

To answer Problem 1, students should look in the row named "kind of paper" for all the presents that have plain paper. [B and D]

They should then determine if present B or D has a ribbon. [Both B and D have a ribbon.] The final clue indicates that Robert's present has a bow. Students can see clearly from their tables that present B had plain paper, a ribbon, and a bow.

Students can continue analyzing the information in the table to determine which presents belong to Mary and William.

Extension
Have students color the presents in the picture. Using the colors and other characteristics, have students write their own clues about the ownership of the presents.

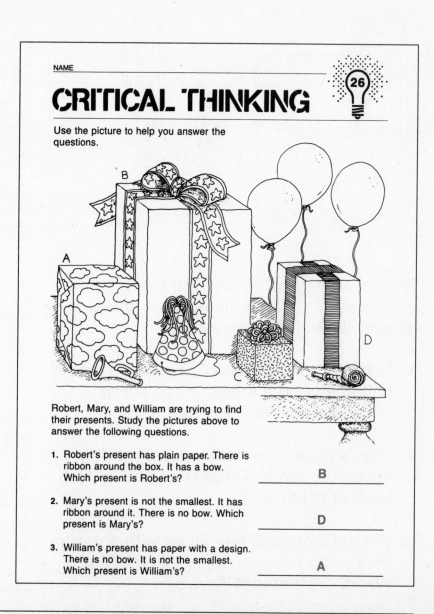

NAME _____

CRITICAL THINKING 26

Use the picture to help you answer the questions.

Robert, Mary, and William are trying to find their presents. Study the pictures above to answer the following questions.

1. Robert's present has plain paper. There is ribbon around the box. It has a bow. Which present is Robert's?   B

2. Mary's present is not the smallest. It has ribbon around it. There is no bow. Which present is Mary's?   D

3. William's present has paper with a design. There is no bow. It is not the smallest. Which present is William's?   A

CRITICAL THINKING

The pictures show the total weight when the same 3 objects are placed on scales in different ways. Study the pictures. Then answer the questions.

1. How much do all three objects weigh together? _____

2. How much does the book and the figure weigh together? _____

3. How much does the toy car weigh? _____

4. How much do the car and the book weigh together? _____

5. How much does the book weigh? _____

6. How much does the toy figure weigh? _____

Teacher Notes

Use with
Objective 27
pages 90–91

Focus
Critical Thinking
   Classifying and Sorting
   Drawing Conclusions

Materials
Scale (optional)
Various sets of three objects
   (optional)

Overview
Students study pictures of three objects on scales and *draw conclusions* about the weight of each object.

Teaching Suggestions
To introduce the activity, ask the following. **Questions:** *Which drawing shows the weight of all three objects?* [The one on the left] *Which drawing shows the weight of the book and the figure together?* [The middle one] *How can you find out how much the toy car weighs?* [Subtract the weight of the book and the figure together from the weight of all three objects.]

Alternate Approach: Allow students to work in small groups with a scale to weigh objects in different groupings, such as the ones shown in the pictures, to find out how much each object weighs.

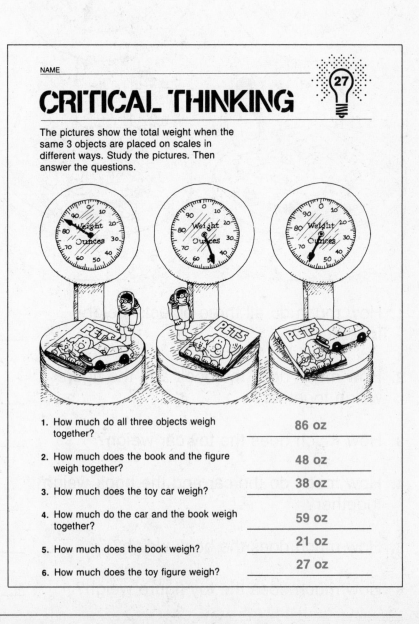

NAME _____

CRITICAL THINKING ⟨27⟩

The pictures show the total weight when the same 3 objects are placed on scales in different ways. Study the pictures. Then answer the questions.

1. How much do all three objects weigh together?   86 oz

2. How much does the book and the figure weigh together?   48 oz

3. How much does the toy car weigh?   38 oz

4. How much do the car and the book weigh together?   59 oz

5. How much does the book weigh?   21 oz

6. How much does the toy figure weigh?   27 oz

VISUAL THINKING

An analogy compares two pairs of objects as in the following example. Write the letter of the figure on the right that correctly completes the analogy on the left.

Example: □ is to ▫, as ○ is to ○.

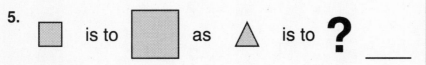

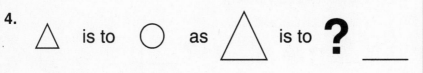

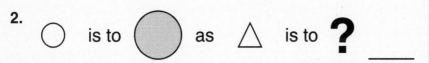

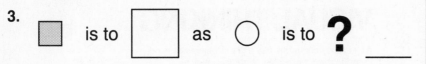

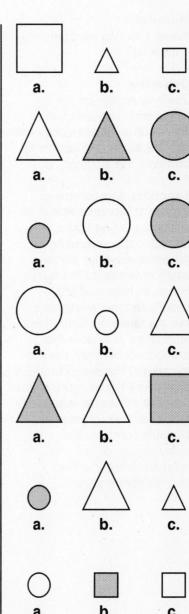

Use with
Objective 28
pages 92–93

Focus
Visual Thinking
   Visual Patterns

Materials
Visual Thinking transparency
   (optional)

Overview
Students recognize the relationship between two figures of a visual analogy and use this same relationship to complete the analogy.

Teaching Suggestions
Explain to students that in an analogy, the first figure is related to the second figure in the same way that the third figure is related to the fourth figure. To help students understand this relationship, ask the following. *Questions: In Problem 1, what is the relationship between the two triangles? [The second triangle is smaller.] Which figure on the right has the same relationship to the square? [c]* Have students complete the remaining problems independently and then discuss their answers.

Extension
Have students work in cooperative groups to create other analogies. Then have the groups exchange their analogies and solve them.

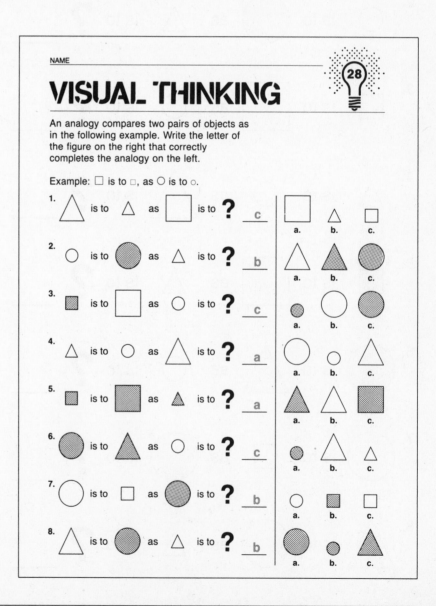

PROBLEM SOLVING

In my wallet, I have coins to pay for any item priced from 1¢ to $1 with exact change.

1. How many different coins are less than $1? List them.

_____

2. What is the least number of coins needed to pay 4¢?

_____

3. What is the least number of coins needed to pay 5¢?

_____

4. What is the least number of coins needed to pay 10¢?

_____

5. What is the least number of coins needed to pay 20¢?

_____

6. What is the least number of coins needed to pay 25¢? 45¢? 50¢?

_____

7. Do I need any more coins for amounts from 51¢ to $1?

_____

8. What is the least number of coins needed to pay for any item from 1¢ to $1 with exact change?

_____

Teacher Notes

Use with
Objective 29
pages 94–95

Focus
Problem Solving
   Use Logical Reasoning

Materials
Play money or real coins

Overview
Students determine the number of each kind of coin needed to pay for any item priced from one cent to one dollar.

Teaching Suggestions
Allow students to work on Problems 1–6, then discuss Problem 7. Point out that in Problem 7 students may assume that they have enough coins to pay the amounts in Problems 2–6. This is a total of nine coins: 4 pennies, 1 nickel, 2 dimes, 1 quarter, and 1 half-dollar.

Alternate Approach: Provide students with play money or real coins. Allow them to work in small groups to count the least number of coins needed to pay for items of various prices and to record the numbers of each kind of coin in a chart until they see that 9 coins is the least number that is needed for any item.

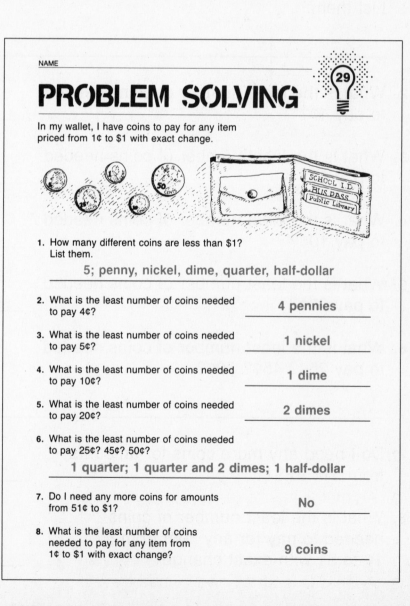

NAME

PROBLEM SOLVING 29

In my wallet, I have coins to pay for any item
priced from 1¢ to $1 with exact change.

1. How many different coins are less than $1?
   List them.
   5; penny, nickel, dime, quarter, half-dollar

2. What is the least number of coins needed
   to pay 4¢?   4 pennies

3. What is the least number of coins needed
   to pay 5¢?   1 nickel

4. What is the least number of coins needed
   to pay 10¢?   1 dime

5. What is the least number of coins needed
   to pay 20¢?   2 dimes

6. What is the least number of coins needed
   to pay 25¢? 45¢? 50¢?
   1 quarter; 1 quarter and 2 dimes; 1 half-dollar

7. Do I need any more coins for amounts
   from 51¢ to $1?   No

8. What is the least number of coins
   needed to pay for any item from
   1¢ to $1 with exact change?   9 coins

CRITICAL THINKING

Decide whether each statement below is
true or false. Write your answers in the
blanks at the right.

A

B

C

D

Examples:
Animal A is black and white.   True _____

Animal D is black and large.   False _____

1. Animal B is small and swims.   _____

2. Animal C is large and white.   _____

3. Animal A is small and spotted.   _____

4. Animal D is white and small.   _____

5. Animal C is small and climbs trees.   _____

Use with
Objective 30
pages 110–113

Focus
Critical Thinking
    Classifying and Sorting
    Using Logic

Overview
Students analyze pictures of familiar animals to determine whether statements about them are true or false.

Teaching Suggestions
Make sure students can name each animal. [A: panda, B: fish, C: squirrel, D: polar bear] *Questions: Which animals are large?* [Panda and polar bear] *Which animals are small?* [Fish and squirrel] Then direct attention to the examples. *Questions: Is animal A black?* [Yes] *Is it white?* [Yes] *Is the statement "Animal A is black and white" a true statement or a false statement?* [True] *Is animal D black?* [No] *Is it small?* [No] *Is the statement "Animal D is black and small" true or false?* [False] *Why?* [Because animal D is not black and not small] Students should be directed to determine the truth of statements from the picture, although they may use any knowledge they have about the animals as well.

Extension
Discuss other characteristics of the pictured animals, such as their feeding habits, where they might live, the likelihood of seeing one near your house, and so on. Students can create their own true or false statements about these or other animals, and exchange papers.

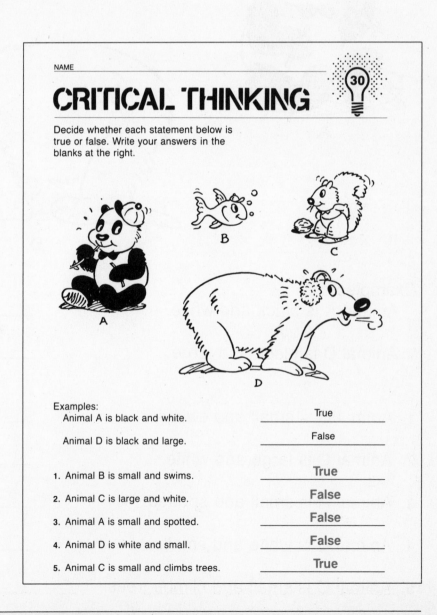

NAME _____

CRITICAL THINKING
30

Decide whether each statement below is true or false. Write your answers in the blanks at the right.

Examples:
    Animal A is black and white.   True

    Animal D is black and large.   False

1. Animal B is small and swims.   True

2. Animal C is large and white.   False

3. Animal A is small and spotted.   False

4. Animal D is white and small.   False

5. Animal C is small and climbs trees.   True

CRITICAL THINKING

Jojo and Ollie live in a large city. Their class went to the science museum. They saw many exhibits and ate lunch in the museum cafeteria.

Decide whether each statement below makes sense. Write *yes* or *no*. If the answer is *no*, write the sentence over so that it makes sense. The first one is done for you.

1. Jojo and Ollie's teacher is 10 years old.

   No. Jojo and Ollie's teacher is

   30 years old.

2. The bus ride to the museum took 1 hour.

   _____

   _____

3. There are 1,000 students in Jojo and Ollie's class.

   _____

   _____

4. The students saw 850 exhibits at the museum.

   _____

   _____

5. Jojo and Ollie's class spent 5 hours at the museum.

   _____

   _____

6. Lunch cost $15 per student at the cafeteria.

   _____

   _____

Use with
Objective 31
pages 114–117

Focus
Critical Thinking
Evaluating Evidence and
Conclusions
Using Number Sense

Overview
Students evaluate numerical
statements to determine
whether they are reasonable or
not.

Teaching Suggestions
To introduce the activity, give
the following example.
Questions: *If I told you there
were 15 carrots in a bag,
would that seem like a
reasonable or possible amount?*
[Yes] *What if I told you there
1,500 carrots in a bag?* [No]
Why not? [1,500 carrots would
fill more than one bag.]

Have students complete
Problems 1–6. Point out that
the answers they give as
reasonable alternatives may
vary, as long as they involve
sensible numbers. After they
have completed the page,
discuss their responses.

Extension
Many tall tales and old legends
exaggerate descriptions and
measurements. For example,
in *Jack and the Beanstalk,* the
beanstalk is tall enough to
touch the clouds, which is not
possible. Have students read a
tall tale and identify the
exaggerated descriptions and
measurements in the tale.

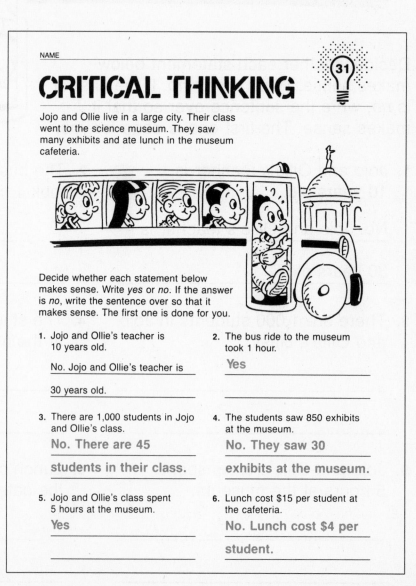

NAME

CRITICAL THINKING 31

Jojo and Ollie live in a large city. Their class
went to the science museum. They saw
many exhibits and ate lunch in the museum
cafeteria.

Decide whether each statement below
makes sense. Write *yes* or *no*. If the answer
is *no*, write the sentence over so that it
makes sense. The first one is done for you.

1. Jojo and Ollie's teacher is
10 years old.

   No. Jojo and Ollie's teacher is

   30 years old.

2. The bus ride to the museum
took 1 hour.

   Yes

3. There are 1,000 students in Jojo
and Ollie's class.

   No. There are 45

   students in their class.

4. The students saw 850 exhibits
at the museum.

   No. They saw 30

   exhibits at the museum.

5. Jojo and Ollie's class spent
5 hours at the museum.

   Yes

6. Lunch cost $15 per student at
the cafeteria.

   No. Lunch cost $4 per

   student.

VISUAL THINKING

32

Marty's father is helping him build a bookcase for his room. They drew the diagram below to help them. Use it to answer the questions.

1. How many pieces of wood will they use to make the bookcase?

_____

2. How many wood screws will they need to buy?

_____

3. Board D is the same size as which other boards?

_____

4. Board C is the same size as which other boards?

_____

5. Which board should they attach to the bookcase last?

_____

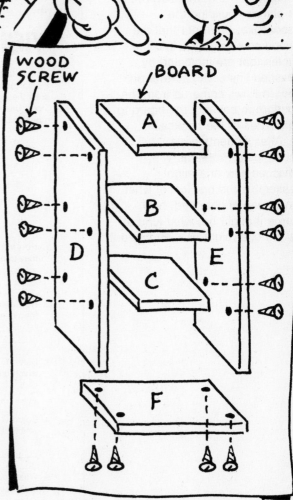

Use with

Objective 32
pages 118–119

Focus

Visual Thinking
  Spatial Perception

Overview

Students use a schematic diagram and interpret visual clues to answer questions about relative sizes, number of parts, and order of assembly.

Teaching Suggestions

Make sure students understand that the diagram is a plan for building the bookcase. Point out that the wood screws will go into the holes that are indicated by dashed lines. The screws on board F will come up from the bottom to connect the board to the sides of the bookcase.

After students have completed Problems 1–5, discuss how one might assemble the bookcase: what tools one might need, how large it might be, what kind of wood one might use, and so on.

Extension

Suggest that students design another piece of furniture, such as a table, chair, or dresser. Encourage them to label all parts, and determine the size and number of pieces necessary to construct their design.

NAME

VISUAL THINKING

Marty's father is helping him build a bookcase for his room. They drew the diagram below to help them. Use it to answer the questions.

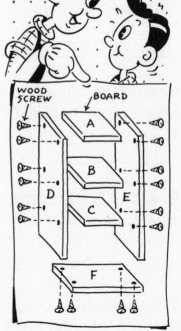

1. How many pieces of wood will they use to make the bookcase?

   6 pieces

2. How many wood screws will they need to buy?

   16 screws

3. Board D is the same size as which other boards?

   E

4. Board C is the same size as which other boards?

   A, B

5. Which board should they attach to the bookcase last?

   F

CRITICAL THINKING

33

Riddle and Columbia Schools are having a physical fitness skills contest day for each grade level.

Mr. Becraft's class scored 213 points for Riddle School. Mrs. Shriver's class scored 363 points, and Ms. Funk's class scored 412 points.

Mrs. Hewitt's class scored 534 points for Columbia School. Mr. Zartman's class scored 254 points. Mr. Poe's class has not finished all the events.

1. How many points did Mr. Becraft's class and Mrs. Shriver's class score together? _____

2. How many points did all three Riddle School classes score? _____

3. How many points did Mrs. Hewitt's and Mr. Zartman's classes score together? _____

4. At least how many points will Mr. Poe's class have to score for Columbia School to win? _____

Use with
Objective 33
pages 120–121

Focus
Critical Thinking
Using Number Sense
Drawing Conclusions

Overview
Students determine the number of points needed to win a skills contest from given information.

Teaching Suggestions
Point out that the information is presented in both the story and the picture.

If students have difficulty with Problems 1–3, ask them to determine what operation they should use for each. [Addition; addition; addition] Then ask the following.
Questions: How many points are still needed for Columbia School to tie the contest? [989 – 788 = 200 points] How many points will they need to win the contest? [201 or more]

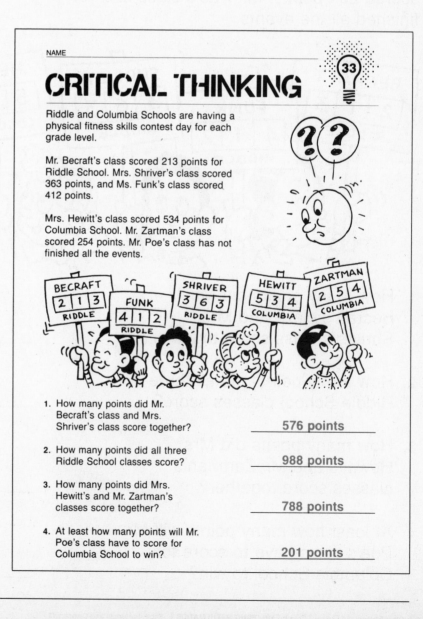

NAME _____

CRITICAL THINKING 33

Riddle and Columbia Schools are having a physical fitness skills contest day for each grade level.

Mr. Becraft's class scored 213 points for Riddle School. Mrs. Shriver's class scored 363 points, and Ms. Funk's class scored 412 points.

Mrs. Hewitt's class scored 534 points for Columbia School. Mr. Zartman's class scored 254 points. Mr. Poe's class has not finished all the events.

BECRAFT 2 1 3 RIDDLE
FUNK 4 1 2 RIDDLE
SHRIVER 3 6 3 RIDDLE
HEWITT 5 3 4 COLUMBIA
ZARTMAN 2 5 4 COLUMBIA

1. How many points did Mr. Becraft's class and Mrs. Shriver's class score together?   **576 points**

2. How many points did all three Riddle School classes score?   **988 points**

3. How many points did Mrs. Hewitt's and Mr. Zartman's classes score together?   **788 points**

4. At least how many points will Mr. Poe's class have to score for Columbia School to win?   **201 points**

VISUAL THINKING

Ring the number of each square that has been divided into 2 parts that match. The first one has been done for you.

 1. 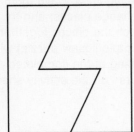   **2.** 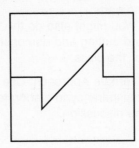   **3.**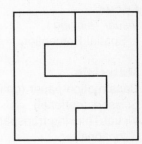

4. 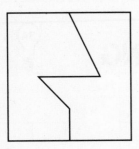   **5.** 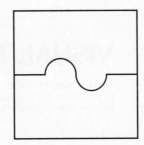   **6.**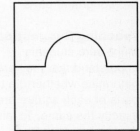

7. 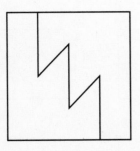   **8.** 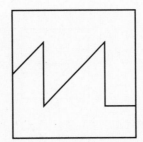   **9.**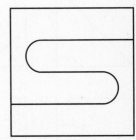

10. 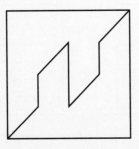   **11.** 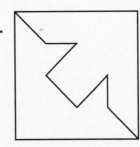   **12.**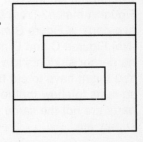

Use with
Objective 34
pages 122–123

Focus
Visual Thinking
Spatial Perception

Materials
Construction paper (optional)
Scissors (optional)
Visual Thinking transparency
(optional)

Overview
Students determine whether
figures have been divided into
two congruent parts.

Teaching Suggestions
Make sure students
understand that they are to
determine whether the two
parts of each square are
exactly the same. To introduce
the lesson, draw these figures
on a piece of paper:

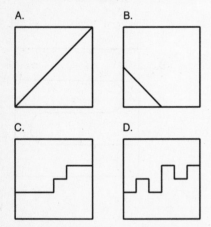

*Questions: Do the two parts of
Figure A match?* [Yes] *Do the
two parts of Figure B match?*
[No] Figures C and D might be
harder for students to visualize.
You might have to cut the
squares to show that for C the
parts are not the same but for
D they are.

If students have difficulty
with the problems on the page,
you might suggest that they
trace the figures and cut out
the parts.

You might also do the tracing
and cutting and demonstrate
for the class.

Alternate Approach: Use the
transparency to elaborate on
the discussion.

Extension
Tell the students to copy these
figures, or create their own,
and cut them along the
dividing lines. Have them
exchange pieces, and try to
match the pieces together (like
a simple jigsaw puzzle) without
looking at the completed
figures on the activity sheet.

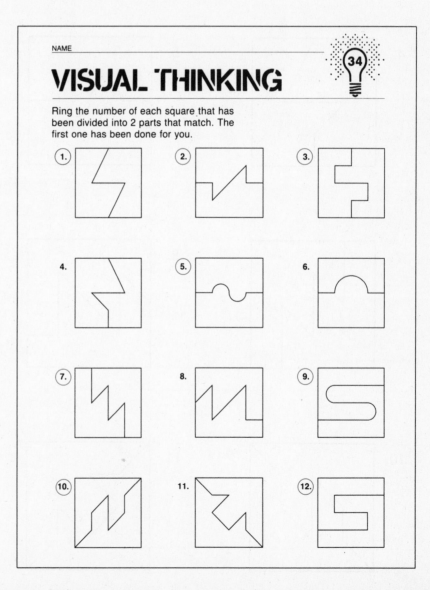

NAME _____

VISUAL THINKING   (34)

Ring the number of each square that has
been divided into 2 parts that match. The
first one has been done for you.

1. 2. 3.
4. 5. 6.
7. 8. 9.
10. 11. 12.

NAME

PROBLEM SOLVING

Becky and Adam were sorting through
photographs to put in the school yearbook.
They found the photograph below.

Becky asked Adam who the people are.
He said, "Jamie is taller than Lee. Pat and
Chris are the same height. Pat is not
wearing an even number."

Finish the table below to help Becky label
the photograph with the students' names.

	1	2	3	4
Jamie	No			
Lee				
Pat				
Chris				

Use with
Objective 35
pages 124–125

Focus
Problem Solving
  Use Logical Reasoning

Overview
Students *use logical reasoning* to identify four children based on indirect information given.

Teaching Suggestions
Point out that the information in the story is not directly related to the children's names. It must be used indirectly to eliminate possibilities and narrow choices. For example, the first statement, "Jamie is taller than Lee," tells that Jamie cannot be wearing Number 1, because the Number 1 child is shorter than any of the other children in the picture. Write "no" in the chart to show that Jamie is not Number 1.

Encourage students to fill in the table as they analyze the information.

If students are having difficulty, go through each clue with them and help them fill in the chart. The second statement, "Pat and Chris are the same height," along with the picture, identifies Pat and Chris as Numbers 2 and 3. The last statement, "Pat is not wearing an even number," identifies Pat as Number 3, so Chris must be Number 2. The clue "Jamie is taller than Lee" identifies Lee as Number 1 and Jamie as Number 4.

Extension
Challenge students to extend the story by adding one more child to the picture. Then have them write additional information in the story that will help identify this child from the other children. For example, the new child might be the same height as Jamie, so students should tell about a characteristic that will distinguish the new person from Jamie.

NAME

PROBLEM SOLVING

Becky and Adam were sorting through photographs to put in the school yearbook. They found the photograph below.

Becky asked Adam who the people are. He said, "Jamie is taller than Lee. Pat and Chris are the same height. Pat is not wearing an even number."

Finish the table below to help Becky label the photograph with the students' names.

	1	2	3	4
Jamie	No	No	No	Yes
Lee	Yes	No	No	No
Pat	No	No	Yes	No
Chris	No	Yes	No	No

DECISION MAKING

36

Dan needs 5 cars to complete his Road Masters collection. The 5 cars cost $2, $3, $3, $4, and $5. Dan only has $9.

1. How much money does Dan have? _____

2. How much do all five cars cost? _____

3. Does Dan have enough money to buy all 5 cars? If not, how much more money does he need? _____

4. Can Dan buy some of the cars? If so, which ones?

_____

5. Which cars do you think Dan should buy and why?

_____

_____

_____

Use with
Objective 36
pages 126–129

Focus
Decision Making

Overview
Students decide which of five model cars to buy with a certain amount of money.

Teaching Suggestions
Have students complete Problems 1–4. If they have difficulty with Problem 3, ask them what operation they must use. [Subtraction] Ask them to explain their answer to Problem 4, and point out that they should list all the cars Dan can buy to spend all of the $9. *Questions: What decision must Dan make?* [He must choose which of the five cars to buy with his $9.] *What must he consider when making his decision?* [Possible answers: How much money he may have in the future, which of the cars he likes best] Have students complete Problem 5 and ask volunteers to explain their decisions. Point out that there are a number of possible choices, and no one right answer.

Extension
Present this twist on the problem to your students. Suppose the store is offering a two-for-one discount, so that Dan can buy one car and get one of equal or lesser value free. Have students explain which cars Dan should buy. [Possible answer: Buy the $3 car and get the other $3 car free; buy the $5 car, and get the $4 car free. He gets 4 cars for $9.]

Ask students the minimum amount Dan would need to get one of each car under the two-for-one discount plan [$10; $5 for the five-dollar and free four-dollar cars, $3 for the two three-dollar cars, and $2 for the two-dollar car]

NAME

DECISION MAKING ⟨36⟩

Dan needs 5 cars to complete his Road Masters collection. The 5 cars cost $2, $3, $3, $4, and $5. Dan only has $9.

1. How much money does Dan have? — $9

2. How much do all five cars cost? — $17

3. Does Dan have enough money to buy all 5 cars? If not, how much more money does he need? — No; $8 more

4. Can Dan buy some of the cars? If so, which ones?
   Possible answer: Yes; the $2, $3, and $4 cars

5. Which cars do you think Dan should buy and why?
   Possible answer: Dan should buy the $4 and $5 car.
   It would be easier to raise a smaller amount of
   money and buy the other 3 cars one at a time.

CRITICAL THINKING

Some of the fastest birds and land animals are listed in the table on the right.

1. Rewrite the list from the fastest to the slowest. Two are done for you.

Animal or bird	Top speed (miles per hour)
Duck hawk	180
Gray fox	40

Animal or bird	Top speed (miles per hour)
Gazelle	50
Hummingbird	60
Jack rabbit	45
Duck hawk	180
Cheetah	70
Golden eagle	120
Gray fox	40

2. How many miles per hour faster is the duck hawk than the golden eagle?

_____

3. How many miles per hour faster is the golden eagle than the hummingbird?

_____

4. A human being can run 20 miles per hour. How much faster can a cheetah run?

_____

Use with
Objective 37
pages 132–133

Focus
Critical Thinking
   Reasoning with Graphs and
   Charts

Overview
Students order information in a
chart on the basis of
magnitude of numbers.

Teaching Suggestions
Make sure students
understand that the chart
shows the top speed of various
animals in miles per hour.
*Questions: Would an animal
that is faster be able to run
more or fewer miles per hour
than an animal that is slower?*
[More] *Which animal on the
chart is the fastest?* [Duck
hawk] *Which animal on the
chart is slowest?* [Gray fox]
Have students complete
Problems 2–4. Ask them to
determine which operation they
should use to find the answers.
[Subtraction]

Point out that the speeds on
the chart are the top speeds of
the animals and that they
cannot travel that fast for long
periods of time.

Extension
Have students research the
animals in the chart and find
other information about them.
You might also have them find
top speeds of other animals
and add these to the table.

NAME _____

CRITICAL THINKING 37

Some of the fastest birds and land animals
are listed in the table on the right.

1. Rewrite the list from the fastest to the
   slowest. Two are done for you.

Animal or bird	Top speed (miles per hour)
Duck hawk	180
Golden eagle	**120**
Cheetah	**70**
Hummingbird	**60**
Gazelle	**50**
Jack rabbit	**45**
Gray fox	40

Animal or bird	Top speed (miles per hour)
Gazelle	50
Hummingbird	60
Jack rabbit	45
Duck hawk	180
Cheetah	70
Golden eagle	120
Gray fox	40

2. How many miles per hour faster
   is the duck hawk than the
   golden eagle?

   <u>60 miles per hour faster</u>

3. How many miles per hour faster
   is the golden eagle than the
   hummingbird?

   <u>60 miles per hour faster</u>

4. A human being can run 20 miles
   per hour. How much faster can a
   cheetah run?

   <u>50 miles per hour faster</u>

VISUAL THINKING

Find the pattern in each row. In the space, write the letter of the next figure in the pattern. Choose from the figures on the right. The first one is done for you.

1. 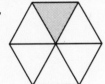   _____c_____

a.

2.  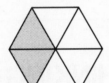 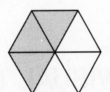 _____

b.

3. 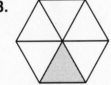  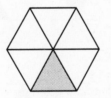 _____

c.

4. 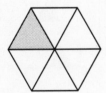 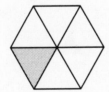 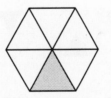 _____

d.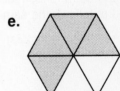

5. 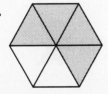 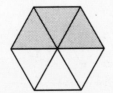 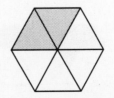 _____

e.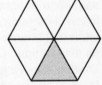

f.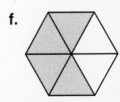

Use with
Objective 38
pages 134–135

Focus
Visual Thinking
  Visual Patterns

Materials
Visual Thinking transparency
  (optional)

Overview
Students recognize the relationships in a *visual pattern* and use this same relationship to complete the pattern.

Teaching Suggestions
Make sure students understand that a visual pattern is a repeating sequence of figures which follow a certain rule. Direct students' attention to Problem 1 as an example. **Question:** *What is the difference between the first and second figures?* [Shading moves to the next section to the right.] Point out that the correct answer, **c,** fits into this pattern.

<u>Alternate Approach:</u> For Problems 2–5, encourage students to describe the pattern in the first three figures, and look for the choice that follows the same pattern.

Extension
Have students draw or describe visual patterns they see around them. For example, tiles, sidewalks, street maps, houses on a block, and so on, may follow visual patterns.

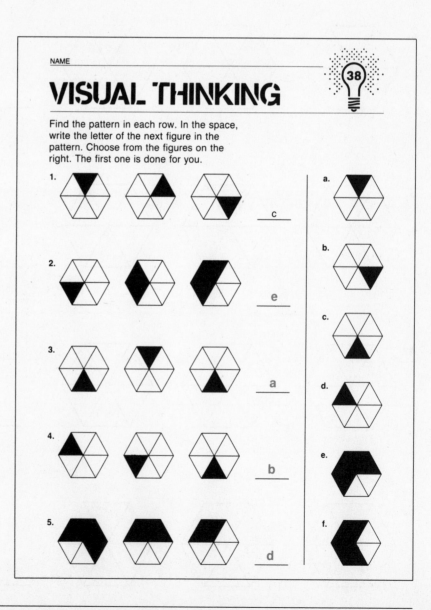

CRITICAL THINKING

Help detective Slim find a secret message by filling in the missing numbers for each exercise below.

1. 4   6   ____   10   ____   14

2. 18   15   12   ____   ____   3

3. 13   ____   9   7   ____   3

4. 25   35   ____   ____   65   75

5. 90   85   80   ____   ____   65

6. 355   345   ____   325   315   ____

7. 850   ____   ____   700   650   600

Now cross out the letter below for each of your answers. The remaining letters spell out the secret message.

12	335	40	15	70	7	11	55	1	6	305
Z	T	N	I	R	C	V	Q	E	B	L

5	45	750	10	16	75	95	330	9	8	800
F	Y	U	W	O	M	R	K	G	A	P

8. Write Detective Slim's secret message in the blank. _____

Teacher Notes

Use with
Objective 39
pages 136–137

Focus
Critical Thinking
  Finding and Using Patterns

Overview
Students recognize the relationships in numerical patterns and use these same relationships to complete the patterns.

Teaching Suggestions
Make sure students understand that each row of numbers in Problems 1–7 forms a number pattern. Each of the consecutive numbers in the row has a certain number either added to or subtracted from it. *Questions: What is the difference between the first two numbers in Problem 1?* [Adding 2] Following this rule, what should the third number be? [8] Tell students to follow this procedure and complete Problem 1. Then have them complete the page independently.

Extension
Ask students to create their own numerical patterns which may be more complicated than those in the activity. Some might like to use more than one operation in a pattern; for example, add 2 to the first number, then subtract 1 from the second number, and so on.

NAME _____

CRITICAL THINKING

Help detective Slim find a secret message by filling in the missing numbers for each exercise below.

1. 4 6 _8_ 10 _12_ 14
2. 18 15 12 _9_ _6_ 3
3. 13 _11_ 9 7 _5_ 3
4. 25 35 _45_ _55_ 65 75
5. 90 85 80 _75_ _70_ 65
6. 355 345 _335_ 325 315 _305_
7. 850 _800_ _750_ 700 650 600

Now cross out the letter below for each of your answers. The remaining letters spell out the secret message.

12	335	40	15	70	7	11	55	1	6	305
X̶	X̶	N	I	X̶	C	X̶	X̶	E	X̶	X̶

5	45	750	10	16	75	95	330	9	8	800
X̶	X̶	X̶	W	O	X̶	R	K	X̶	X̶	X̶

8. Write Detective Slim's secret message in the blank.   ___Nice work___

T39

NAME _____

PROBLEM SOLVING

40

Lisa, Roy, and Edward collect stamps.
One person has 305 stamps, one has
674 stamps, and one has 427 stamps.

1. Which person has the most stamps? _____

2. Who has 369 fewer stamps than Lisa? _____

3. How many stamps does each
   person have?

   Lisa: _____ Edward: _____ Roy: _____

Problem Solving and Critical Thinking/EXPLORING MATHEMATICS © Scott, Foresman and Company/3   Use after pages 138–139.

Use with

Objective 40
pages 138–139

Focus

Problem Solving
 Use Logical Reasoning

Overview

Students *use logical reasoning* to identify how many stamps belong to each of three children.

Teaching Suggestions

Make sure students understand that they must use the information both in the story and in the picture to determine the number of stamps each child has. To complete Problem 1, students need to recognize that since Roy and Edward's stamps together total only slightly more than Lisa's alone, they can reason that she has more stamps than either of the boys. *Questions: How many stamps does Lisa have?* [674] *What must you do to find the number of stamps Edward has?* [Subtract 369 from 674.] Have students complete Problems 2 and 3.

Extension

Questions: What information was most helpful in solving the problems? [Possible answer: Lisa's statement, the number of stamps] *What information was least helpful?* [That Roy has an odd number of stamps] *Why?* [There are two odd numbers.]

PROBLEM SOLVING

Solve the following problems about time. You may use a clock or calendar.

1. Eric goes to bed at 7 o'clock. He thought he had set the alarm for 8 o'clock the next morning. Eric was sleeping for only 1 hour when his alarm rang. Why did it go off so soon?

_____

2. A clock stops running. How many times a day will it show the correct time? _____

3. On December 31 Ginny waved good-bye to her friend Minnie and said, "See you next year!" Ginny saw Minnie the next day. How can this be possible?

_____

Use with

Objective 41
pages 150–153

Focus

Problem Solving
    Use Logical Reasoning

Materials

Demonstration standard clock

Overview

Students use their knowledge of A.M. and P.M. time to solve problems.

Teaching Suggestions

Discuss the concept of A.M. and P.M. with students. *Questions: How many hours are shown on the standard clock face?* [12 hours] *How many times each day must the hour hand go around the clock?* [2 times] Explain that A.M. is used for the hours between midnight and noon, and that P.M. is used for the hours between noon and midnight.

In Problem 1, explain that when Eric went to bed at 7:00 P.M., he set the alarm for 8:00. The next time the hour hand moved to 8:00, it was 8:00 P.M., not 8:00 A.M.

In Problem 2, be sure students understand that a clock shows the same time twice each day—once for A.M. and once for P.M. Use the demonstration clock to show 7:00. Then move the hour hand around the face of the clock twelve times to show the passing of twelve hours. *Question: What time does the clock show after the hour hand has moved around the face of the clock twelve times?* [7:00]

In Problem 3, explain that a new year begins on January 1 of each year.

Extension

Ask students to write three time problems of their own. When students are finished, ask them to exchange papers with a partner. Encourage students to work together to clarify and answer the problems.

NAME _____

PROBLEM SOLVING 41

Solve the following problems about time. You may use a clock or calendar.

1. Eric goes to bed at 7 o'clock. He thought he had set the alarm for 8 o'clock the next morning. Eric was sleeping for only 1 hour when his alarm rang. Why did it go off so soon?

    He did not distinguish between A.M. and P.M. time.

2. A clock stops running. How many times a day will it show the correct time?

    Two times a day

3. On December 31 Ginny waved good-bye to her friend Minnie and said, "See you next year!" Ginny saw Minnie the next day. How can this be possible?

    The next day was January 1 of the next year.

DECISION MAKING

Here is your chance to make up
your very own special month!
Answer the questions below.

1. Which of the 12 months would you most
   like to change?

   _____

2. List three or more things you would like to
   change about this month.

   _____

   _____

3. Which one of the things listed above would
   you most like to change? Why?

   _____

   _____

4. Make up names for 3 new holidays in your
   month. Give the date for each holiday and
   tell what that day celebrates.

Name	Date	Celebrates

Use with
Objective 42
pages 154–155

Focus
Decision Making

Materials
Crayons (optional)
Drawing paper (optional)

Overview
Students use their knowledge of the calendar to make decisions about changing one of the existing months.

Teaching Suggestions
Review the calendar by asking students to identify the days of the week and the months of the year. Discuss students' likes and dislikes for certain months, weeks, and/or days. *Question: In what ways might you change a month, a week, or a day?* [Accept reasonable responses.] Discuss how it might be fun to change the names and rearrange the order of the months and/or days, to have fewer days in a week, and to make new holidays.

Alternate Approach: Work as a group to create a new calendar for the current month. Ask students to provide fun names for the existing month and days of the week, to designate the number of days in each week (and thus in the month), to specify the order of the days in each week, and to create new holidays for the month.

Extension
Suggest that students draw a calendar for their own special month. Display a sample monthly calendar for students. Provide crayons and drawing paper with which students may draw their calendar. After students have made their calendars, list the changes they have made and vote on those changes to determine which ones are the most popular.

NAME _____

DECISION MAKING 42

Here is your chance to make up your very own special month! Answer the questions below.

1. Which of the 12 months would you most like to change?

    Possible answer: February

2. List three or more things you would like to change about this month.

    Possible answers: Change name to Fabulary; add

    days; shorten weeks to 5 days

3. Which one of the things listed above would you most like to change? Why?

    Possible answer: Change name to Fabulary so it

    sounds like a fun month

4. Make up names for 3 new holidays in your month. Give the date for each holiday and tell what that day celebrates.

    Possible answers:

Name	Date	Celebrates
My Day's Eve	Feb. 11	Day before my birthday
My Day	Feb. 12	My birthday
After My Day	Feb. 13	Day after my birthday

CRITICAL THINKING

Art is helping to move items out of the basement. The basement doorway is 32 inches wide and 80 inches high.

1. Art needs to move a desk that is 60 inches long, 37 inches wide, and 29 inches high. Will the desk fit through the doorway? Explain.

2. Art built a doghouse for his dog. It is 30 inches wide, 33 inches long, and 24 inches high. Will the doghouse fit through the doorway? Explain.

3. The doorway of the doghouse is 18 inches high. Art's dog is 20 inches tall. Will he fit through the doorway of the doghouse? Explain.

Teacher Notes

Use with
Objective 43
pages 156–157

Focus
Critical Thinking
  Developing Alternatives

Materials
Bookshelf
Oversized book
Rulers
Scissors

Overview
Students develop alternative approaches for fitting certain objects through openings that appear to be too small.

Teaching Suggestions
Measure the height of the bookshelf and write the measurement on the chalkboard. Then, using a book that is taller than the height of the shelf, measure the height of the oversized book and record its measurement on the board.
Questions: Will the book fit on the shelf? [No] *Can you think of a way that you might be able to fit the book on the shelf?* [Yes, if it is placed flat]

In Problem 1, students may assume that the desk cannot fit through the doorway because it is wider than the doorway. Encourage students to find an alternate solution. *Question: How could you turn the desk so it would fit through the doorway?* [Turn it on its side.]

In Problem 3, remind students that height is measured from head to feet when standing tall.
Question: How might Art's dog be able to fit into his doghouse even though he is taller than the doorway of the doghouse? [The dog can lower his head or crawl through the opening.] Reinforce the point that alternative solutions often can be found for problems.

Extension
Art needs to move a board that is 81 inches long, 81 inches wide, and 1/4 inch thick out of the basement. Ask students if the board will fit through the doorway and have them explain their answers. [Yes; if he tilts the board, it will fit.]

NAME

CRITICAL THINKING

Art is helping to move items out of the basement. The basement doorway is 32 inches wide and 80 inches high.

1. Art needs to move a desk that is 60 inches long, 37 inches wide, and 29 inches high. Will the desk fit through the doorway? Explain.

   Yes; it will have to be turned on its side.

2. Art built a doghouse for his dog. It is 30 inches wide, 33 inches long, and 24 inches high. Will the doghouse fit through the doorway? Explain.

   Yes; it is not as wide as the doorway.

3. The doorway of the doghouse is 18 inches high. Art's dog is 20 inches tall. Will he fit through the doorway of the doghouse? Explain.

   Yes; he will have to lower his head.

VISUAL THINKING

Order the following line segments from shortest to longest. Do not measure the segments. The first one is done for you.

1.

| 2 | 3 | 1 | 4 |

2.

| □ | □ | □ | □ |

3.

| □ | □ | □ | □ |

4.

| □ | □ | □ | □ |

5.

| □ | □ | □ | □ |

Use after pages 158–159.

Use with
Objective 44
pages 158–159

Focus
Visual Thinking
 Visual Patterns

Materials
Visual Thinking transparency
 (optional)

Overview
Students visualize the relationship between given line segments and rank them in order from shortest to longest.

Teaching Suggestions
Draw the following set of lines on the chalkboard:

Ask students to rank the lines in order from shortest to longest. Students should have little difficulty ranking the vertical segments. Then draw the following set of lines on the board:

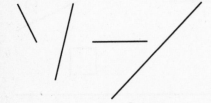

Students may have more difficulty ranking the segments in this set. Explain that it is more difficult to judge the length of segments when they are tilted. Tell students that it may help if they compare two segments at a time.

Questions: Of the first two segments, which one is shorter? [The first segment] *Of the first segment and the third segment, which is shorter?* [The first segment] *Is the first segment shorter than the fourth segment?* [Yes] Encourage students to use the same process to order the three remaining segments.

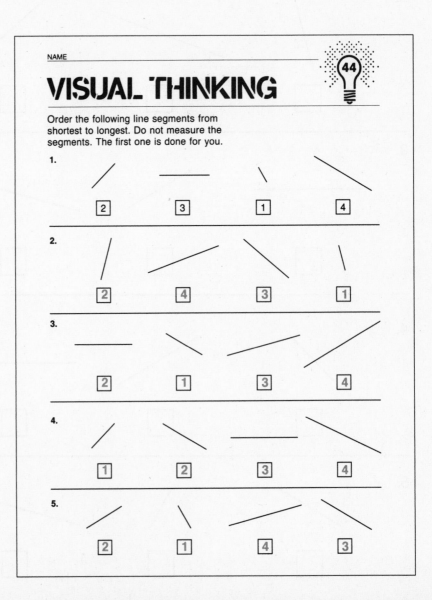

NAME

VISUAL THINKING 44

Order the following line segments from shortest to longest. Do not measure the segments. The first one is done for you.

1.   2   3   1   4

2.   2   4   3   1

3.   2   1   3   4

4.   1   2   3   4

5.   2   1   4   3

PROBLEM SOLVING

Felipe drew a map showing roads for his model cars.

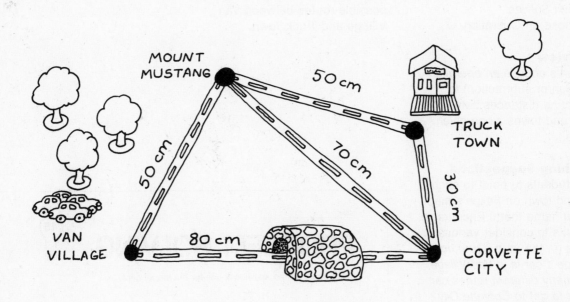

1. What is the shortest distance from Van
   Village to Corvette City by way of Mount
   Mustang? _____

2. How much shorter is it from Van Village to
   Corvette City if a car does not go through
   Mount Mustang? _____

3. How far would a car travel from Van
   Village to Corvette City if it goes through
   Mount Mustang and Truck Town? _____

4. How much shorter is it from Van Village to
   Corvette City if a car does not go through
   Mount Mustang and Truck Town, but goes
   directly there? _____

Use with

Objective 45
pages 160–161

Focus

Problem Solving
  Choose an Operation

Overview

Students *choose an operation* (addition or subtraction) to determine distances between cities and towns along given routes.

Teaching Suggestions

Ask students to point to each city and town on Felipe's map as you name them. Encourage students to consider various routes on the map. *Question: If Felipe's car is in Van Village, how many different routes can it take to get to Corvette City?* [3 routes]

For Problem 1, be sure students see that there are two routes from Van Village to Corvette City that pass through Mount Mustang. *Questions: How would you find out which of the two routes is the shortest?* [Add the distance between each city.] *If you wanted to know how much shorter one route is than another, what would you do?* [Find the distance for each route. Then subtract the shorter distance from the longer to find the difference.]

Extension

Tell students to use Felipe's map to determine the shortest distance between any two places. Note that there are four possible routes between Van Village and Truck Town.

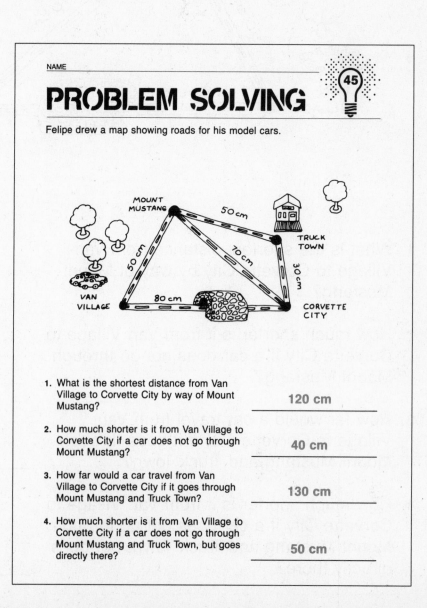

NAME

PROBLEM SOLVING

Felipe drew a map showing roads for his model cars.

1. What is the shortest distance from Van Village to Corvette City by way of Mount Mustang?

   120 cm

2. How much shorter is it from Van Village to Corvette City if a car does not go through Mount Mustang?

   40 cm

3. How far would a car travel from Van Village to Corvette City if it goes through Mount Mustang and Truck Town?

   130 cm

4. How much shorter is it from Van Village to Corvette City if a car does not go through Mount Mustang and Truck Town, but goes directly there?

   50 cm

VISUAL THINKING

Look around your classroom.
Without using a ruler, find 5 items
that are about a meter in length,
5 that are less than a meter, and
5 that are greater than a meter.

	Meter-length	Less than a meter	Greater than a meter
1.			
2.			
3.			
4.			
5.			

6. How did you figure the length of each
   item without measuring?

_____

Use with
Objective 46
pages 164–165

Focus
Visual Thinking
  Spatial Perception

Materials
Meter stick
String
Visual Thinking transparency
  (optional)

Overview
Students observe different classroom objects and categorize them according to length.

Teaching Suggestions
Before students begin the page, display a meter stick for them to observe. Allow time for students to visualize its length and compare it to objects in the room. *Questions: What objects in the classroom are less than a meter in length?* [Accept reasonable responses.] *What objects are greater than a meter in length?* [Accept reasonable responses.] Encourage students to consider only straight-line lengths.

Alternate Approach: Allow students who are having difficulty visualizing the lengths of objects in the classroom to use the meter stick to measure them. If additional meter lengths are needed, cut pieces of string the length of a meter and distribute as needed.

Extension
Play a class guessing game relative to a meter. Ask a student to select an object in the room that is less than a meter in length. Then have other students take turns naming objects in the room that are less than a meter in length. The student who correctly identifies the object goes next. Then play the game using objects that are about a meter in length or greater than a meter.

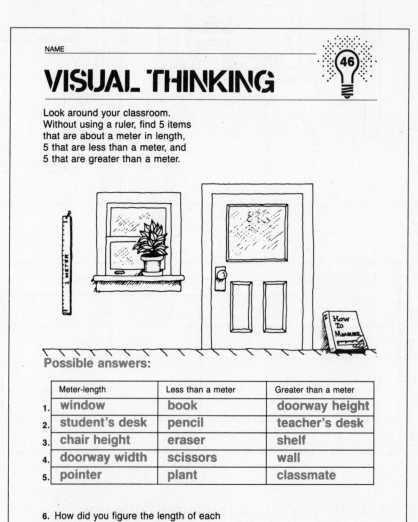

NAME _____

VISUAL THINKING

46

Look around your classroom. Without using a ruler, find 5 items that are about a meter in length, 5 that are less than a meter, and 5 that are greater than a meter.

Possible answers:

	Meter-length	Less than a meter	Greater than a meter
1.	window	book	doorway height
2.	student's desk	pencil	teacher's desk
3.	chair height	eraser	shelf
4.	doorway width	scissors	wall
5.	pointer	plant	classmate

6. How did you figure the length of each item without measuring?

  Possible answer: Estimate

PROBLEM SOLVING

Barbara stacked some blocks in
the shape of a staircase.

1. How many blocks are used in 2 stairs?
   3 stairs? 4 stairs?

   _____

2. Complete the table below to show the
   answers to Problem 1.

Number of stairs	1	2	3	4
Total number of blocks in staircase	1			

3. Find the total number of blocks used
   if the staircase is 5 stairs high.

   _____

4. How many blocks did Barbara use if
   the highest step was 10 blocks high?

   _____

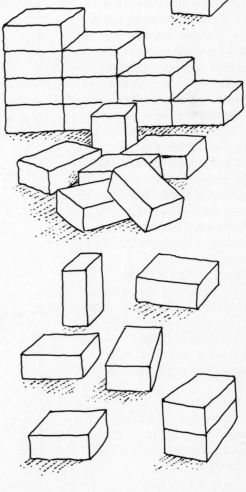

Number of stairs	1	2	3	4	5	6	7	8	9	10
Total number of blocks in staircase	1	3	6	10	15	21	28	36	45	55

+2 +3 +4 +5 +6 +7 +8 +9 +10

Use with
Objective 47
pages 166–167

Focus
Problem Solving
  Make a Table
  Find a Pattern

Overview
Students *make a table* to *find a pattern* for determining the total number of blocks in a staircase built of toy blocks.

Teaching Suggestions
For Problem 1, ask students how they can determine the number of blocks in 2 stairs. Students should suggest that they can count the blocks in the picture, or they can add 1 + 2. Have students use either method to determine the number of blocks in 3 and 4 stairs. Help students *find a pattern* in the table for Problem 2. **Questions:** *How many blocks were added to the number of blocks in 1 stair to make 2 stairs?* [2] *How many blocks were added to the number of blocks in 2 stairs to make 3 stairs?* [3] *How many blocks were added to the number of blocks in 3 stairs to make 4 stairs?* [4]

For Problem 3, have students extend the pattern. **Questions:** *How many blocks do you think will be added to the number of blocks in 4 stairs to make 5 stairs?* [5] *How many blocks will there be then?* [15]

For Problem 4, have students use the pattern to extend the table to 10 stairs like the example in the next column.

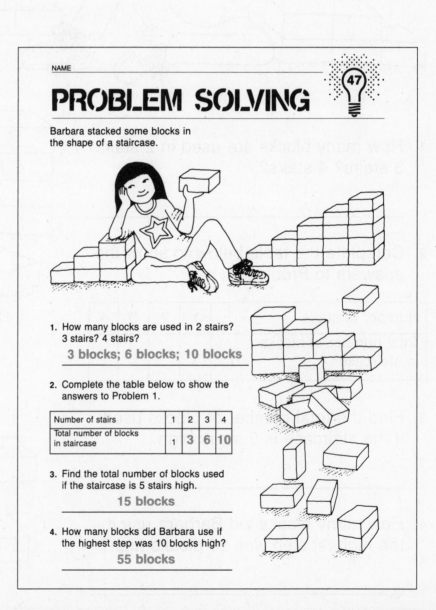

NAME

PROBLEM SOLVING

Barbara stacked some blocks in the shape of a staircase.

1. How many blocks are used in 2 stairs? 3 stairs? 4 stairs?

   3 blocks; 6 blocks; 10 blocks

2. Complete the table below to show the answers to Problem 1.

Number of stairs	1	2	3	4
Total number of blocks in staircase	1	3	6	10

3. Find the total number of blocks used if the staircase is 5 stairs high.

   15 blocks

4. How many blocks did Barbara use if the highest step was 10 blocks high?

   55 blocks

CRITICAL THINKING

Here are a few special rectangles. When you find their perimeters you will see what makes them special.

1.

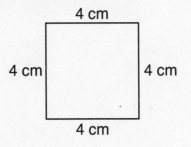

4 cm

4 cm   4 cm

4 cm

_____

2.

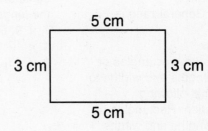

5 cm

3 cm   3 cm

5 cm

_____

3.

6 cm

2 cm   2 cm

6 cm

_____

4.

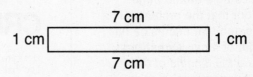

7 cm

1 cm   1 cm

7 cm

_____

5. What is special about the perimeter of the figures above?

_____

6. Use the space below to draw two *different* special rectangles that have perimeters of 12 centimeters.

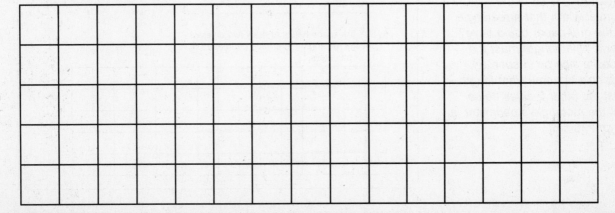

Use with

Objective 48
pages 168–169

Focus

Critical Thinking
   Making Generalizations

Overview

Students study rectangles of different lengths and widths to discover the following generalization: Rectangles of different lengths and widths may have the same perimeter.

Teaching Suggestions

Direct students' attention to the first rectangle on the page. Point out that the rectangle is a square and that each side has a length of 4 cm. *Questions: How are the lengths of the other three rectangles related?* [Each length increases by 1 cm.] *How are their widths related?* [Each width decreases by 1 cm.] *What might you predict about the perimeter of each figure?* [The perimeters are equal.] Ask students to verify their predictions by completing Problems 1 through 4. Then have them complete Problems 5 and 6.

Alternate Approach: Assist students who are having difficulty with Problem 6. *Questions: What is the shortest width that a rectangle on the grid paper could have?* [1 cm] *What length must the opposite side be in such a rectangle?* [1 cm] *What length must the other 2 sides be so that the rectangle's perimeter is 12 cm?* [5 cm]

Extension

Tell students to draw the family of all rectangles having a perimeter of 32 cm. Remind students that only whole centimeters may be used for the lengths and widths. [8 × 8, 7 × 9, 6 × 10, 5 × 11, 4 × 12, 3 × 13, 2 × 14, 1 × 15]

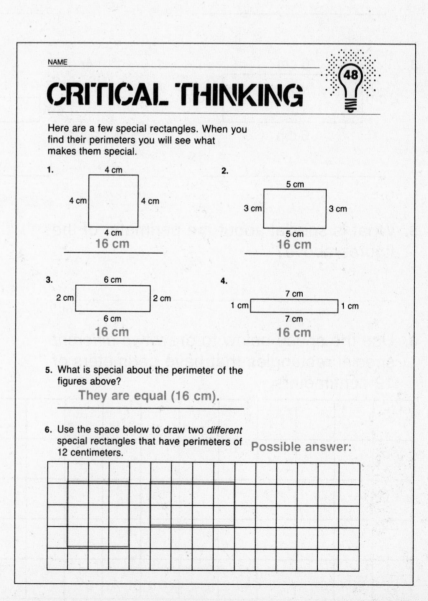

NAME

CRITICAL THINKING 48

Here are a few special rectangles. When you find their perimeters you will see what makes them special.

1.
4 cm
4 cm   4 cm
4 cm
16 cm

2.
5 cm
3 cm   3 cm
5 cm
16 cm

3.
6 cm
2 cm   2 cm
6 cm
16 cm

4.
7 cm
1 cm   1 cm
7 cm
16 cm

5. What is special about the perimeter of the figures above?
   They are equal (16 cm).

6. Use the space below to draw two *different* special rectangles that have perimeters of 12 centimeters.

Possible answer:

CRITICAL THINKING

1. The figures below all have perimeters of 12 centimeters. Find the area of each.

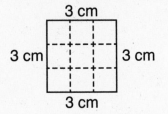

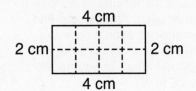

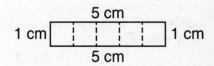

a. _____

b. _____

c. _____

2. What shape is the figure above that has the greatest area?

_____

3. The figures below all have perimeters of 16 centimeters. Find the area of each.

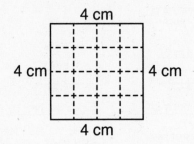

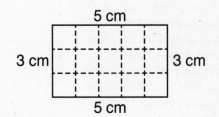

a. _____

b. _____

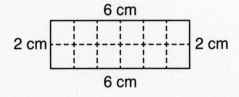

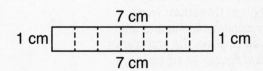

c. _____

d. _____

4. What shape is the figure in Problem 3 that has the greatest area?

_____

5. If a square and a rectangle have the same perimeter, which has the greater area?

_____

Use with
Objective 49
pages 170–171

Focus
Critical Thinking
   Making Generalizations
   Finding/Extending/Using
      Patterns

Overview
Students study rectangles of equal perimeter to discover the following: Although the perimeters may be equal, the square has the largest area.

Teaching Suggestions
This activity is related to the previous one, but does not depend on it. If students have not completed the previous activity, you may want to introduce the present activity in the manner described in the Teaching Suggestions on page T48. Students who have completed the previous activity should be able to complete the present activity without further instruction.

Alternate Approach: If students are having difficulty, remind them that the area of a figure is the number of square centimeters needed to cover the figure. *Question: How many square centimeters are needed to cover the first row of the first figure?* [3 sq cm] Repeat the question for the second and third rows. *Question: How many square centimeters are needed to cover the first figure?* [3 + 3 + 3 = 9 sq cm] Students may use the same strategy for the remaining problems.

Extension
Ask students to solve the following problem. Gene has 100 feet of fencing. He wants to use the fencing to enclose a garden plot. What shape and dimensions should he make the plot so it contains the greatest area? [A square, 25 ft by 25 ft]

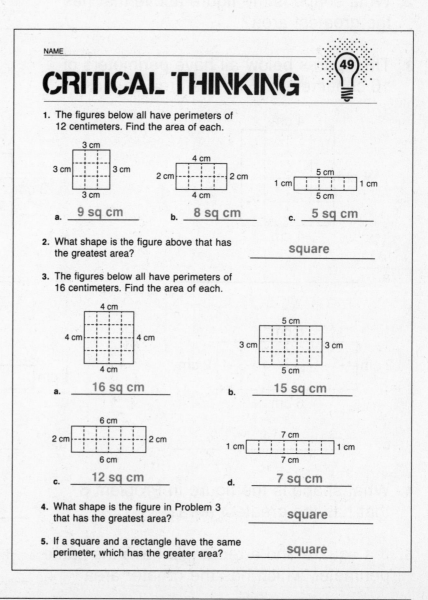

NAME

CRITICAL THINKING
49

1. The figures below all have perimeters of 12 centimeters. Find the area of each.

   3 cm
   3 cm   3 cm
   3 cm
   a. __9 sq cm__

   4 cm
   2 cm 2 cm
   4 cm
   b. __8 sq cm__

   5 cm
   1 cm   1 cm
   5 cm
   c. __5 sq cm__

2. What shape is the figure above that has the greatest area?   __square__

3. The figures below all have perimeters of 16 centimeters. Find the area of each.

   4 cm
   4 cm   4 cm
   4 cm
   a. __16 sq cm__

   5 cm
   3 cm   3 cm
   5 cm
   b. __15 sq cm__

   6 cm
   2 cm   2 cm
   6 cm
   c. __12 sq cm__

   7 cm
   1 cm   1 cm
   7 cm
   d. __7 sq cm__

4. What shape is the figure in Problem 3 that has the greatest area?   __square__

5. If a square and a rectangle have the same perimeter, which has the greater area?   __square__

PROBLEM SOLVING

Answer the following questions to help you find how many 7's are used to number the pages of a 100-page book.

PAGING MR. 7!

I'M MR. 7 – WHY ARE YOU PAGING ME?

MR. 7

16

17

1. What number is on the first page? The last page?

_____

2. How may 7's are used to number page 16? Page 17? Page 77?

_____

3. Use the table at the right to count the number of 7's that were used in each group of pages. How many 7's were used to number all the pages?

_____

4. Use the table to count the number of 6's that were used to number the book. How many were there?

_____

Group of pages	Number of Sevens	Number of Sixes
1– 9		
10–19		
20–29		
30–39		
40–49		
50–59		
60–69		
70–79		
80–89		
90–99		
100		

Use with
Objective 50
pages 172–173

Focus
Problem Solving
Make a Table
Find a Pattern

Overview
Students examine the digits used to write the numbers 1–100 to determine how many 7s are needed.

Teaching Suggestions
For Problem 3, have students complete the table by listing the numbers containing the digit 7 for each group of pages. Students can then count the number of 7s.

Encourage students to complete Problem 4 without listing the numbers.

Questions: Which groups of pages need only one 6 to number? [1–9, 10–19, 20–29, 30–39, 40–49, 50–59, 70–79, 80–89, 90–99] *Which group of pages requires more than one 6 to number?* [60–69]

Extension
Have students find the number of each of the other digits needed to number a 100-page book. [For the digits 2–9, the number needed is the same, 20. Twenty-one 1s are needed, and only eleven 0s are needed.]

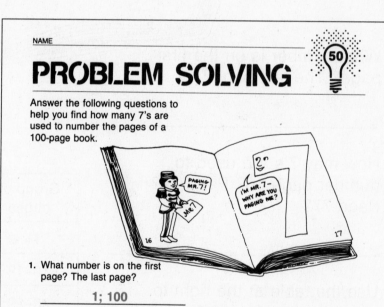

NAME

PROBLEM SOLVING 50

Answer the following questions to help you find how many 7's are used to number the pages of a 100-page book.

1. What number is on the first page? The last page?

    1; 100

2. How may 7's are used to number page 16? Page 17? Page 77?

    0; 1; 2

3. Use the table at the right to count the number of 7's that were used in each group of pages. How many 7's were used to number all the pages?

    20

4. Use the table to count the number of 6's that were used to number the book. How many were there?

    20

Group of pages	Number of Sevens	Number of Sixes
1– 9	1	1
10–19	1	1
20–29	1	1
30–39	1	1
40–49	1	1
50–59	1	1
60–69	1	11
70–79	11	1
80–89	1	1
90–99	1	1
100	0	0

PROBLEM SOLVING

Use the thermometers to help you answer the following questions.

1. On Monday morning, the temperature inside the schoolroom was 20°C. The day got very hot and by noon the temperature had risen 10°C. What was the temperature of the schoolroom at noon?

_____

2. Kimmy's mother is heating water on the stove to make pasta. The water is now 180°F. How many more degrees will the temperature have to rise in order for the water to boil?

_____

3. Manuel's room is 72°F. How many degrees over freezing is this?

_____

4. The temperature outside is 3°C. How many degrees will the temperature have to drop for water to freeze?

_____

5. If the temperature drops from 5°F to -2°F, how far is the drop?

_____

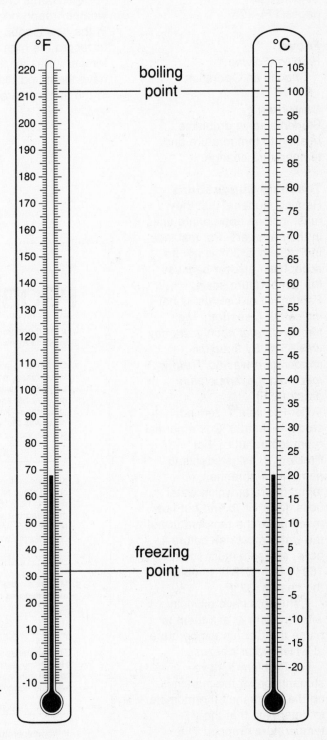

Use with
Objective 51
pages 174–175

Focus
Problem Solving
  Choose an Operation

Overview
Students solve problems relating to temperature and temperature change.

Teaching Suggestions
Remind students that they must include appropriate units in their answers. For instance, in Problem 1, 30° is not an acceptable answer because the temperature scale, Fahrenheit or Celsius, is not indicated. **Question:** *The temperature at noon yesterday was 65°F. By 3 P.M. the temperature was 60°F. How much did the temperature drop?* [5°F]

For Problem 1, remind students that 20°C is a normal room temperature. For Problem 2, ask students to name the Fahrenheit temperature at which water boils. [212°F] To find out how much more the temperature of the water must rise before it boils, students must subtract 180°F from 212°F to obtain the answer, 32°F.

If students have difficulty with Problem 4, ask them to name the Celsius temperature at which water freezes.

For Problem 5, have students count the markings on the Fahrenheit thermometer to determine that the temperature dropped 7°F.

Extension
Have students check the weather report on television or in the newspaper. Ask students to record the high and low temperatures for the day. Then have them find the difference in the temperatures for the day.

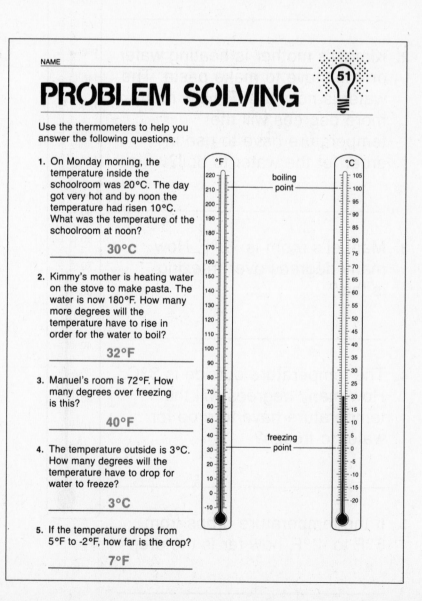

NAME _____

PROBLEM SOLVING
51

Use the thermometers to help you answer the following questions.

1. On Monday morning, the temperature inside the schoolroom was 20°C. The day got very hot and by noon the temperature had risen 10°C. What was the temperature of the schoolroom at noon?

   30°C

2. Kimmy's mother is heating water on the stove to make pasta. The water is now 180°F. How many more degrees will the temperature have to rise in order for the water to boil?

   32°F

3. Manuel's room is 72°F. How many degrees over freezing is this?

   40°F

4. The temperature outside is 3°C. How many degrees will the temperature have to drop for water to freeze?

   3°C

5. If the temperature drops from 5°F to -2°F, how far is the drop?

   7°F

CRITICAL THINKING

Color the shapes at the bottom and side of the page. Then cut them out.

Place the shapes in the squares so that each column and each row has no like colors and no like shapes.

Color in your answer on the grid. There is more than one correct answer.

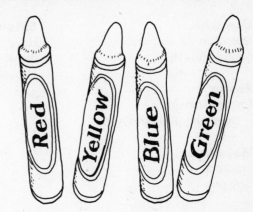

Red Yellow Blue Green

Color red

R   R

R   R

Color yellow

Y   Y

Y   Y

Color green

G   G

G   G

Color blue

B   B

B   B

Use with
Objective 52
pages 186–187

Focus
Critical Thinking
Developing Alternatives

Materials
Scissors
Crayons

Overview
Students arrange shapes according to a rule.

Teaching Suggestions
Have the students color the shapes and cut them out.

You may want to do this activity as a class. If so, make a grid of four rows and four columns on the chalkboard or overhead. Display the cut-out shapes. Have a student volunteer arrange the shapes on the grid so that in each column and each row there are no like colors and no like shapes. Have other students arrange the shapes in alternate ways.

Extension
Have a contest to see who can discover the greatest number of possible arrangements.

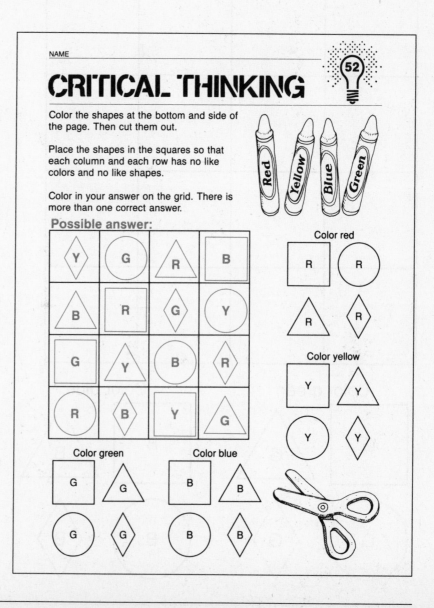

NAME

CRITICAL THINKING

Color the shapes at the bottom and side of the page. Then cut them out.

Place the shapes in the squares so that each column and each row has no like colors and no like shapes.

Color in your answer on the grid. There is more than one correct answer.

Possible answer:

VISUAL THINKING

Karen needs to cut each stack of papers on the dotted lines to make bookmarks. Write the number of bookmarks she will get from each stack of papers.

First, Karen used a stack of 2 sheets.

1.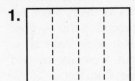

_____

2.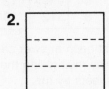

_____

3.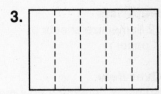

_____

Next, she used a stack of 3 sheets.

4.

_____

5.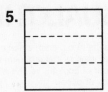

_____

6.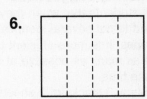

_____

Finally, she used a stack of 4 sheets.

7.

_____

8.

_____

9.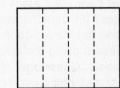

_____

Before Karen cut the 3 sheets on the right, she punched holes in them as shown.

10. How many bookmarks have 1 hole? _____

11. How many bookmarks have 2 holes? _____

12. How many holes are there in all? _____

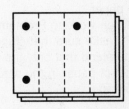

Use after pages 188–191.

Use with
Objective 53
pages 188–191

Focus
Visual Thinking
   Visual Patterns

Materials
12 same-size sheets of
   paper

Overview
Students determine how many
rectangular shapes will result
from cutting apart stacks of
paper.

Teaching Suggestions
Tell students that when they
need to cut several identical
shapes, it is more efficient to
cut as many as possible at the
same time.

   Show 3 stacks of 2 sheets of
paper. **Questions:** *How many
rectangles will we have if we
cut 1 stack into 2 pieces?* [4]
*How many will we have if we
cut 1 stack into 3 pieces?* [6]
*What if we cut 1 stack into 4
pieces?* [8] Demonstrate by
cutting the stacks each time.

   Repeat using 2 stacks of
3 sheets. **Questions:** *How
many rectangles will we have if
we cut this stack into 2 pieces?*
[6] *How many rectangles will
we have if we cut the stack into
4 pieces?* [12]

   Have students predict the
number of pieces that will
result before actually cutting
the paper.

   When working Problems
1–7, make sure that students
understand that only the top
sheet of paper in the stack is
showing.

Alternate Approach: Make a
table to show how many pieces
result from cutting each stack.

Number of pieces cut	Number of sheets		
	2	3	4
2	4	6	8
3	6	9	12
4	8	12	16

Point out that each answer can
be obtained by multiplying the
number of sheets by the
number of pieces cut.

Extension
Have students cut a sheet of
paper in half. Have them form
a stack of two sheets with the
two halves and cut the stack in
half again. Have them put the
four pieces together and cut
this stack in half. Have them
continue this as many times as
they can, recording the number
of pieces after each stack is
cut. [First cut, 2 pieces; second
cut, 4 pieces; third cut,
8 pieces; and so on]

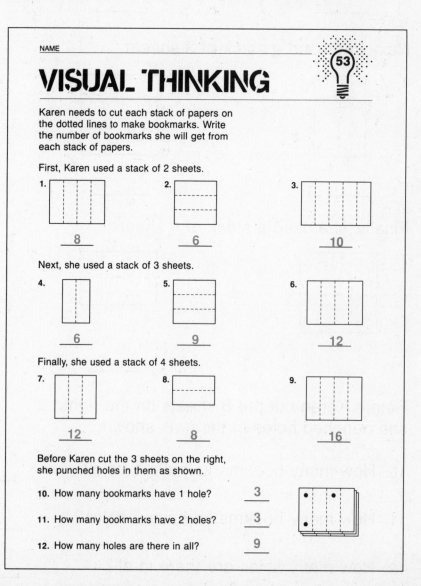

NAME _____

VISUAL THINKING 53

Karen needs to cut each stack of papers on
the dotted lines to make bookmarks. Write
the number of bookmarks she will get from
each stack of papers.

First, Karen used a stack of 2 sheets.

1. ___8___   2. ___6___   3. ___10___

Next, she used a stack of 3 sheets.

4. ___6___   5. ___9___   6. ___12___

Finally, she used a stack of 4 sheets.

7. ___12___   8. ___8___   9. ___16___

Before Karen cut the 3 sheets on the right,
she punched holes in them as shown.

10. How many bookmarks have 1 hole?   ___3___

11. How many bookmarks have 2 holes?   ___3___

12. How many holes are there in all?   ___9___

PROBLEM SOLVING

Brian has 5 chains with 4 links each. He also has 4 loose links. Brian wants the 5 chains and 4 loose links joined into 1 chain of 24 links.

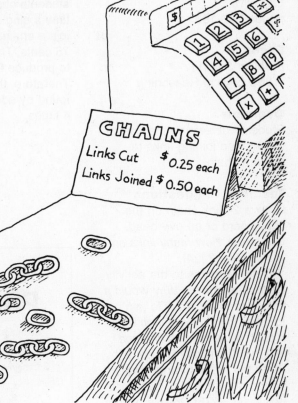

CHAINS
Links Cut $0.25 each
Links Joined $0.50 each

1. How much would it cost to cut one of the loose links and use it to join 2 chains? How many links would be in the new chain?

_____

2. How much would it cost to cut the remaining loose links? How much would it cost to join the remaining 3 chains and the chain made in Problem 1?

_____

3. How many links are in the chain made in Problem 2? What would be the total cost to make the chain?

_____

 Use after pages 192–193.

Use with

Objective 54
pages 192–193

Focus

Problem Solving
  Use Logical Reasoning

Overview

Students determine the cost of cutting and joining links to make a chain.

Teaching Suggestions

Draw a 24-link chain on the chalkboard or an overhead. *Question: How many links are in this chain?* [24]

  Refer students to the activity page. *Questions: Why would a link need to be cut?* [To join it to other links] *How much does it cost to cut a loose link and join it to 2 chains?* [75 cents] Write the problem and solution on the chalkboard or overhead. [25 + 50 = 75] *Draw a picture* of the new chain. *Question: How many links are in this chain?* [9 links]

  Draw 3 chains of 4 links each. *Question: How much will it cost to join these 3 chains and the chain of 9 links?* [$1.50] Point out that the links will be joined in 3 places. *Question: How many links are in the chain?* [24] Be sure that students include the links used to join each chain in solving the problem. *Question: How can we find out the total cost of the chain?* [By adding $0.75 + $0.75 + $1.50; The total cost is $3.00.]

Alternate Approach: Have students observe that each time a single link is used to join a chain, the cost is 75 cents. This is done 4 times to produce the 24-link chain. Therefore, the total cost can be found by adding 75 cents 4 times.

Extension

Have students make up similar problems for a partner to solve. Students' problems should involve larger numbers of chains, links, and cuts.

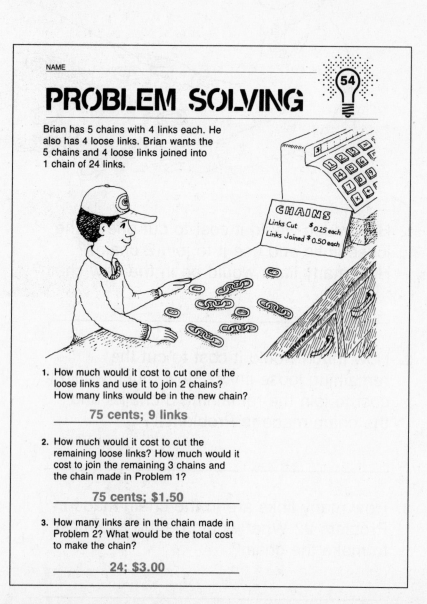

NAME

PROBLEM SOLVING

Brian has 5 chains with 4 links each. He also has 4 loose links. Brian wants the 5 chains and 4 loose links joined into 1 chain of 24 links.

CHAINS
Links Cut $0.25 each
Links Joined $0.50 each

1. How much would it cost to cut one of the loose links and use it to join 2 chains? How many links would be in the new chain?

   75 cents; 9 links

2. How much would it cost to cut the remaining loose links? How much would it cost to join the remaining 3 chains and the chain made in Problem 1?

   75 cents; $1.50

3. How many links are in the chain made in Problem 2? What would be the total cost to make the chain?

   24; $3.00

VISUAL THINKING

The single block on the left has all 6 sides showing. The two blocks on the right have only 5 sides showing, since they are touching on 1 side each. Use these ideas and the pictures to answer the questions.

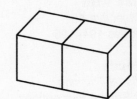

1. How many sides does the middle block have showing? How many sides does each end block have showing?

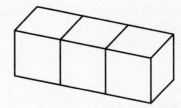

_____

2. How many sides does each block have showing?

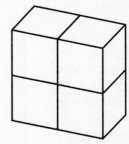

_____

3. How many sides does each block have showing?

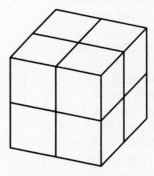

_____

4. How many blocks have 3 sides showing? How many have 2 sides showing?

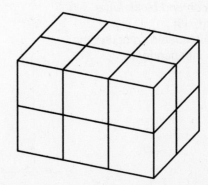

_____

Teacher Notes

Use with
Objective 55
pages 194–195

Focus
Visual Thinking
  Spatial Perception

Materials
12 unit cubes or
  snap-together blocks
Visual Thinking transparency
  (optional)

Overview
Students determine the
number of sides showing on
blocks situated in various
arrangements.

Teaching Suggestions
Hold up a block and ask how
many sides it has. [6] Then put
two blocks together so that one
side of each is touching.
*Question: How many sides of
each block are showing?* [5]
Count the sides with the class.

   For Problem 1, put three
blocks together. *Questions:
How many sides can you see
on the middle block?* [4] *How
many of the middle block's
sides are touching other
blocks?* [2] Point out that the
total number of sides (6) minus
the number of sides touching
other blocks (2) equals the
number of sides that show. (4)
*Question: How many sides
does each end block have
showing?* [5]

   Have students complete the
activity independently.

Alternate Approach: Have
students use cubes or blocks
to help them solve the
problems. If they make models
and put them on a table, make
sure they realize that the side
that is on the table is
considered a side that is
showing because it would
"show" if it were lifted off the
table.

Extension
Ask students how many blocks
they would have to put
together in a row so there are
38 sides showing. [9] Repeat
using different numbers of
blocks.

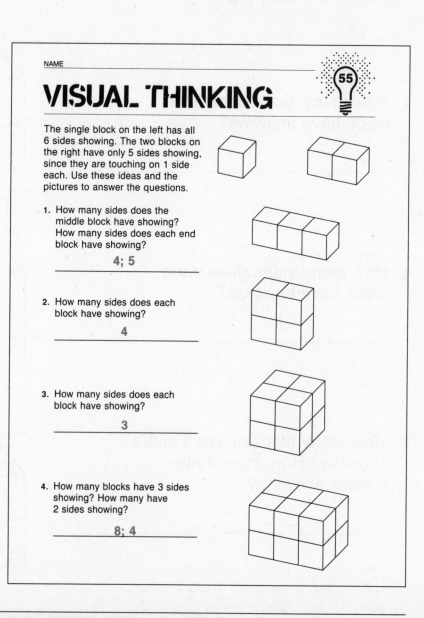

NAME _____

VISUAL THINKING
55

The single block on the left has all
6 sides showing. The two blocks on
the right have only 5 sides showing,
since they are touching on 1 side
each. Use these ideas and the
pictures to answer the questions.

1. How many sides does the
   middle block have showing?
   How many sides does each end
   block have showing?

   _____ 4; 5 _____

2. How many sides does each
   block have showing?

   _____ 4 _____

3. How many sides does each
   block have showing?

   _____ 3 _____

4. How many blocks have 3 sides
   showing? How many have
   2 sides showing?

   _____ 8; 4 _____

56

PROBLEM SOLVING

A colony of penguins has formed 7 groups
on separate pieces of ice. The 7 groups
form a pattern. The first 4 are shown below.

Fill in the table below to find out how many
penguins are in Group 7.

	Group 1	Group 2	Group 3	Group 4	Group 5	Group 6	Group 7
Number of penguins							

1. How many penguins are in Group 7?

_____

2. What pattern did you use to find the
number of penguins in Group 7?

_____

Use after pages 196–197.

Use with
Objective 56
pages 196–197

Focus
Problem Solving
    Make a Table
    Find a Pattern

Overview
Students *make a table* to *find a pattern.*

Teaching Suggestions
Refer students to the picture on the activity page. Tell them that the groups of penguins form a pattern. ***Questions: What pattern is formed by these groups of penguins?*** [The number of the previous group is doubled.] *How might we organize this information?* [By making a table]

Remind students that a table is a good way to organize data. Then have them look at the table. ***Questions: Following the pattern, how many penguins are in Group 5?*** [16] *How many are in Group 6?* [32] Have students complete the table to solve the problems.

Extension
Using the same pattern, have students continue the table to find out how many penguins would be in groups 8, 9, and 10. [128; 256; 512]

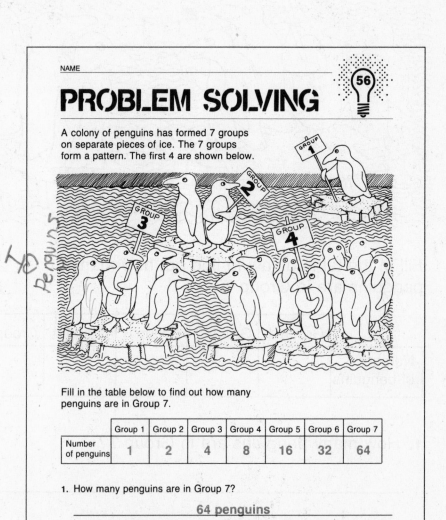

NAME

PROBLEM SOLVING

56

A colony of penguins has formed 7 groups on separate pieces of ice. The 7 groups form a pattern. The first 4 are shown below.

Fill in the table below to find out how many penguins are in Group 7.

	Group 1	Group 2	Group 3	Group 4	Group 5	Group 6	Group 7
Number of penguins	1	2	4	8	16	32	64

1. How many penguins are in Group 7?

    64 penguins

2. What pattern did you use to find the number of penguins in Group 7?

    Double the number of the previous group.

PROBLEM SOLVING

57

Vanessa and Jessica live on the same street 9 blocks from each other. Vanessa left her house and began riding her bike toward Jessica's house. Jessica left her house and began jogging toward Vanessa's house at the same time.

1 BLOCK

Vanessa rides 2 blocks on her bike in the same amount of time that Jessica jogs 1 block. Use the drawing and solve the problems below to find out how many blocks each girl had traveled when they met.

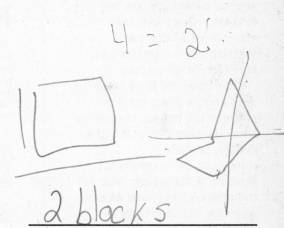

1. How far will Vanessa have ridden after Jessica has jogged 1 block?

   2 blocks

2. After Jessica has jogged 1 block, what is the total blocks traveled by the girls?

   3 blocks

3. After Jessica has jogged 2 blocks, what is the total blocks traveled by the girls?

   6 blocks

4. How many blocks will each girl have traveled when they meet?

   Vanessa: 3 _____   Jessica: 6 _____

Use with
Objective 57
pages 200–201

Focus
Problem Solving
   Draw a Picture

Overview
Students *draw pictures* to solve problems.

Teaching Suggestions
Have students use the drawing at the top of the page and label one house as Jessica's and the other house as Vanessa's.

   After students read the second paragraph, ask the following. *Question: How many times as fast can Vanessa ride as Jessica can jog?* [Two times as fast]

   Then have students move their pencils along the line between the houses in order to show the positions of the girls in each problem.

   Have students complete Problem 4. *Question: Who will have traveled the most blocks when the two girls meet?* [Vanessa]

Alternate Approach: Have students *make a table* to show the relationship of blocks traveled.

Blocks traveled by:				
Jessica	1	2	3	4
Vanessa	2	4	6	8
Total	3	6	9	12

Extension
Have students solve the following problem. Mark is trying to climb a rugged mountain on a very windy day. For each 3 steps he moves forward, he moves 1 step back. At this rate, how many steps will Mark take to end 21 steps ahead of his starting point?
[39 steps]

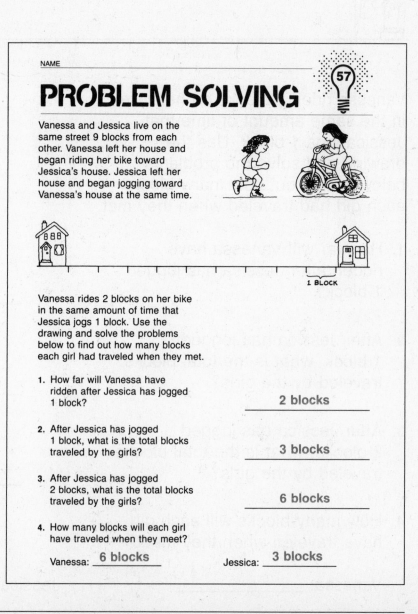

NAME

PROBLEM SOLVING   57

Vanessa and Jessica live on the same street 9 blocks from each other. Vanessa left her house and began riding her bike toward Jessica's house. Jessica left her house and began jogging toward Vanessa's house at the same time.

1 BLOCK

Vanessa rides 2 blocks on her bike in the same amount of time that Jessica jogs 1 block. Use the drawing and solve the problems below to find out how many blocks each girl had traveled when they met.

1. How far will Vanessa have ridden after Jessica has jogged 1 block?   **2 blocks**

2. After Jessica has jogged 1 block, what is the total blocks traveled by the girls?   **3 blocks**

3. After Jessica has jogged 2 blocks, what is the total blocks traveled by the girls?   **6 blocks**

4. How many blocks will each girl have traveled when they meet?

   Vanessa: _____**6 blocks**_____   Jessica: _____**3 blocks**_____

PROBLEM SOLVING

Koko the Clown is putting up a tightrope in the shape of a square. She wants each side to be 9 feet long. She wants a post every 3 feet. Solve the problems below to find out how many posts and how much rope Koko used.

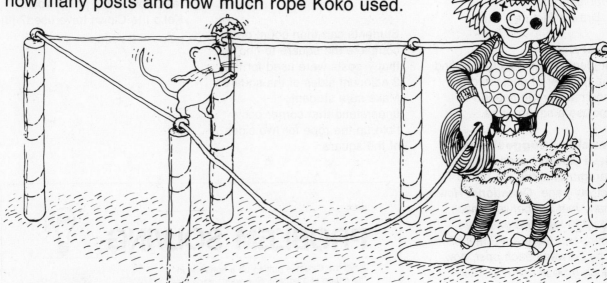

1. How many posts will Koko use for the first 3 feet of rope on a side?

_____

2. How many posts are needed for the first 6 feet of rope on a side?

_____

3. How many feet of rope are held up by 4 posts?

_____

4. How many posts does Koko need for 2 sides of the square that meet?

_____

5. How many posts in all does she need for the square?

_____

6. How much rope does she need for the square?

_____

Use with
Objective 58
pages 202–203

Focus
Problem Solving
  Draw a Picture

Overview
Students *draw a picture* to find the number of posts and the length of a rope needed to enclose a square area.

Teaching Suggestions
Have students read the paragraph at the top of the activity page. *Questions: How many feet are between each post?* [3 feet] *If 3 posts are used, and there are 3 feet of rope between each post, how much rope is used?* [6 feet]

   Explain that sometimes a problem can be easily solved by drawing a picture. Have students *draw a picture* of the rope measuring 3 feet in length. *Question: Since there is a post every 3 feet, how many posts are used?* [2] For Problem 2, students can continue drawing another 3 feet of rope and notice that they have to add only one more post. Continuing in this way, they will find that 4 posts are needed for 9 feet of rope.

   Have students begin to draw the square in Problem 4. Since they know that each side of the square is 9 feet long, and that there is a post every 3 feet, they can draw 3 lengths of 3 feet for each side of the square like the drawing in the next column.

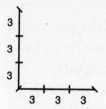

Students can then count or complete the square to find that 7 posts were used for the 2 adjacent sides of the square. Make sure students understand that corner posts hold up the rope for two sides of the square.

Extension
Have students solve the following problem. If the square tightrope were 6 feet on each side, with a post every 3 feet, how many posts would Koko the Clown have used? [8]

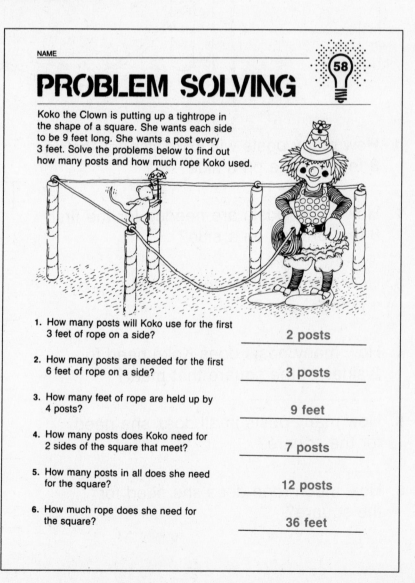

NAME _____

PROBLEM SOLVING

58

Koko the Clown is putting up a tightrope in the shape of a square. She wants each side to be 9 feet long. She wants a post every 3 feet. Solve the problems below to find out how many posts and how much rope Koko used.

1. How many posts will Koko use for the first 3 feet of rope on a side? **2 posts**

2. How many posts are needed for the first 6 feet of rope on a side? **3 posts**

3. How many feet of rope are held up by 4 posts? **9 feet**

4. How many posts does Koko need for 2 sides of the square that meet? **7 posts**

5. How many posts in all does she need for the square? **12 posts**

6. How much rope does she need for the square? **36 feet**

VISUAL THINKING

Think about how to separate the large blocks into 4 groups of 4 squares each, using the shape given. For example, the shape above the block on the right was used to divide it into the 4 outlined groups.

Use the shapes above the blocks to separate them into 4 groups of 4 squares each. Outline or color each group of 4 squares.

shape

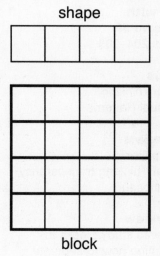

block

1.

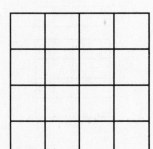

2.

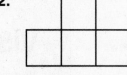

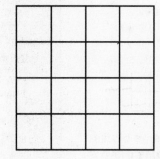

3.

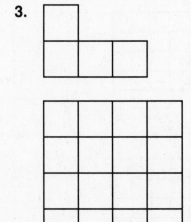

4.

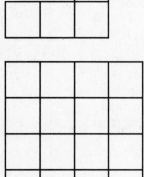

Use with
Objective 59
pages 204–205

Focus
Visual Thinking
   Visual Patterns

Materials
Grid paper
Visual Thinking transparency
   (optional)

Overview
Students study blocks to determine how to separate them into 4 congruent shapes.

Teaching Suggestions
On the chalkboard or an overhead, have students draw shapes that can be made by using 4 squares. Possible answers might include:

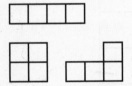

Then draw several large blocks that contain 16 squares. Have students use the 4 square shapes to demonstrate different ways to separate the large block into 4 groups of 4 squares each.

Alternate Approach: Have students use grid paper to cut out 4 congruent shapes like each example on the activity page. Then have them show how to fit the shapes together to make a block.

Extension
Have students show ways to separate blocks of 36 squares into 6 groups of 6 squares each.

NAME _____

VISUAL THINKING

Think about how to separate the large blocks into 4 groups of 4 squares each, using the shape given. For example, the shape above the block on the right was used to divide it into the 4 outlined groups.

shape

Use the shapes above the blocks to separate them into 4 groups of 4 squares each. Outline or color each group of 4 squares.

block

Possible answers:

1.

2.

3.

4.

DECISION MAKING

Ronald, Tyrone, and Sasha are planning a race route for the Kids Run-for-Fun Race. The race must start and finish on the spot marked **X** on the map below.

Use the map below and the following information to plan their route.

- The route should be 14 to 16 blocks.
- The route must pass each of their houses.
- The route cannot cross over itself.
- The route cannot go down any block more than once.

Draw a possible race route that you think they should run.

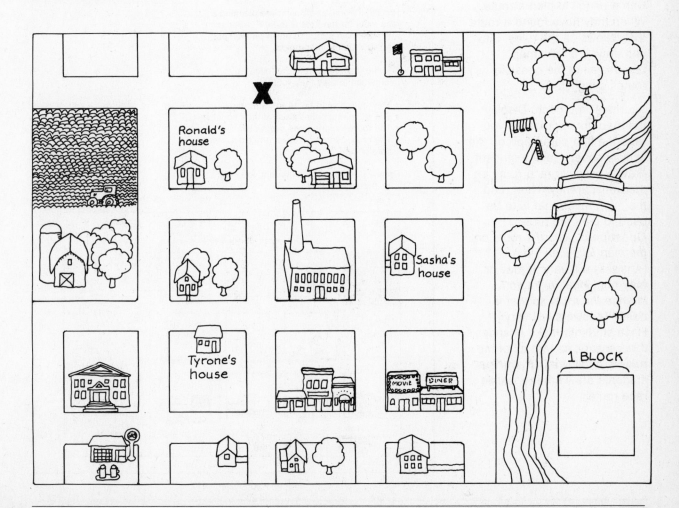

Use with
Objective 60
pages 206–207

Focus
Decision Making

Materials
Overhead transparency of the
map on the activity page
Tracing paper

Overview
Students use information to
determine a possible race
route.

Teaching Suggestions
You might suggest that
students use tracing paper
over the map or draw lightly
with a pencil to plan a route.
When they have found a route
that follows all the rules, they
can draw it on the map.
Discuss all of the possible
routes suggested.

Alternate Approach: Display
the map on a screen as you
read the first paragraph on the
activity sheet. Have a student
draw a possible race route on
the transparency. Then read
the information that is to be
used to plan the route.
*Questions: Does the route on
the map follow all the rules?*
[Answers will vary. It may or
may not.] *How might you
change the route so that it
does?* [Answers will vary.]
Have students make changes,
if necessary, so that all of the
rules are followed. Then have
students draw other possible
race routes.

Extension
Have students draw maps and
write rules to follow in order to
plan a race route. Then have
them exchange their papers
with a partner and draw the
race route described in the
rules.

NAME

DECISION MAKING

Ronald, Tyrone, and Sasha are planning a
race route for the Kids Run-for-Fun Race.
The race must start and finish on the spot
marked **X** on the map below.

Use the map below and the following
information to plan their route.

- The route should be 14 to 16 blocks.
- The route must pass each of their houses.
- The route cannot cross over itself.
- The route cannot go down any block more
  than once.

Draw a possible race route that you think
they should run.
Possible answer:

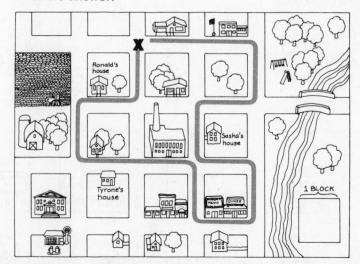

CRITICAL THINKING

The five fastest runners in the School Olympics Race were Leslie, Pat, Lee, Chris, and Cary.

- Leslie finished 4 seconds ahead of Pat.
- Pat finished 1 second behind Chris.
- Cary finished 1 second ahead of Leslie.
- Lee finished 8 seconds behind Cary.

Write the name of each runner on the correct ribbon.

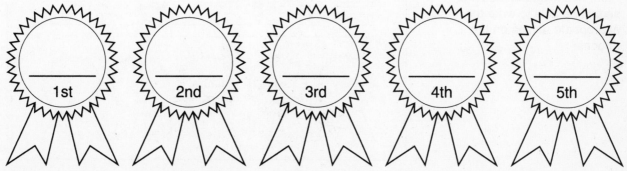

1st   2nd   3rd   4th   5th

Use with

Objective 61
pages 208–209

Focus

Critical Thinking
   Ordering and Sequencing

Overview

Students use information to find the order that runners finish in a race.

Teaching Suggestions

You might do this activity as a class. Draw a line on the chalkboard or overhead transparency and mark off 12 equal segments to represent seconds. Be sure that students understand which end of the line is the front and which end is the back. Write Leslie's name at one of the points. *Questions: Read the first clue. Where should you put Pat's name?* [Behind Leslie's by 4 seconds] *Read the second clue. What does this tell you about Chris's position?* [Chris is between Leslie and Pat, and one second ahead of Pat.] Continue in this way until all of the names are on the line.

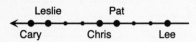

From this diagram, students should be able to write the appropriate names on the ribbons.

Extension

Have students determine how many seconds Cary finished ahead of Pat [5], how many seconds Lee was behind Leslie [7], and how many seconds Chris was ahead of Lee [4].

NAME

CRITICAL THINKING

61

The five fastest runners in the School Olympics Race were Leslie, Pat, Lee, Chris, and Cary.

- Leslie finished 4 seconds ahead of Pat.
- Pat finished 1 second behind Chris.
- Cary finished 1 second ahead of Leslie.
- Lee finished 8 seconds behind Cary.

Write the name of each runner on the correct ribbon.

VISUAL THINKING

62

Count the blocks in each picture. Some blocks are hidden behind others. Picture them when you are counting. There are no empty spaces hidden behind blocks.

1.

_____

2.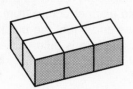

_____

3.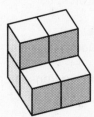

_____

4.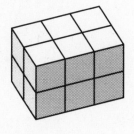

_____

5.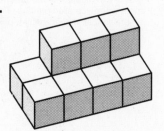

_____

6.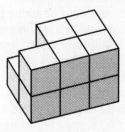

_____

7.

_____

8.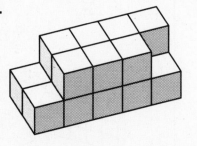

_____

9.

_____

Use after pages 220–221.

Use with
Objective 62
pages 220–221

Focus
Visual Thinking
. Spatial Perception

Materials
24 small blocks for each
 student
Visual Thinking transparency
 (optional)

Overview
Students use *spatial perception*
to count the numbers of blocks
in various arrangements.

Teaching Suggestions
Have a student volunteer take
a "handful" of cubes and
create a structure. Have a
second volunteer describe the
structure (noting such things
as the number of layers and
shape of each layer) and guess
how many cubes were used.
Together, have them check the
answer by counting cubes.
Repeat with other students,
and have them discuss how
they made their guesses.

 Draw one cube on the
chalkboard showing only three
faces.

 Ask students to describe the
part of the cube that is not
showing. Then extend the
drawing to show two cubes,
side-by-side. Have students
discuss the sides that are not
showing.

Alternate Approach: Students
with difficulty visualizing may
make each structure from
cubes and count the blocks as
the structure is built.

Extension
Have students imagine the
blocks were glued together in
pairs as shown on the
chalkboard drawing. Ask them
to think about building each
picture using only "double
blocks." Have students
determine which pictures on
the page could not be built,
and how many "double
blocks" would be required to
build the ones that can be
built.

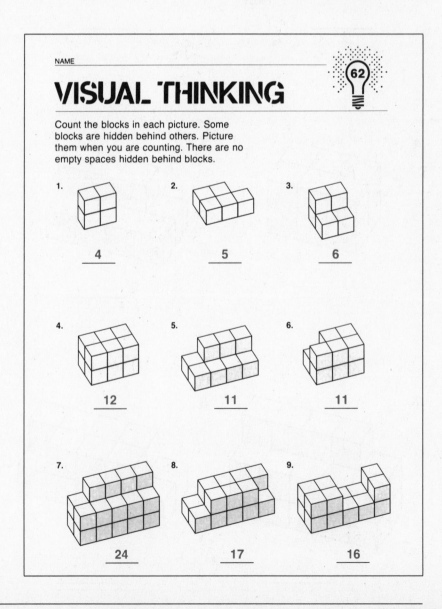

NAME _____

VISUAL THINKING (62)

Count the blocks in each picture. Some
blocks are hidden behind others. Picture
them when you are counting. There are no
empty spaces hidden behind blocks.

1. 4

2. 5

3. 6

4. 12

5. 11

6. 11

7. 24

8. 17

9. 16

PROBLEM SOLVING

Michael is shopping for new school clothes. He would like to make as many outfits as he can from the items of clothing that he buys.

1. How many shirts and how many pairs of pants will he need to make one outfit?

_____

2. If Michael buys 1 shirt and 2 pairs of pants, how many different outfits will he have?

_____

3. Complete the table below to find how many shirts and how many pairs of pants Michael will need to buy to have 12 different outfits.

Number of shirts	Number of pants	Number of outfits
1	1	
1	2	
2	2	
2	3	
2	4	
3		12

4. How many different outfits would you have if you had 2 jackets, 3 shirts, and 4 pairs of pants? (Hint: Notice that you multiplied to get the total number of outfits for the table.)

_____

Teacher Notes

Use with
Objective 63
pages 222–223

Focus
Problem Solving
   Make a Table

Overview
Students find numbers of outfits by combining different numbers of shirts, pants, and jackets.

Teaching Suggestions
Tell students that you are thinking of a shape; either it is a triangle or it is a square. On the chalkboard, draw an equilateral triangle and a square.

Next tell students that the shape is either shaded, dotted, or blank inside. Have volunteers draw the possible shapes on the chalkboard and then describe the possibilities [Shaded triangle, dotted triangle, empty triangle, shaded square, dotted square, empty square].

Have students complete Problems 1 and 2 and describe the outfits [Dotted shirt, plaid pants; dotted shirt, striped pants]. *Question: How many outfits could Michael make if he has 2 shirts and 1 pair of pants?* [2]

As students complete the table in Problem 3, have them describe outfits they can make and discuss how they can be sure they listed all the possibilities. *Question: How else might Michael buy shirts and pants so that he has 12 outfits?* [Possible answers: 2 shirts and 6 pants; 4 shirts and 3 pants]

After Problem 4, have students discuss why there are twice as many outfits when 2 jackets are included [Each jacket can be paired with each of the 12 outfits].

NAME _____

PROBLEM SOLVING

63

Michael is shopping for new school clothes. He would like to make as many outfits as he can from the items of clothing that he buys.

1. How many shirts and how many pairs of pants will he need to make one outfit?

   1 shirt and 1 pair of pants

2. If Michael buys 1 shirt and 2 pairs of pants, how many different outfits will he have?

   2 different outfits

3. Complete the table below to find how many shirts and how many pairs of pants Michael will need to buy to have 12 different outfits.

Number of shirts	Number of pants	Number of outfits
1	1	1
1	2	2
2	2	4
2	3	6
2	4	8
3	4	12

4. How many different outfits would you have if you had 2 jackets, 3 shirts, and 4 pairs of pants? (Hint: Notice that you multiplied to get the total number of outfits for the table.)

   24 different outfits

PROBLEM SOLVING

Janice, Barbara, Lynn, and Margaret each own a cat. The cats' names are Juggles, Bingo, Lovey, and Muff. Each cat's name begins with a letter different from the first letter of its owner's name.

Bingo's owner is one of Margaret's best friends. Janice doesn't know Muff's owner, but she took care of Lynn's cat, Juggles, while Lynn was on vacation.

Look back to the story to solve the problems.

1. Who owns Juggles? _____

2. Can Janice own Muff? _____

3. Can Margaret own Muff? _____

4. Who owns Muff? _____

5. Can Margaret own Bingo? _____

6. Who owns Bingo? _____

7. Who owns which cat?

_____

_____

Use with

Objective 64
pages 224–225

Focus

Problem Solving
Use Logical Reasoning
Make a Table

Overview

Students use and organize information about cats and owners to determine who can or cannot own each cat.

Teaching Suggestions

Have students read the story and describe the situation in their own words. Have them predict what they think they are going to be asked to find [Who owns each cat]. *Question: Do you already know any of the cats' owners?* [Yes, Lynn's cat is Juggles.]

To help students organize their work, suggest that they use a table like the one below. Explain to the students that they can fill in the table using the clues. Write *yes* in the table to show that Lynn owns Juggles. *Questions: Can any of the other children own Juggles?* [No] *Does Lynn own any of the other cats?* [No] Write *no* in the rest of Lynn's row and in the column for Juggles to show this.

CATS				
OWNERS	Juggles	Bingo	Lovey	Muff
Janice	no			
Barbara	no			
Lynn	yes	no	no	no
Margaret	no			

Question: Can Barbara own Bingo? Why? [No; names begin with the same letter.] *What else does that tell you about the owners?* [Margaret does not own Muff and Janice does not own Juggles.]

Continue through the story until the table is complete. Students should note that if a column or row has 3 *no*s, the final entry must be *yes.* If a column or row has 1 *yes,* the other entries must be *no.*

CATS				
OWNERS	Juggles	Bingo	Lovey	Muff
Janice	no	yes	no	no
Barbara	no	no	no	yes
Lynn	yes	no	no	no
Margaret	no	no	yes	no

Extension

For each question on the page, have students identify which statement in the story justifies their answer. Have students discuss how the table helped them organize their findings.

NAME

PROBLEM SOLVING
64

Janice, Barbara, Lynn, and Margaret each own a cat. The cats' names are Juggles, Bingo, Lovey, and Muff. Each cat's name begins with a letter different from the first letter of its owner's name.

Bingo's owner is one of Margaret's best friends. Janice doesn't know Muff's owner, but she took care of Lynn's cat, Juggles, while Lynn was on vacation.

Look back to the story to solve the problems.

1. Who owns Juggles? _____ Lynn
2. Can Janice own Muff? _____ No
3. Can Margaret own Muff? _____ No
4. Who owns Muff? _____ Barbara
5. Can Margaret own Bingo? _____ No
6. Who owns Bingo? _____ Janice
7. Who owns which cat?

Lynn owns Juggles, Janice owns Bingo, Margaret owns Lovey, Barbara owns Muff

CRITICAL THINKING

Read the story below. Use the information to fill in the missing pounds in Tables 1 through 4.

Claire and her cat weigh 51 pounds together. Claire's cat weighs 10 pounds. When Claire holds her cat and Cory's chicken, they weigh 57 pounds together. Cory and his chicken weigh 66 pounds together. Cory and his collie weigh 105 pounds together.

		Pounds
1.	Claire + cat	51
	Cat	10
	Claire	

		Pounds
2.	Claire + cat + chicken	57
	Claire + cat	51
	Chicken	

		Pounds
3.	Cory + Chicken	66
	Chicken	
	Cory	

		Pounds
4.	Cory + Collie	105
	Cory	
	Collie	

Use with
Objective 65
pages 226–227

Focus
Critical Thinking
Using Logic

Overview
Students use information to fill in tables and *use logic* to draw conclusions about weights of children and animals.

Teaching Suggestions
Read through the story together. Have volunteers identify the characters in the story and list them on the chalkboard. Then, for each character, ask students to tell something they know about its weight.

Direct students' attention to the tables. Have a volunteer check the story or the chalkboard to verify each weight that is already filled in. Have them complete Tables 1 and 2. **Questions:** *In Table 3, where will you find the weight of the chicken?* [It is the answer from Table 2.] *In Table 4, where will you find Cory's weight?* [It is the answer from Table 3.]

When students have completed the tables, have a volunteer identify which operation was used to calculate the final weight in each table. [Subtraction] Record the weights on the chalkboard. Have volunteers record the names in order of weight, from lightest to heaviest.

Extension
Make tables and record the information to find the children's weight in this story. Together, Al, Barb, and Carol weigh 150 pounds. Barb, Carol, and Don weigh 140 pounds altogether. If Al weighs 70 pounds and Barb weighs 50 pounds, what are Carol's weight and Don's weight? [Carol weighs 30 pounds and Don weighs 60 pounds.]

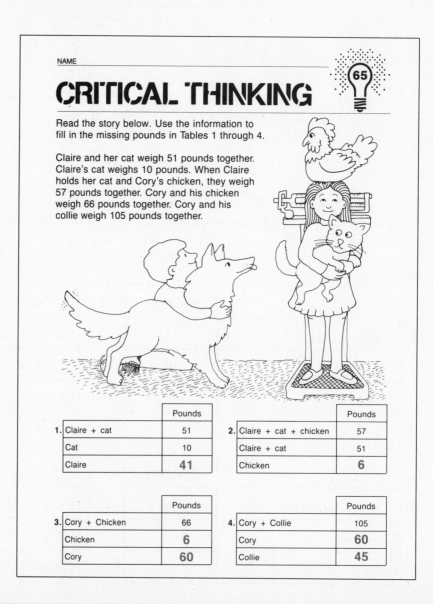

NAME

CRITICAL THINKING 65

Read the story below. Use the information to fill in the missing pounds in Tables 1 through 4.

Claire and her cat weigh 51 pounds together. Claire's cat weighs 10 pounds. When Claire holds her cat and Cory's chicken, they weigh 57 pounds together. Cory and his chicken weigh 66 pounds together. Cory and his collie weigh 105 pounds together.

1.

	Pounds
Claire + cat	51
Cat	10
Claire	41

2.

	Pounds
Claire + cat + chicken	57
Claire + cat	51
Chicken	6

3.

	Pounds
Cory + Chicken	66
Chicken	6
Cory	60

4.

	Pounds
Cory + Collie	105
Cory	60
Collie	45

VISUAL THINKING

An analogy compares two pairs of objects as in the following example.

| a large square | is to | a small square | as | a large circle | is to | a small circle |

Ring the letter of the figure on the right that will correctly complete the analogy on the left.

1. ☐ is to ■ as ◯ is to **?**

   a.   b.   c.   d.

2. ◯ is to ◯ as ⬡ is to **?**
   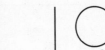
   a.   b.   c.   d.

3. is to as is to **?**

   a.   b.   c.   d.

4. is to as is to **?**

   a.   b.   c.   d.

5. 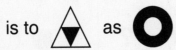 is to as is to **?**

   a.   b.   c.   d.

Use with
Objective 66
pages 230–231

Focus
Visual Thinking
   Visual Patterns

Overview
Students recognize the relationship between two figures of a visual analogy and use this same relationship to complete the analogy.

Teaching Suggestions
Explain that analogies help us discover patterns or relationships. We try to find how two objects are alike and how they are different. Then we show how other objects are alike and different in the same ways. *Questions: In the example, how are the first two objects alike and different?* [They are the same shape, but the second is smaller.] *How are the third and fourth objects related?* [Each is the same shape, but the fourth object is smaller.]

Draw an equilateral triangle on the chalkboard. Ask a student to follow the pattern in the example and draw another figure. They should draw a smaller equilateral triangle.

Have students read the directions and look at a few items. Ask them to explain in their own words what they are to do. [Students must decide how the first two objects are related. They then consider the third object and choose a fourth object—from the ones shown—that is related to the third object in the same way.]

Allow time for students to complete the page. Then have them fold back the page on the vertical line, so that the answers do not show.

For each problem, have a volunteer describe how the second object is related to the first: How the objects are alike and different. Have a second volunteer describe what type of object would compare in the same way with the third object.

Students may unfold their papers to check their responses. Then ask them to identify a reason why each of the other choices would not be correct.

Extension
For each problem, have students add a third pair of objects that follow the given pattern.

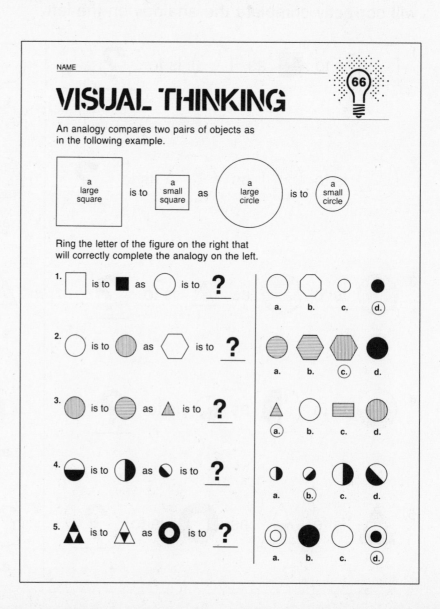

DECISION MAKING

Marlene and Lisa are having a party. They would like to buy a Fun-Time party bag. They cannot decide which bag to choose from the 2 different selections. There will be 25 people at the party.

$15.50

$12.50

Fun-Time Party Bag A	Fun-Time Party Bag B
10 whistles	5 whistles
15 toy cars	7 toy cars
12 balloons	10 balloons
12 mini-books	8 mini-books
8 comic books	10 comic books
_____ Total	_____ Total

1. How many items (if any) would be left over from Bag A if each person received one item? Two items?

2. How many items (if any) would be left over from Bag B if each person received one item? Two items?

3. Marlene and Lisa want to give away any leftover items as prizes. Which bag do you think they should choose? How many prizes should they give away? Explain.

Use with

Objective 67
pages 232–235

Focus

Decision Making

Overview

Given a choice of two sets of small gift items, students decide which set provides enough favors for 25 people at the party and enough leftovers for prizes.

Teaching Suggestions

Have students read the story and describe the situation, including a reason for buying a Fun-Time bag. Ask volunteers to compare the bags item-by-item, using a complete sentence for each statement. For example, Bag A contains two times as many whistles as Bag B. Have students determine the total number of items in each bag and the difference in price.

Have students discuss which items make the best prizes and how they might distribute all the items among the 25 guests.

Allow students time to answer Problems 1 and 2 and to reach a decision in Problem 3. Have several volunteers explain their reasoning for choosing Bag A and have several tell why they chose Bag B.

Students may discuss advantages and disadvantages of having the same favors or prizes for everyone. ***Question: What is the least number of party bags you would need to buy so that every guest had at least one of each item?*** [4 *A*s (to have enough comic books) and 5 *B*s (to have enough whistles)]

Extension

Have students design a Fun-Time Party Bag C. They must determine which items to include, how many of each item, and how much to charge for the entire bag. Have them write a short paragraph giving the reasons for their decisions.

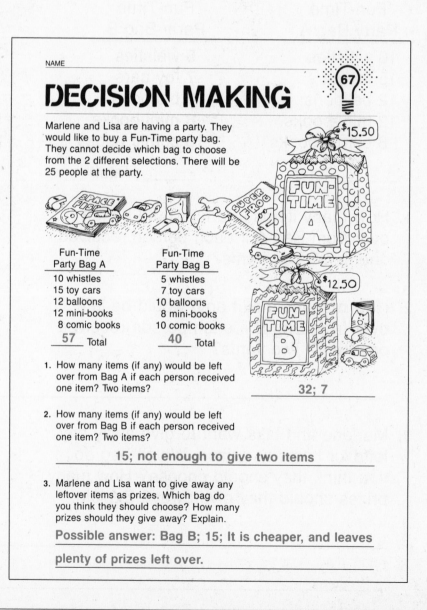

NAME

DECISION MAKING

67

Marlene and Lisa are having a party. They would like to buy a Fun-Time party bag. They cannot decide which bag to choose from the 2 different selections. There will be 25 people at the party.

$15.50

Fun-Time Party Bag A	Fun-Time Party Bag B
10 whistles	5 whistles
15 toy cars	7 toy cars
12 balloons	10 balloons
12 mini-books	8 mini-books
8 comic books	10 comic books
57 Total	40 Total

$12.50

1. How many items (if any) would be left over from Bag A if each person received one item? Two items?

    32; 7

2. How many items (if any) would be left over from Bag B if each person received one item? Two items?

    15; not enough to give two items

3. Marlene and Lisa want to give away any leftover items as prizes. Which bag do you think they should choose? How many prizes should they give away? Explain.

    Possible answer: Bag B; 15; It is cheaper, and leaves

    plenty of prizes left over.

PROBLEM SOLVING

68

Read the story and answer the questions below. Fran the farmer has feed bins for her chickens. By using 1 bin, she can feed 4 chickens.

If 2 bins are put together, as in the picture, she can feed 6 chickens.

1. Complete the table for each number of bins put together.

Number of bins	1	2	3	4		
Number of chickens	4	6				

2. Every time Fran adds a bin, the number of chickens she can feed increases by how many?

_____

3. If 12 bins are put together in a row, how many chickens can Fran feed?

_____

Use with
Objective 68
pages 236–237

Focus
Problem Solving
Make a Table
Find a Pattern

Overview
Students may draw pictures to help them understand how chickens can be arranged for eating. Then they *make a table* and *find a pattern* to solve the problem.

Teaching Suggestions
Draw a square on the chalkboard. Put an X at each side and announce that 4 children are sitting at a play table, 1 on each side.

Then draw a second, separate table and ask how many in all can now be seated. [8] *Questions: Suppose the tables are right next to each other and only one child sits on each side of a square table. How many in all can be seated? Explain.* [6; When the tables are put together, 2 children lose their places.]

Direct students' attention to the story. Have student volunteers draw pictures for 3 bins and for 4 bins, and determine the number that can be fed. [3 bins feed 8; 4 bins feed 10]

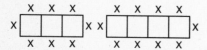

Questions: How many chicks do you predict 5 bins will feed? 6 bins? [12; 14]

For Problem 3, students should notice that the number of chicks increases by 2 for each new bin. Some may notice other relationships: The number of chicks is 2 times the number of bins plus 2 (for the chicks on the ends); or the number of chicks is 2 times the number that is one more than the number of bins.

Extension
Suppose Fran could feed 2 chickens on each side of a bin. How many chickens could she feed if 10 bins were put together in a row? [44] *Draw a picture* or *make a table* to show your results.

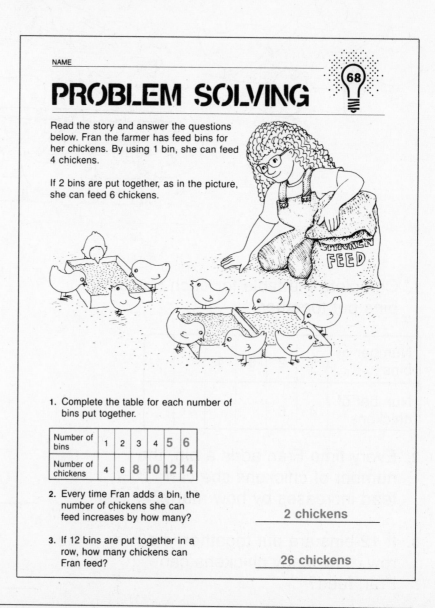

NAME _____

PROBLEM SOLVING

(68)

Read the story and answer the questions below. Fran the farmer has feed bins for her chickens. By using 1 bin, she can feed 4 chickens.

If 2 bins are put together, as in the picture, she can feed 6 chickens.

1. Complete the table for each number of bins put together.

Number of bins	1	2	3	4	5	6
Number of chickens	4	6	8	10	12	14

2. Every time Fran adds a bin, the number of chickens she can feed increases by how many?

_____ 2 chickens

3. If 12 bins are put together in a row, how many chickens can Fran feed?

_____ 26 chickens

VISUAL THINKING

Imagine that you slide one of the two shapes
on the left on top of the other one. Do not
turn or flip the figures. Which figure on the
right will you get? Ring the letter of the answer.

1.

a.   b.   c.   d.

2.

a.   b.   c.   d.

3.

a.   b.   c.   d.

4.

a.   b.   c.   d.

5.

a.   b.   c.   d.

Use with
Objective 69
pages 238–239

Focus
Visual Thinking
  Spatial Perception

Materials
Tracing paper
Visual Thinking transparency
  (optional)

Overview
Students study two shapes to determine which of four figures shows them overlapped on each other.

Teaching Suggestions
Ask two volunteers to draw large, simple shapes, such as circles or rectangles, on the board or overhead projector. Have the other students draw a sketch showing how the two shapes might look if one was put on top of the other in some way. Discuss several of these sketches.

   After students have answered each problem, have them explain their reasoning. Have a volunteer tell why each alternative choice would not be correct. Students may wish to use tracing paper to compare alternatives and resolve disagreements about sizes or orientations of the figures.

Alternate Approach: Trace the simple shapes in each problem on an overhead transparency. Then superimpose these shapes onto the combined figures on the optional overhead transparency to determine if they are correct.

Extension
Have students trace or copy one of the "unused" choices from each problem on the activity sheet to create 5 similar items of their own. On their own paper, have them separate the two shapes and then create their own multiple choice answers. Students may trade papers to try other students' problems.

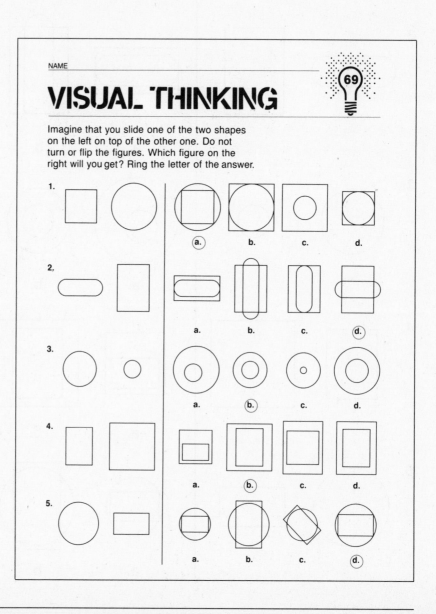

NAME

VISUAL THINKING
69

Imagine that you slide one of the two shapes on the left on top of the other one. Do not turn or flip the figures. Which figure on the right will you get? Ring the letter of the answer.

VISUAL THINKING

Ring the letter of the figure on the right that
matches the figure on the left.

1.

a.　　　　b.　　　　c.　　　　d.

2.

a.　　　　b.　　　　c.　　　　d.

3.

a.　　　　b.　　　　c.　　　　d.

4.

a.　　　　b.　　　　c.　　　　d.

5.

a.　　　　b.　　　　c.　　　　d.

6.

a.　　　　b.　　　　c.　　　　d.

Use with

Objective 70
pages 254–257

Focus

Visual Thinking
  Spatial Perception

Overview

Students compare figures to determine which one is the same as the given figure.

Teaching Suggestions

Encourage students to study each drawing carefully. Point out that in all cases the basic shape of each figure in a row is the same. Have students look for details that make each different from the given figure. Some students will see that some figures are obviously wrong. In so doing, they narrow down the possibilities.

  Question: What should you do first for each problem? [Study the figure on the left.] Encourage students to note the details of lines and shading. *Question: What should you do next?* [Carefully study each of the possible choices.]

  By a combination of eliminating obviously wrong figures and carefully studying the others, students should be able to choose the correct figure in all problems.

Alternate Approach: For some students you may want to do one row together. *Questions: In Problem 1, which choices are obviously wrong?* [Choice **c** has a tree rather than a feather, and choice **d** has no lines on the hat.] *What is different about choice* **a**? [The hat has no band.] *What choice is left?* [Choice **b**] *Is choice* **b** *exactly like the main figure?* [Yes]

Extension

Have students create similar problems. Encourage them to be creative in their designs. Also, have them make some problems more difficult by changing the orientation of the choices.

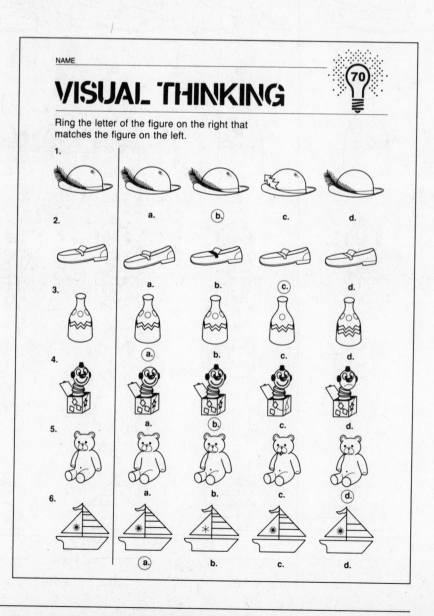

NAME

VISUAL THINKING   70

Ring the letter of the figure on the right that matches the figure on the left.

PROBLEM SOLVING

Mr. Allen's class is making a city picture from paper shapes. The class will make apartment buildings, houses, garages, and cars like those pictured. The students need to find out how many shapes of each kind they need to make each object. Complete the table to show the information the students need to know.

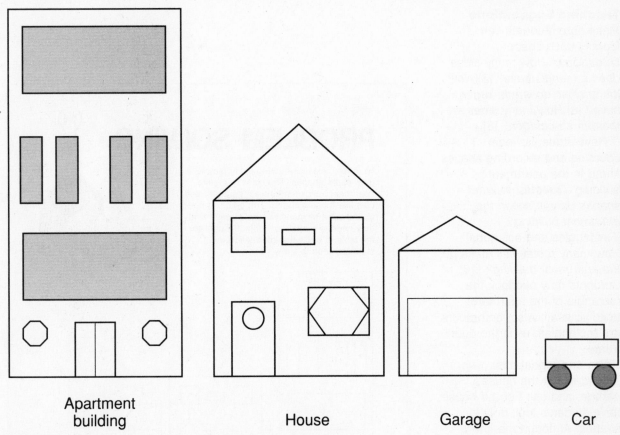

Apartment building   House   Garage   Car

Building	Circles	Squares	Triangles	Rectangles	Hexagons	Octagons
Apartment						
House						
Garage						
Car						

Use with
Objective 71
pages 258–261

Focus
Problem Solving
  Make a Table

Overview
Students *make a table* to organize information.

Teaching Suggestions
Make sure students can identify each shape.
Questions: *How many sides does a triangle have?* [3] *How many sides does a hexagon have?* [6] *How many sides are there in an octagon?* [8]
  Have students begin counting and recording shapes found in the apartment building. **Questions:** *What shapes do you see in the apartment building?* [Rectangles and octagons] *How many rectangles make up the apartment building?* [10; Students may overlook the rectangle of the apartment building itself. Also, both doors are rectangles, as is the door frame.]
  You can repeat this procedure for the house, garage, and car. For the house, have students look only for shapes. Although the lower window of the house could be formed from a rectangle and a hexagon, count it as four triangles, one rectangle, and one hexagon. Remind students that squares are "special" rectangles, and should also be counted as such. Thus, the house has 6 rectangles, 3 of which are squares.

Alternate Approach: For some students you may wish to work through the table in a more orderly way. Start with the apartment building and look for each shape in the order they appear in the table.

Extension
Have students make intricate designs using the six shapes in this activity. Encourage them to put shapes inside other shapes and through other shapes. Have other students count the numbers of each shape.

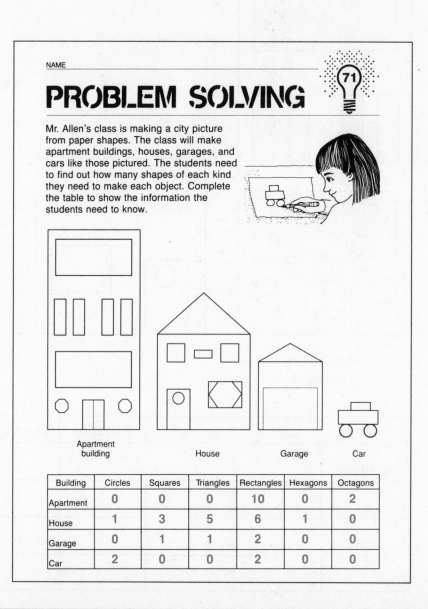

NAME

PROBLEM SOLVING

71

Mr. Allen's class is making a city picture from paper shapes. The class will make apartment buildings, houses, garages, and cars like those pictured. The students need to find out how many shapes of each kind they need to make each object. Complete the table to show the information the students need to know.

Apartment building   House   Garage   Car

Building	Circles	Squares	Triangles	Rectangles	Hexagons	Octagons
Apartment	0	0	0	10	0	2
House	1	3	5	6	1	0
Garage	0	1	1	2	0	0
Car	2	0	0	2	0	0

VISUAL THINKING

Angles that form square corners are called right angles. Sometimes two smaller angles can be put together to form a right angle, like this:

↙ and ∨ gives ↙

Ring the number of each pair of angles that form a right angle when they are put together.

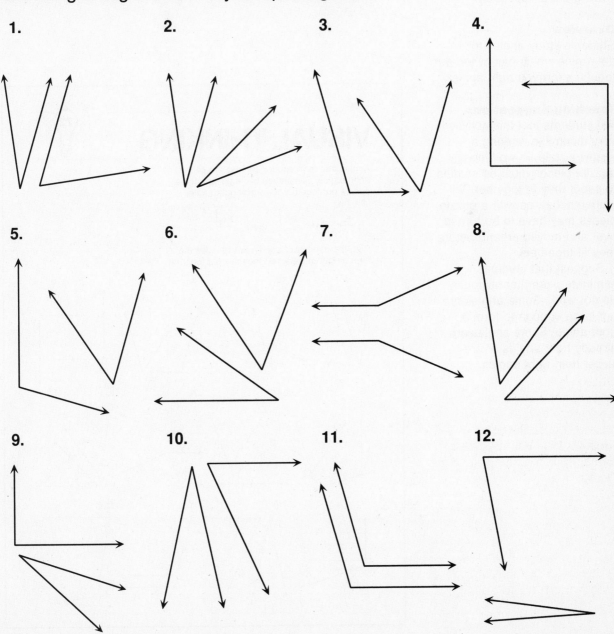

1.   **2.**   **3.**   **4.**

5.   **6.**   **7.**   **8.**

9.   **10.**   **11.**   **12.**

Use with
Objective 72
pages 262–263

Focus
Visual Thinking
    Spatial Perception

Materials
Visual Thinking transparency
    (optional)
Tracing paper (optional)

Overview
Students study angles to determine which pair, when put together, forms a right angle.

Teaching Suggestions
Tell students that this activity is very much like working a jigsaw puzzle. In working a puzzle, pieces must be studied to see if they fit together. Tell students that, as with a puzzle, pieces may have to be turned over and moved around before they fit together.

Suggest that students eliminate pairs that obviously do not work. Some angles are not large enough to form a right angle. Some angles are already right angles or are larger than right angles.

Alternate Approach: Suggest that students trace each pair of angles on tracing paper and cut them out. Then they can put each pair of angles together to see which form right angles. This could be a final step after eliminating the obviously wrong pairs.

Extension
Have students tell about activities they may have done at home that involve putting pieces together to form a whole object. [Possible answers: Doing jigsaw puzzles, building models, and gluing a broken object back together]

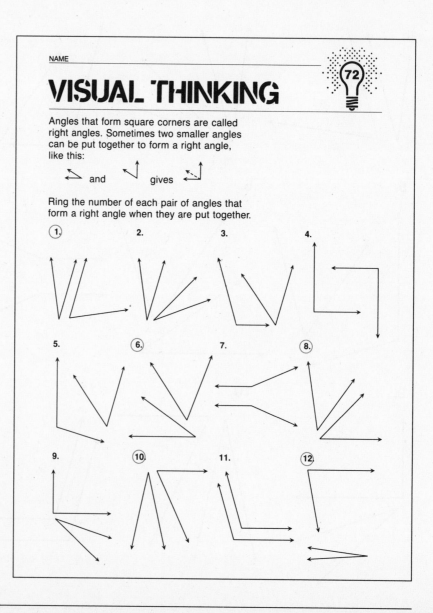

NAME

VISUAL THINKING

72

Angles that form square corners are called right angles. Sometimes two smaller angles can be put together to form a right angle, like this:

and   gives

Ring the number of each pair of angles that form a right angle when they are put together.

1.   2.   3.   4.

5.   6.   7.   8.

9.   10.   11.   12.

PROBLEM SOLVING

Rita Rhodes is driving from her home in
Santa Maria to her job in San Luis.

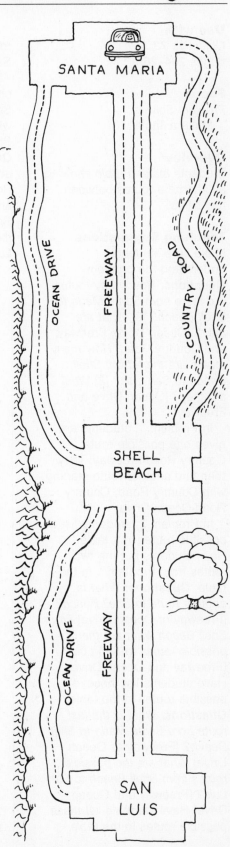

1. One route Rita can take is the Country
Road to Shell Beach and then the
Freeway to San Luis. Name another route
to San Luis taking the Country Road first.

_____

2. Complete the table to list all the different
routes from Santa Maria to San Luis. How
many different routes are there?

Santa Maria to Shell Beach	Shell Beach to San Luis
Country Road	

_____

3. If there was also a Country Road from
Shell Beach to San Luis, how many ways
would there be for Rita Rhodes to drive to
her job?

_____

Use with
Objective 73
pages 264–265

Focus
Problem Solving
Make a Table

Overview
Students *make a table* showing all alternate routes between two cities.

Teaching Suggestions
Make sure students understand the problem. ***Questions:*** *How many routes are there from Santa Maria to Shell Beach?* [3] *What are they?* [Ocean Drive, Freeway, and Country Road] *How many routes are there from Shell Beach to San Luis?* [2] *What are they?* [Ocean Drive and Freeway]

In Problem 1, students are given one possible route, Country Road-Freeway. They then find another route starting with Country Road, Country Road-Ocean Drive.

In Problem 2, students list all possible routes in a table. Have students put the two routes from Problem 1 in the table. ***Questions:*** *What is another route to Shell Beach?* [Freeway or Ocean Drive] *From Shell Beach what are the possible routes to San Luis?* [Freeway and Ocean Drive] Have students list these possible routes in the table. ***Questions:*** *What is the last route from Santa Maria to Shell Beach?* [Freeway or Ocean Drive] *What are the possible routes from Shell Beach to San Luis?* [Freeway and Ocean Drive] Have students list these possible routes in the *table.*

Combining both sets of routes gives 6 routes from Santa Maria to San Luis.

In Problem 3, students must combine each route from Santa Maria to Shell Beach with the Country Road from Shell Beach to San Luis. ***Questions:*** *What routes are added?* [Ocean Drive-Country Road, Freeway-Country Road, and Country Road-Country Road] *How many routes are there from Santa Maria to San Luis?* [3 × 3 = 9]

Extension
Have the students add a third town, Morro Bay, below San Luis on the picture. Have them assume there is one road from San Luis to Morro Bay and ask them how many different routes there are between Santa Maria and Morro Bay. [6] Repeat this question for 2, 3, and 4 roads between San Luis and Morro Bay. [2 roads: 12 routes; 3 roads: 18 routes; 4 roads: 24 routes]

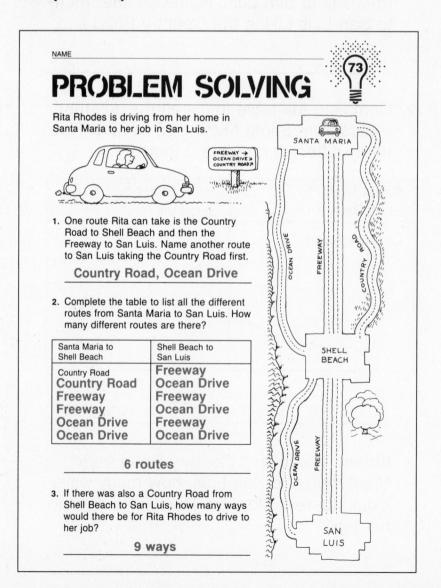

NAME

PROBLEM SOLVING 73

Rita Rhodes is driving from her home in Santa Maria to her job in San Luis.

FREEWAY →
OCEAN DRIVE →
COUNTRY ROAD ↗

1. One route Rita can take is the Country Road to Shell Beach and then the Freeway to San Luis. Name another route to San Luis taking the Country Road first.

Country Road, Ocean Drive

2. Complete the table to list all the different routes from Santa Maria to San Luis. How many different routes are there?

Santa Maria to Shell Beach	Shell Beach to San Luis
Country Road	Freeway
Country Road	Ocean Drive
Freeway	Freeway
Freeway	Ocean Drive
Ocean Drive	Freeway
Ocean Drive	Ocean Drive

_____ **6 routes**

3. If there was also a Country Road from Shell Beach to San Luis, how many ways would there be for Rita Rhodes to drive to her job?

_____ **9 ways**

CRITICAL THINKING

74

Kenji, Sara, Steve, and Maria are making a mobile. For the mobile they will cut out a circle, a square, a triangle, and a rectangle. Each of them will cut out one shape for the mobile. Kenji must decide who will cut out each shape. Kenji knows the following facts.

- Sara cuts triangles well.
- Steve cuts long straight lines best.
- Maria cuts nice rounded curves.
- Kenji can cut all kinds of shapes.

On each shape, write the name of the person who should cut it out.

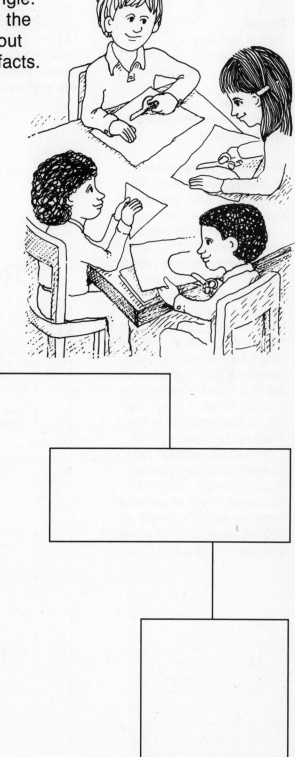

Use with
Objective 74
pages 266–267

Focus
Critical Thinking
    Using Logic
    Classifying and Sorting

Overview
Students assign tasks based on known skills.

Teaching Suggestions
Students must analyze the strengths of each person. *Question: Since Sara cuts triangles well, which shape should she cut out?* [Triangle] *Since Maria cuts nice rounded curves, which shape should she cut out?* [Circle] *If Steve cuts long straight lines best, which shapes could he cut out?* [Rectangle, square, or triangle] *Since Sara should cut out the triangle, which shape should Steve cut out?* [Rectangle or square] Some students may assign the rectangle to Steve since he cuts long straight lines well. *Questions: What shapes could Kenji cut out?* [Circle, triangle, square, or rectangle] *Which shape should Kenji cut out?* [Rectangle or square, depending on which one Steve cuts out]

Extension
Have students discuss other situations in which decisions can be made based on the skills of individuals. [Possible answers: Hiring a person for a job, choosing members for a sports team, assigning tasks for a group project]

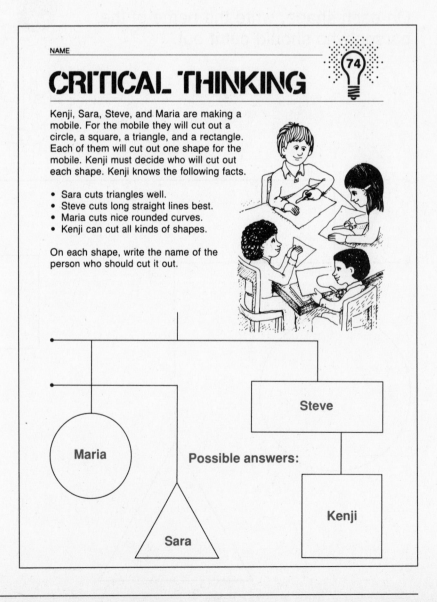

NAME _____

CRITICAL THINKING 74

Kenji, Sara, Steve, and Maria are making a mobile. For the mobile they will cut out a circle, a square, a triangle, and a rectangle. Each of them will cut out one shape for the mobile. Kenji must decide who will cut out each shape. Kenji knows the following facts.

- Sara cuts triangles well.
- Steve cuts long straight lines best.
- Maria cuts nice rounded curves.
- Kenji can cut all kinds of shapes.

On each shape, write the name of the person who should cut it out.

Steve

Possible answers:

Maria

Kenji

Sara

CRITICAL THINKING

75

Mr. Omaki's class is setting up a classroom library. Each student has looked at the books, and the class has made some notes about the books.

1. Help Mr. Omaki's class sort their books. Below each book, write FT if a book is a fairy tale, AN if a book is about animals, AD if a book is an adventure, and MY if a book is a mystery.

2. Draw an X over each note about the books that is not correct.

3. How many of each type of book are there in the classroom library?

FT: _____ AN: _____

AD: _____ MY: _____

Notes about our books.
1. Most of the books are fairy tales.
2. There are no books about animals.
3. All of the adventure books are about boys
4. The fewest books are mystery books
5. There are no books about girls.

_____

_____

_____

_____

_____

_____

_____

_____

_____

_____

_____

_____

Use with
Objective 75
pages 270–271

Focus
Critical Thinking
 Classifying and Sorting

Overview
Students *classify* books based on their content.

Teaching Suggestions
Discuss the importance of *classifying* books. **Question: *What are some advantages of classifying books?*** [It gives a basis for organizing books on shelves and makes finding a certain type of book easier.] Make sure students understand the four book classifications used in the activity. **Question: *How can you decide which type each book is?*** [The title indicates what the book is about and thus how to classify it.]

 For Problem 2, students must determine the number of books in each classification and use titles to make additional assumptions about the contents of some books. **Questions: *For Note 3, how do you know the adventure books are about boys?*** [All the adventure book titles contain boys' names.] *Are there any books about girls?* [Yes, *Cinderella* and *Juanita's Mysterious Message*] *How do you know?* [Juanita is a girl's name; Cinderella was a girl.]

Extension
Have students find out how books are classified in their school library or their local public library. Have them learn about the Dewey decimal system, which classifies books by subjects.

 Have students discuss other objects that are often classified, such as newspaper classified ads, and living organisms.

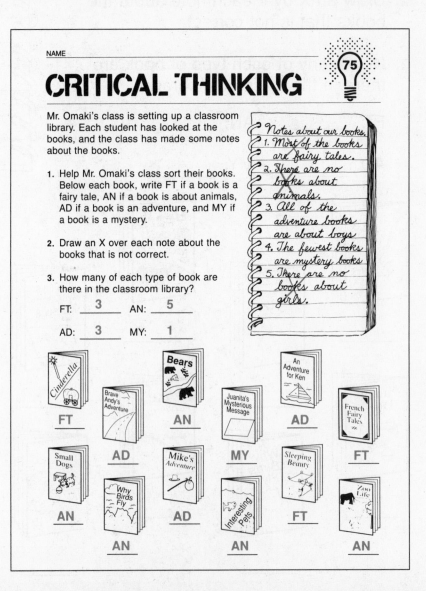

NAME

CRITICAL THINKING
75

Mr. Omaki's class is setting up a classroom library. Each student has looked at the books, and the class has made some notes about the books.

1. Help Mr. Omaki's class sort their books. Below each book, write FT if a book is a fairy tale, AN if a book is about animals, AD if a book is an adventure, and MY if a book is a mystery.

2. Draw an X over each note about the books that is not correct.

3. How many of each type of book are there in the classroom library?

FT: __3__ AN: __5__

AD: __3__ MY: __1__

Notes about our books.
1. *Most of the books are fairy tales.*
2. *There are no books about animals.*
3. *All of the adventure books are about boys.*
4. *The fewest books are mystery books*
5. *There are no books about girls.*

Cinderella — **FT**
Brave Andy's Adventure — **AD**
Bears — **AN**
Juanita's Mysterious Message — **MY**
An Adventure for Ken — **AD**
French Fairy Tales — **FT**
Small Dogs — **AN**
Why Birds Fly — **AN**
Mike's Adventure — **AD**
Interesting Pets — **AN**
Sleeping Beauty — **FT**
Zoo Life — **AN**

PROBLEM SOLVING

76

Jamie's little brother, Paulo, built a tower of blocks. There were 10 layers of blocks in the tower. Paulo used 40 blocks to build the tower. Use the information below to find out how many blocks were in each layer. Then write the number of blocks on each layer of the tower.

- Every layer has more than one block.
- Pairs of layers have the same number of blocks as shown in the diagram below.
- Layers I and J (at the bottom) have six blocks each.

Layer A
Layer B
Layer C
Layer D
Layer E
Layer F
Layer G
Layer H
Layer I
Layer J

Use with
Objective 76
pages 272–273

Focus
Problem Solving
   Use Logical Reasoning

Overview
Students determine the number of blocks in each layer of a tower using information about the layers.

Teaching Suggestions
Make sure students understand the information given in the paragraph and in the clues. *Questions: How many blocks are in each of layers I and J?* [6] *What does the diagram indicate about the blocks in layers G and H?* [They have the same number of blocks and they have fewer blocks than layers I and J.] *What relationship do you see about each pair of layers?* [Each pair has fewer blocks than the pair below it.] *How many blocks did Paulo use in all?* [40] With this information, students can *use logical reasoning* to determine the number of blocks in each layer.

Extension
Have students determine other possible arrangements of the 40 blocks in 10 layers without the conditions given and the arrangement shown.

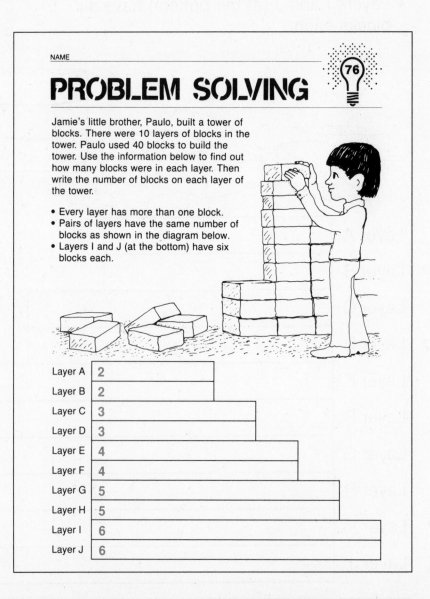

NAME _____

PROBLEM SOLVING   76

Jamie's little brother, Paulo, built a tower of blocks. There were 10 layers of blocks in the tower. Paulo used 40 blocks to build the tower. Use the information below to find out how many blocks were in each layer. Then write the number of blocks on each layer of the tower.

- Every layer has more than one block.
- Pairs of layers have the same number of blocks as shown in the diagram below.
- Layers I and J (at the bottom) have six blocks each.

Layer A	2
Layer B	2
Layer C	3
Layer D	3
Layer E	4
Layer F	4
Layer G	5
Layer H	5
Layer I	6
Layer J	6

NAME _____

DECISION MAKING

Glenda is getting ready for her Friends' Club meeting. She is going to bring something to drink. Each club member signed up for what he or she wanted to drink. She took this sign-up sheet to the store.

At the store, Glenda found that drinks were on sale. Each drink comes in packages according to this sign.

Sign-up Sheet

Raul – Milk
Steve – Apple juice or orange juice
Maria – Orange juice
Glenda – Apple juice
Shari ~ Orange juice
Sam – Milk or apple juice
Beth – Orange juice
Michael – Apple juice or Orange juice

SALE!   SALE!

Milk	Apple Juice	Orange Juice
1-pack	2-pack	4-pack
	3-pack	

SAVE SAVE SAVE SAVE

1. If you were Glenda, how many sale packs of each drink would you buy?

   Milk: _____

   Apple Juice: _____

   Orange Juice: _____

2. Complete the table to show who would get each kind of drink.

	Milk	Apple Juice	Orange Juice
Club Members			

Use with
Objective 77
pages 274–275

Focus
Decision Making

Overview
Students organize given information to determine a combination of items which will satisfy specific requirements.

Teaching Suggestions
To make the given information easier to see, encourage students to organize it in a table. They might list, under each drink, the names of the persons requesting it and highlight the names of persons making only one choice.

Milk	Apple	Orange
Sam RAUL	Sam Steve Michael GLENDA	Steve Michael MARIA SHARI BETH

Questions: What milk packs could be purchased? [Either one 1-pack if someone had another drink, or two 1-packs] *Since four people are listed under apple juice, what packs could be purchased for them?* [Two 2-packs; one 3-pack if one person had another drink; one 2-pack if two people had another drink] *Could Glenda buy two 2-packs of apple juice?* [No, this choice would leave only three people under orange juice.]

Since five people could drink orange juice, what should be purchased? [One 4-pack with one person having another drink] Either Steve or Michael will get orange juice. The other will get apple juice.

Based on their choices, have students fill in the table in Problem 2. Another possible answer is 1-pack milk (Raul), 3-pack apple juice (Glenda, Steve, Sam), and 4-pack orange juice (Maria, Shari, Beth, Michael).

Extension
Have students assign prices for each of the drink packs. Then determine which packs to purchase in order to spend the lowest possible amount and still give everyone their choices.

NAME _____

DECISION MAKING

77

Glenda is getting ready for her Friends' Club meeting. She is going to bring something to drink. Each club member signed up for what he or she wanted to drink. She took this sign-up sheet to the store.

Sign-up Sheet
Raul – Milk
Steve – Apple juice or orange juice
Maria – Orange juice
Glenda – Apple juice
Shari – Orange juice
Sam – Milk or apple juice
Beth – Orange juice
Michael – Apple juice or orange juice

At the store, Glenda found that drinks were on sale. Each drink comes in packages according to this sign.

SALE! SALE!

| Milk 1-pack | Apple Juice 2-pack 3-pack | Orange Juice 4-pack |

SAVE SAVE SAVE SAVE

Possible answer:

1. If you were Glenda, how many sale packs of each drink would you buy?

Milk: _____ two 1-packs _____

Apple Juice: _____ one 2-pack _____

Orange Juice: _____ one 4-pack _____

2. Complete the table to show who would get each kind of drink.

	Milk	Apple Juice	Orange Juice
Club Members	Raul Sam	Glenda Michael	Maria Shari Beth Steve

CRITICAL THINKING

Dan wrote a letter to his grandmother in England about the first time he washed his dog Willy. Dan knows that the metric system is used in England, and he wanted to show his grandmother how good he was at metric measurement. Since he wanted to check the spellings, he left blanks for the metric units.

Help Dan finish the letter by writing in the correct metric unit for each amount. Choose milliliters, liters, centimeters, or meters.

Dear Grandma,

    I gave my dog, Willy, a bath yesterday.
He did not want a bath, so I had to run about
15 _____ before I caught him. Then I put
his 100 _____ dog leash on him and hooked
it to his doghouse.

    I filled the washtub with 15 buckets of water.
Each bucket held 2 _____, so the tub held
30 _____ of water. Then I added a small amount,
only 12 _____ of "Sudsy Pup" soap.

    When I put Willy in the tub, he splashed out most
of the water, so I put in 20 _____ more. Finally
he was clean and dry! Then we both had a big
200 _____ drink of water after
Willy's bath was over.

                    Love,
                    Dan

Use with
Objective 78
pages 276–277

Focus
Critical Thinking
   Using Number Sense

Overview
Students determine which metric units to use to describe given quantities.

Teaching Suggestions
Review the metric units given with students. *Questions: Which of the units are for measuring length?* [Centimeter and meter] *Which length unit is longer?* [A meter is longer than a centimeter.] *How many centimeters are in one meter?* [100] *Which units are for measuring volume?* [Milliliter and liter] *How many milliliters make 1 liter?* [1,000]

   To correctly fill in the blanks in the letter, students must determine which type of measurement is being made and the unit to use for the amount indicated.

Alternate Approach: If students have difficulty determining which units to use, guide them through the letter. *Questions: What is being measured in the sentence with the first blank?* [Distance Dan ran] *Which unit is used to measure how far a person runs?* [Meter] Guide students similarly to fill in the remaining blanks in the letter.

Extension
Have students write stories that contain measuring mistakes. Mistakes could be with the amounts, units, or both for a given measurement. Have students exchange stories and find and correct the mistakes.

NAME _____

CRITICAL THINKING

Dan wrote a letter to his grandmother in England about the first time he washed his dog Willy. Dan knows that the metric system is used in England, and he wanted to show his grandmother how good he was at metric measurement. Since he wanted to check the spellings, he left blanks for the metric units.

Help Dan finish the letter by writing in the correct metric unit for each amount. Choose milliliters, liters, centimeters, or meters.

Dear Grandma,
   I gave my dog, Willy, a bath yesterday.
He did not want a bath, so I had to run about
15 __meters__ before I caught him. Then I put
his 100 __centimeter__ dog leash on him and hooked
it to his doghouse.
   I filled the washtub with 15 buckets of water.
Each bucket held 2 __liters__, so the tub held
30 __liters__ of water. Then I added a small amount,
only 12 __milliliters__ of "Sudsy Pup" soap.
   When I put Willy in the tub, he splashed out most
of the water, so I put in 20 __liters__ more. Finally
he was clean and dry! Then we both had a big
200 __milliliter__ drink of water after
Willy's bath was over.
                        Love,
                        Dan

VISUAL THINKING

A balance scale has two pans. When each pan holds the same weight, the pans will balance. Each balance scale below has some objects on the left side. Write the letter of the objects that should be on the right side to make the pans balance.

1.

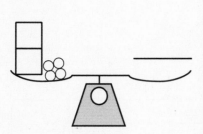

2.

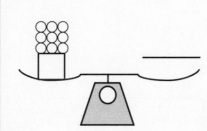

A.

3.

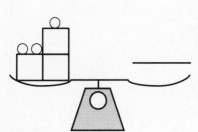

4.

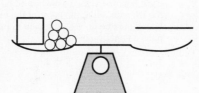

B.

C.

5.

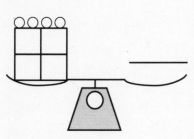

6.

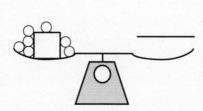

D.

E.

7.

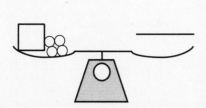

8.

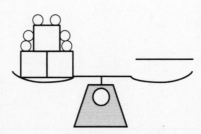

F.

G.

H.

Use with
Objective 79
pages 278–279

Focus
Visual Thinking
   Spatial Perception

Overview
Students choose objects to balance given objects on a balance scale.

Teaching Suggestions
Point out to students that each side of these balances must contain identical objects for the sides to hang evenly. Point out that knowing the weight of each square or circle is not important, just that both sides are the same. *Questions: What must be on the right to balance one square on the left? [One square] What must be on the right to balance one circle? [One circle] How can you determine what will balance the squares and circles in Problem 1? [Count the number of squares and circles, then find that number of squares and circles in the list of choices.]* Many students should be able to determine the matches by sight. They can see that Problem 1 has two squares and four circles and that choice E has two squares and four circles.

Alternate Approach: If students are having difficulty, suggest that they write below each left pan the number of squares and circles. Then have them write the number of squares and circles beside each choice. Then students match the numbers of squares and circles.

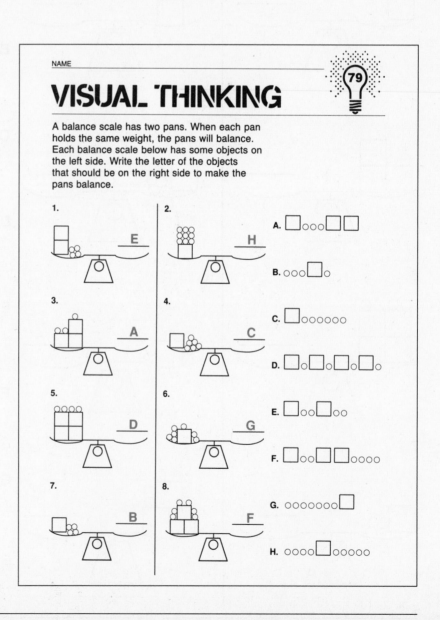

PROBLEM SOLVING

Tim, Dave, Janet, and Louise each read a book about a different animal. The four animals were a tiger, a dog, a jaguar, and a lion.

No one has a name that begins with the same letter as the name of the animal he or she read about.

No one has a name with the same number of letters as the name of the animal he or she read about.

Tim did not read about the jaguar.

1. Could Tim have read about the tiger? _____

2. Could Tim have read about the dog? _____

3. Which animal did Tim read about? _____

4. Which animal did Janet read about? _____

5. Which animal did each person read about?

_____

Use after pages 280-281.

Teacher Notes

Use with
Objective 80
pages 280–281

Focus
Problem Solving
Use Logical Reasoning
Make a Table

Overview
Students determine which animal each of four students reads about based on given information.

Teaching Suggestions
Point out that the book each child read can be found by determining which ones he or she did not read. In Problem 1, students reason that Tim did not read about the tiger because *tiger* begins with the same letter as his name.

In Problem 2, students reason that Tim did not read a book about a dog since *dog* has the same number of letters as his name. For Problem 3, students read the clue, "Tim did not read about the jaguar." Thus, Tim must have read about a lion.

In Problem 4, students reason that Janet did not read about the tiger since *Janet* and *tiger* have five letters each. They can also eliminate *jaguar* since both *jaguar* and *Janet* begin with the letter *j*. The only choice left is that Janet read about the dog.

In Problem 5, students reason that Louise did not read about the jaguar since *Louise* and *jaguar* have six letters each. Louise must have read about the tiger. Thus, Dave must have read about the jaguar.

Alternate Approach: Students might organize the information by *making a table* like the example in the next column. Have them list the animal names on the side of the table and the children's names across the top of the table. Have students put an *X* in a blank if that person did not read the book and an *O* in the blank if the person read the book.

	Tim	Dave	Janet	Louise
tiger	X	X	X	O
dog	X	X	O	X
jaguar	X	O	X	X
lion	O	X	X	X

NAME _____

PROBLEM SOLVING

Tim, Dave, Janet, and Louise each read a book about a different animal. The four animals were a tiger, a dog, a jaguar, and a lion.

No one has a name that begins with the same letter as the name of the animal he or she read about.

No one has a name with the same number of letters as the name of the animal he or she read about.

Tim did not read about the jaguar.

1. Could Tim have read about the tiger? _____ No

2. Could Tim have read about the dog? _____ No

3. Which animal did Tim read about? _____ lion

4. Which animal did Janet read about? _____ dog

5. Which animal did each person read about?
   Tim, lion; Dave, jaguar; Janet, dog; Louise, tiger

T80

VISUAL THINKING

Look at each figure on the left. Then ring the letter of the group of figures on the right that could be rearranged to make the figure on the left.

1.

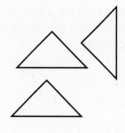
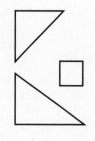
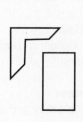

    a.   **b.**   **c.**   **d.**

2.

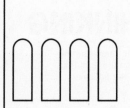

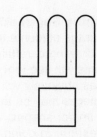

    a.   **b.**   **c.**   **d.**

3.

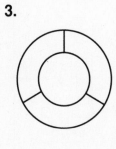

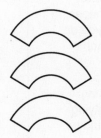
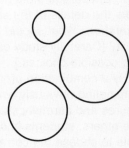

    a.   **b.**   **c.**   **d.**

4.

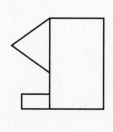
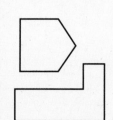
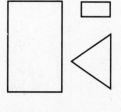
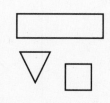
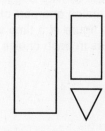

    a.   **b.**   **c.**   **d.**

Use with
Objective 81
pages 282–283

Focus
Visual Thinking
  Visual Patterns

Materials
Visual Thinking transparency
  (optional)

Overview
Students study groups of
shapes to determine which
group, when put together,
forms the given shape.

Teaching Suggestions
Encourage students to study
each drawing carefully. Some
students will see that some
choices obviously will not work.
The pieces may be the wrong
sizes and/or shapes.
  Question: *In doing each
problem, what should you do
first?* [Study the figure on the
left.] Encourage students to
note the details of the shapes.
Question: *What should you do
next?* [Carefully study each of
the possible choices.]
  By a combination of
eliminating obviously wrong
figures and carefully studying
the others, students should be
able to choose the correct
figure in all the problems.
  If students have difficulty
with the activity, suggest that
they match one part of the
given figure at a time with the
shapes in each choice.

Alternate Approach: Suggest
that students trace each choice
on another piece of paper and
cut them out. Then they can
put the pieces together to see
which forms the shape on the
left. This could be a final step
after eliminating the obviously
wrong choices.

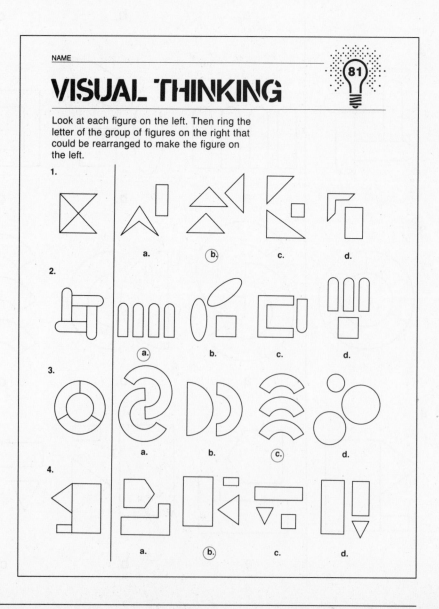

NAME

VISUAL THINKING 81

Look at each figure on the left. Then ring the
letter of the group of figures on the right that
could be rearranged to make the figure on
the left.

1.
  a.   b.   c.   d.

2.
  a.   b.   c.   d.

3.
  a.   b.   c.   d.

4.
  a.   b.   c.   d.

PROBLEM SOLVING

Four friends lined up for lunch. Bob is right in front of Ann. Jane and Ann are in front of Dan. There is one person in line between Dan and Bob.

1. On the diagram below, show where Bob is in line.

BACK |————————•————————| FRONT
              Ann

2. Show where Dan is in line.

3. Complete the diagram by showing where Jane is in line.

4. Five friends lined up. Ed, Fran, Gail, and Hoyt are behind Ike. Gail is right in front of Fran. Fran is behind Hoyt. There is one person between Ike and Ed. Show their order on the diagram below.

BACK |————————————————•————| FRONT
                          Ike

Use with
Objective 82
pages 284–285

Focus
Problem Solving
   Draw a Diagram
   Use Logical Reasoning

Overview
Students determine the order of children as they stand in a line.

Teaching Suggestions
Make sure students understand the difference between "in front of" and "right in front of." *Questions: If Ted is in front of Fred, can there be anyone between them?* [Yes] *If Ned is right in front of Jed, can anyone be between them?* [No] *In Problem 1, can there be anyone between Ann and Bob?* [No]

Encourage students to refer to the activity introduction several times as they determine the answers to Problems 1–3. *Question: For Problem 1, where is Bob?* [Right in front of Ann] Have students put "Bob" under the dot in front of Ann.

Question: What do you know about Dan? [Jane and Ann are in front of him.] Since students know where Ann is, Dan's position can be determined and marked. *Question: Where must Jane be in the line?* [Right in front of Bob] Encourage students to check Jane's position by making sure all statements are correct with the positions as marked.

Have students complete Problem 4 using the same procedure.

Alternate Approach: If students have difficulty with this activity, have them act out the problem. Use four students in Problems 1–3 and five students in Problem 4 to line up according to the information given. Also, students could use pieces of paper labeled with the names of the children. They can easily move the paper according to the information.

Extension
Have students solve the following problem. Tell them that in this problem the sentences are not given in the order they are used. Four friends lined up in front of Jim. Ron was next to Sally. Pete was between Jim and Sue. Sally was right in front of Sue. Find their order. [Jim, Pete, Sue, Sally, Ron]

NAME

PROBLEM SOLVING 82

Four friends lined up for lunch. Bob is right in front of Ann. Jane and Ann are in front of Dan. There is one person in line between Dan and Bob.

1. On the diagram below, show where Bob is in line.

BACK   Dan Ann **Bob Jane**   FRONT

2. Show where Dan is in line.

3. Complete the diagram by showing where Jane is in line.

4. Five friends lined up. Ed, Fran, Gail, and Hoyt are behind Ike. Gail is right in front of Fran. Fran is behind Hoyt. There is one person between Ike and Ed. Show their order on the diagram below.

BACK   **Fran Gail Ed Hoyt** Ike   FRONT

VISUAL THINKING

Lori and Gretchen are sharing a garden. They want each part to be exactly the same size and shape.

Here are 2 ways they can share the garden.

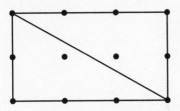 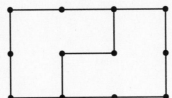

1. Which of these 4 ways shows parts that are exactly the same size and shape? Ring the letter.

   a.   b.   c.   d.

2. Which of these 4 ways shows parts that are not the same size? Ring the letter.

   a.   b.   c.   d.

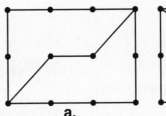 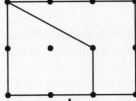

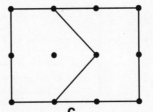 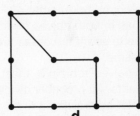

3. Draw lines and color your drawing to show 2 other ways Lori and Gretchen could share the garden.

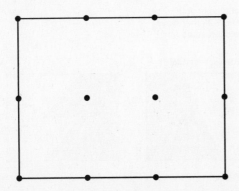 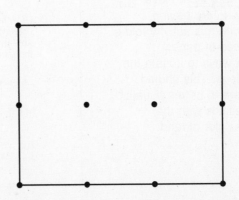

Use with
Objective 83
pages 296–299

Focus
Visual Thinking
   Spatial Perception

Materials
Square sheets of paper
Visual Thinking transparency
   (optional)

Overview
Students compare figures to determine which are the same size and shape.

Teaching Suggestions
To solve Problems 1 and 2, some students may find it helpful to "connect the dots" to form the squares and triangles that make up each half of the diagrams. They can then count the number of shapes in both halves of each figure to see if the areas are the same.

   To solve Problem 3, most students will probably divide the plot by drawing a line either parallel to the length or parallel to the width of the rectangle. Explain that these are correct solutions, but encourage them to be creative with their answers.

Alternate Approach: Have students who are having difficulty with this activity fold a square piece of paper 3 different ways to imitate the girls' gardens. This should enable them to better visualize the possibilities with the rectangular plot of land.

Extension
Sketch 3 hexagons on a piece of grid paper. Have students use colored pencils and divide the first into 2 equal area garden plots, the second into 3, and the third into 6 equal plots.

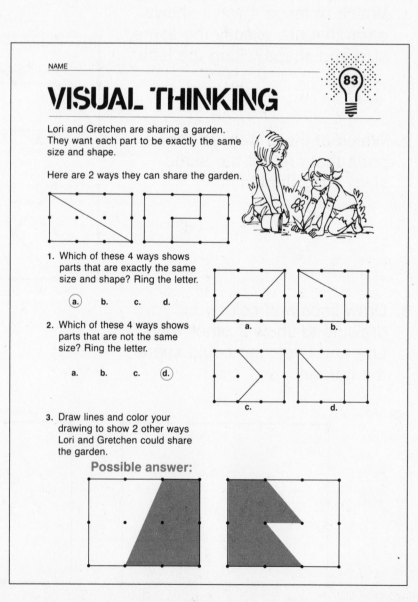

NAME _____

VISUAL THINKING
83

Lori and Gretchen are sharing a garden. They want each part to be exactly the same size and shape.

Here are 2 ways they can share the garden.

1. Which of these 4 ways shows parts that are exactly the same size and shape? Ring the letter.

   (a.)   b.   c.   d.

2. Which of these 4 ways shows parts that are not the same size? Ring the letter.

   a.   b.   c.   (d.)

   a.   b.   c.   d.

3. Draw lines and color your drawing to show 2 other ways Lori and Gretchen could share the garden.

   Possible answer:

PROBLEM SOLVING

Of these beads, 1 red bead is the same length as 2 blue beads. The beads snap together to make different chains.

There is 1 way to make a chain that is 1 blue bead long.

There are 2 ways to make a chain that is 2 blue beads long.

There are 3 ways to make a chain that is 3 blue beads long.

1. Predict the number of different ways you can make a chain that is the same length as 4 blue beads. Check your prediction by drawing all the ways.

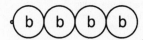

2. Draw pictures to show all the ways to make a chain that is 5 blue beads long.

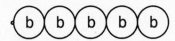

3. Fill in the table. Look for a pattern and predict how many different chains are the same length as 6 blue beads.

Chain length (in blue beads)	1	2	3	4	5	6
Number of different chains	1	2	3			

Use with
Objective 84
pages 300–303

Focus
Problem Solving
Draw a Picture
Make a Table
Find a Pattern

Overview
Students predict the number of ways beads can be combined to form chains of equal length and then *find a pattern* to predict the length for a given number of beads.

Teaching Suggestions
Some students may make incorrect predictions for Problem 1 based on the apparent pattern shown by the examples. The pattern seems to be that the number of blue bead chains increases by 1 each time a bead is added to the length. Students will realize, however, that this is not the pattern when they draw the pictures of 5 possible blue chains in Problem 1.

For Problem 1, make sure that students count the chain with 4 blue beads as a possibility. Remind students that 1 red bead is the same length as 2 blue beads.

Encourage students to systematically *draw the pictures* in Problem 2.

Some students may need help in solving Problem 3. After they have completed the table for lengths of 1 through 5 blue beads, write the sequence of numbers for "Number of different chains" on the chalkboard. Have students try to *find a pattern*.

If necessary, give them a hint, such as asking how the numbers are related to previous numbers. Once they see that each number, beginning with the third is the sum of the preceding 2 numbers, they should be able to predict the number of different chains for a length of 6 blue beads as 5 + 8, or 13.

Extension
Ask students how many blue beads make one inch. [3] Then ask them how many blue beads they would need to make a bracelet and have them extend the table to find the number of different ways they could make this bracelet using blue and/or red beads. [4-in. (12 blue beads), 233 ways; 5-in. (15 blue beads), 987 ways; 6-in. (18 blue beads) 4,181 ways; 7-in. (21 blue beads), 17,711 ways]

NAME _____

PROBLEM SOLVING

Of these beads, 1 red bead is the same length as 2 blue beads. The beads snap together to make different chains.

There is 1 way to make a chain that is 1 blue bead long.

There are 2 ways to make a chain that is 2 blue beads long.

There are 3 ways to make a chain that is 3 blue beads long.

1. Predict the number of different ways you can make a chain that is the same length as 4 blue beads. Check your prediction by drawing all the ways.

2. Draw pictures to show all the ways to make a chain that is 5 blue beads long.

3. Fill in the table. Look for a pattern and predict how many different chains are the same length as 6 blue beads.

Chain length (in blue beads)	1	2	3	4	5	6
Number of different chains	1	2	3	5	8	13

DECISION MAKING

You are planning games for the school outdoor field day. Use these facts to help you plan a schedule for field day.

- We want as many students to participate as possible.
- There are 24 students in each of two classes.
- There will be 2 games being played at once at all times.
- Teams can be formed from only one class at a time.

1. Complete the table below.

Event	Number in 1 team	Number of teams	Students left over
Volleyball	6	4	
Badminton	4	6	
Softball	9	2	
Basketball	5	4	
Soccer	11	2	
Kickball	8	3	

2. Complete the schedule below.

Time	Events
10:00 A.M.–11:30 A.M.	
12:30 P.M.–2:00 P.M.	
2:00 P.M.–3:30 P.M.	

Use with
Objective 85
pages 304–305

Focus
Decision Making

Overview
Students identify and analyze options to make a hypothetical sports day schedule.

Teaching Suggestions
To complete the table in Problem 1, students must multiply the number of students per team as shown in Column 1 by the number of teams in Column 2. This number is then subtracted from the total number of students in one class, which is 24.

To complete the schedule, students should choose combinations that include the most number of students participating at one time.
Question: Why is a combination of softball and basketball not a reasonable choice? [This combination leaves out 10 students.]

Extension
Have students assume that teams can be formed from both classes at one time. In this case, there would be 48 students. Have them rework the table in the first problem so that a minimum number of students are left over for each sport. For example, in softball, the number of teams would increase to 5, leaving 3 students left over.

NAME _____

DECISION MAKING

 85

You are planning games for the school outdoor field day. Use these facts to help you plan a schedule for field day.

- We want as many students to participate as possible.
- There are 24 students in each of two classes.
- There will be 2 games being played at once at all times.
- Teams can be formed from only one class at a time.

1. Complete the table below.

Event	Number in 1 team	Number of teams	Students left over
Volleyball	6	4	0
Badminton	4	6	0
Softball	9	2	6
Basketball	5	4	4
Soccer	11	2	2
Kickball	8	3	0

2. Complete the schedule below.

Possible answer:

Time	Events
10:00 A.M.–11:30 A.M.	Volleyball Softball
12:30 P.M.–2:00 P.M.	Badminton Basketball
2:00 P.M.–3:30 P.M.	Soccer Kickball

PROBLEM SOLVING

86

Johnny picked fewer than 40 apples from his tree. He sorted them into 6 equal groups. Then he changed his mind and divided them into 4 equal groups. If he had picked 1 more apple, he could have divided them into 5 equal groups.

1. Could Johnny have picked 40 apples?
   18 apples? 8 apples?

   ___ ___ ___

2. List all the numbers less than 40 that can be equally divided by 6.

   ___ ___ ___ ___ ___ ___

3. Which of the answers to Problem 2 can be equally divided by 4?

   ___ ___ ___

4. How many apples did Johnny pick?

   _____

5. Tina picked fewer than 30 apples and divided them into 5 equal groups. If she ate 1 apple, she could divide the remaining apples into 4 equal groups. How many apples did she pick?

   _____

Teacher Notes

Use with
Objective 86
pages 306–307

Focus
Problem Solving
Try and Check
Use Logical Reasoning

Overview
Students examine numbers to see if they are divisible by different divisors.

Teaching Suggestions
Have students explain their answers to Problem 1. If they appear to have guessed, help them to conclude that 40 is not divisible by 6, and the problem states that Johnny picked fewer than 40 apples; 18 is not divisible by 4; and 8 is not divisible by 6.

Alternate Approach: If students are having difficulty with the activity, pose the following questions to help them better understand the nature of the activity. *Questions: If Johnny had 12 apples and divided them into 2 equal groups, how many apples would be in each group?* [6 apples] *Could he divide 12 apples into 4 equal groups? How many would be in each group?* [Yes; 3 apples] *Could he divide 12 apples into 5 equal groups? Why?* [No, 12 is not divisible by 5.]

For Problem 5, have students list all numbers less than 30 that are divisible by 5 and subtract 1 from each to find which new numbers are divisible by 4.

Extension
Write these numbers on the chalkboard and tell the students that each number is divisible by 4: 28, 40, 72, 88, 96, 128, 340, 872, 1,288, and 5,696.

Have students determine whether or not 14, 24, 64, 144, 522, 912, 2,524, and 22,420 are divisible by 4. Before dividing, encourage students to look for a pattern in the numbers that are on the chalkboard. Some students may realize that a number is divisible by 4 if the number named by the last two digits is divisible by 4.

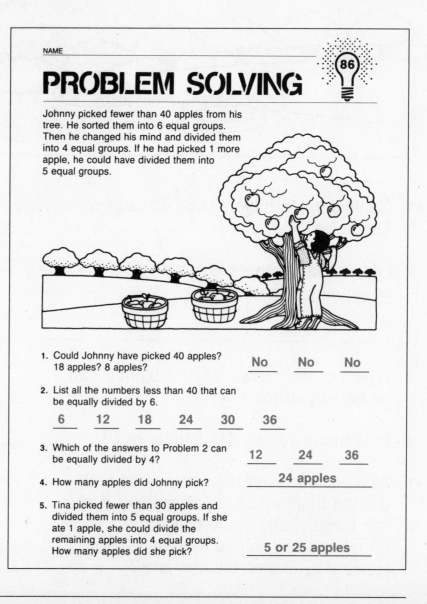

NAME

PROBLEM SOLVING 86

Johnny picked fewer than 40 apples from his tree. He sorted them into 6 equal groups. Then he changed his mind and divided them into 4 equal groups. If he had picked 1 more apple, he could have divided them into 5 equal groups.

1. Could Johnny have picked 40 apples? 18 apples? 8 apples?

   No   No   No

2. List all the numbers less than 40 that can be equally divided by 6.

  6   12   18   24   30   36

3. Which of the answers to Problem 2 can be equally divided by 4?

  12   24   36

4. How many apples did Johnny pick?

  24 apples

5. Tina picked fewer than 30 apples and divided them into 5 equal groups. If she ate 1 apple, she could divide the remaining apples into 4 equal groups. How many apples did she pick?

  5 or 25 apples

PROBLEM SOLVING

Sarah sees 7 circus clowns in the parade.
Some clowns are on bicycles and some are
on tricycles. Sarah counted 16 wheels.

1. Could Sarah have seen 1 bicycle and
   6 tricycles?

   _____

2. Finish completing the table to show all
   the possible combinations of bicycles
   and tricycles.

Number of bicycles	Number of tricycles	Number of wheels
1	6	

3. How many bicyles did Sarah see? How
   many tricycles?

   _____   _____

Use with
Objective 87
pages 308–309

Focus
Problem Solving
Use Logical Reasoning
Make a Table

Materials
Round buttons or coins
(optional)

Overview
Students determine various
combinations of bicycles and
tricycles that have a total of
16 wheels.

Teaching Suggestions
Make sure students
understand this activity by
posing these questions.
*Questions: How many wheels
does a bicycle have?* [2] *How
many does a tricycle have?* [3]

To solve Problem 1, students
must determine if 16 wheels
can be divided among
1 bicycle and 6 tricycles. Two
wheels plus 6 times 3 wheels
does not equal 16 wheels.

Have students *make a table.*
Remind students that Sarah
saw 7 clowns; thus the number
of bicycles and tricycles in
each combination must equal 7.

After students answer
Problem 3, ask the following.
*Questions: How many of the
16 wheels were on the
bicycles? Were on the
tricycles?* [10; 6]

<u>Alternate Approach</u>: Have
students use round buttons or
coins to make the various
combinations of cycles that
Sarah may have seen.

Extension
Have students solve the
following problem. Suppose
Sarah saw 8 clowns on either
bicycles or tricycles. Have
them list all the combinations
and the number of wheels
possible with 8 clowns.

Solution:

Number of bicycles	Number of tricycles	Number of wheels
1	7	23
2	6	22
3	5	21
4	4	20
5	3	19
6	2	18
7	1	17

NAME _____

PROBLEM SOLVING (87)

Sarah sees 7 circus clowns in the parade.
Some clowns are on bicycles and some are
on tricycles. Sarah counted 16 wheels.

1. Could Sarah have seen 1 bicycle and
6 tricycles? _____ **No**

2. Finish completing the table to show all
the possible combinations of bicycles
and tricycles.

Number of bicycles	Number of tricycles	Number of wheels
1	6	20
2	5	19
3	4	18
4	3	17
5	2	16
6	1	15

3. How many bicycles did Sarah see? How
many tricycles?

5 bicycles   **2 tricycles**

PROBLEM SOLVING

The students at Washington Elementary School are presenting the play, "Go Fish." In the school, there are 3 third-grade classes, 4 fourth-grade classes, and 3 fifth-grade classes.

1. Miss Chavez's class will line up as a school of fish in the shape of a triangle. If the back line has 10 students, the next line has 8 students, then 6 students, and so on, does Miss Chavez have enough students to make the triangle? There are 31 students in the class.

_____

_____

2. If there are 28 students in Mr. Jeffrey's class, can each student be part of a giant octopus? (Hint: Each leg of a student can be one octopus leg.)

_____

_____

3. Fewer than 25 students are in the final scene. When they are put in groups of 3, there are 2 students left over. In groups of 4, there are 3 students left over. How many students could there be in the final scene?

_____

  Use after pages 312-313.

Use with
Objective 88
pages 312–313

Focus
Problem Solving
Try and Check
Find a Pattern

Overview
Students determine whether or not various class sizes meet certain numerical requirements.

Teaching Suggestions
For Problem 1, make sure students *find a pattern* in the number of "fish" in each row of the triangle. Following the pattern of 2 fewer students in each successive row, she would use 10 + 8 + 6 + 4 + 2, or 30 students. Then if a student is put at the top or tip of the triangle, all 31 students would be used.

Have students read Problem 2. **Question:** *How many legs does an octopus have?* [8] Lead students to conclude that each octopus is made of 4 students.

Alternate Approach: Some students may find it easier to solve the first two problems by drawing pictures.

For Problem 3, have students list all the multiples of both 3 and 4 that are less than 25. Multiples of 3 include 3, 6, 9, 12, 15, 18, 21, and 24. Multiples of 4 are 4, 8, 12, 16, 20, and 24. Have students *try and check* each of the numbers to see which are possible solutions.

Extension
Have students suppose that each third-grade class has 28 students; each fourth-grade class has 22; and each fifth-grade class has 32. Have students compute the number of octopuses that could be made using all the students in the classes. [There are 84 third graders, 88 fourth graders, and 96 fifth graders, or a total of 268 students. Sixty-seven octopuses could be made.]

NAME _____

PROBLEM SOLVING

The students at Washington Elementary School are presenting the play, "Go Fish." In the school, there are 3 third-grade classes, 4 fourth-grade classes, and 3 fifth-grade classes.

1. Miss Chavez's class will line up as a school of fish in the shape of a triangle. If the back line has 10 students, the next line has 8 students, then 6 students, and so on, does Miss Chavez have enough students to make the triangle? There are 31 students in the class.

   <u>Yes. If the tip of the triangle has 1 student, she will</u>

   <u>use all 31 students: 10 + 8 + 6 + 4 + 2 + 1 = 31.</u>

2. If there are 28 students in Mr. Jeffrey's class, can each student be part of a giant octopus? (Hint: Each leg of a student can be one octopus leg.)

   <u>Yes. To have 8 legs, each octopus needs 4 students.</u>

   <u>There are enough for 7 octopuses.</u>

3. Fewer than 25 students are in the final scene. When they are put in groups of 3, there are 2 students left over. In groups of 4, there are 3 students left over. How many students could there be in the final scene?

   <u>There are either 11 students or 23 students.</u>

VISUAL THINKING

In this game, 8 children form a circle, face inward, and hold hands. Two children make an arch with their arms. Without letting go, the other children go under the arch.

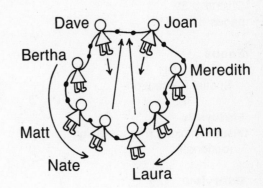

1. If Dave and Joan make the first arch, and then Nate and Laura are the first to go under, will the children be facing inward or outward?

_____

2. Write names on the drawing to show each child's new place.

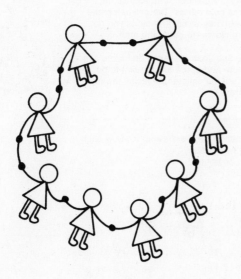

Use with
Objective 89
pages 314–315

Focus
Visual Thinking
  Spatial Perception

Materials
Visual Thinking transparency
  (optional)

Overview
Students recognize the relationship in a *visual pattern* and use this same relationship to complete the pattern.

Teaching Suggestions
You might have 8 students volunteer to be the children in the activity. Have students follow the instructions given to solve the problem. Note that 2 of the children going under the arch will also have to duck under their own arms.

Students should notice that in the resulting arrangement, the 8 children are in the same position relative to one another. For example, Meredith is still between Joan and Ann, Joan is still between Meredith and Dave, and so on.

Alternate Approach: You can also use the optional Visual Thinking transparency to do this activity as a group.

NAME _____

VISUAL THINKING

In this game, 8 children form a circle, face inward, and hold hands. Two children make an arch with their arms. Without letting go, the other children go under the arch.

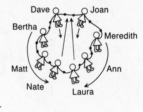

1. If Dave and Joan make the first arch, and then Nate and Laura are the first to go under, will the children be facing inward or outward?

Outward

2. Write names on the drawing to show each child's new place.

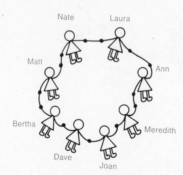

PROBLEM SOLVING

Decide which operation you could use to answer each question. Then fill in the boxes with "easy" numbers. Trade papers with a friend and compare answers.

Ring **A** if you will add, **S** if you will subtract, **M** if you will multiply, or **D** if you will divide. Then find the answer.

1. Lois bought ☐ tickets for the school play. Each ticket cost ☐ dollars. How much did the tickets cost?

   M D A S _____

2. The Math Club has ☐ members. This is 2 more than the Science Club. How many members are in the Science Club?

   M D A S _____

3. The speech team has twice as many members as the chess team. If there are ☐ speech team members, how many members are on the chess team?

   M D A S _____

4. Glenna has 30 pencils to share equally among her ☐ friends. How many pencils does each person get?

   M D A S _____

Use with

Objective 90
pages 316–317

Focus

Problem Solving
  Choose an Operation

Overview

Students decide which of 4 operations to use when solving various problems.

Teaching Suggestions

Tell students to use whole numbers less than 20 for these problems. Also explain that each student must solve his or her own problems *before* trading papers with another student. ***Questions:*** *Is there only one way to solve Problem 1? Explain.* [Students should realize that either multiplication or addition can be used to solve this problem.]

  For Problem 4, if the number of pencils is not divisible by the number of friends, have students also include the number of pencils that are left over.

Extension

Have students write other simple problems like these but allow them to include examples in which the answers are not whole numbers.

NAME _____

PROBLEM SOLVING

Decide which operation you could use to answer each question. Then fill in the boxes with "easy" numbers. Trade papers with a friend and compare answers.

Ring **A** if you will add, **S** if you will subtract, **M** if you will multiply, or **D** if you will divide. Then find the answer.

Possible answers:

1. Lois bought ⬛5⬛ tickets for the school play. Each ticket cost ⬛3⬛ dollars. How much did the tickets cost?

    Ⓜ D A S   15 dollars

2. The Math Club has ⬛10⬛ members. This is 2 more than the Science Club. How many members are in the Science Club?

    M D A Ⓢ   8 members

3. The speech team has twice as many members as the chess team. If there are ⬛20⬛ speech team members, how many members are on the chess team?

    M Ⓓ A S   10 members

4. Glenna has 30 pencils to share equally among her ⬛3⬛ friends. How many pencils does each person get?

    M Ⓓ A S   10 pencils

CRITICAL THINKING

In these puzzles, pairs of outside numbers can be multiplied together to get the inside products. Fill in the missing numbers to complete the example.

In the puzzles below, 1 puzzle cannot be completed, 1 can be completed in many ways, and the others can be completed in exactly 1 way. Finish the puzzles to decide which is which.

Think 3 × ? = 15

×	4	☐
3	12	15
5	☐	☐

Think 5 × 4 = ?

1.

×	4	10
2	☐	☐
3	☐	☐

2.

×	4	☐
6	☐	18
☐	28	☐

3.

×	☐	☐
☐	18	24
5	☐	☐

4.

×	4	☐
☐	☐	15
5	☐	35

5.

×	☐	☐
☐	4	8
☐	5	10

6.

×	☐	8
7	☐	☐
9	54	☐

Use with
Objective 91
pages 318–319

Focus
Critical Thinking
   Using Number Sense

Overview
Students use their knowledge of multiplication tables to complete various puzzles.

Teaching Suggestions
Do the example as a group. Have student volunteers determine the missing values.
   Have students read Problem 3. *Questions: What are possible answers to the puzzle?* [Other than the solution shown, students might choose 2 rather than 6. Then the answers would be 9, 12, 45, and 60.] *If you put a 3 in the box under the multiplication sign, what answers would you get?* [6, 8, 30, and 40]

Alternate Approach: Have students write equations for each pair of numbers to facilitate their solving the puzzles. For example, in Problem 1, equations include: $2 \times 4 = x, x = 8; 2 \times 10 = x, x = 20$; and so on.

Extension
Make and distribute similar puzzles with problems that involve division, subtraction, and addition.

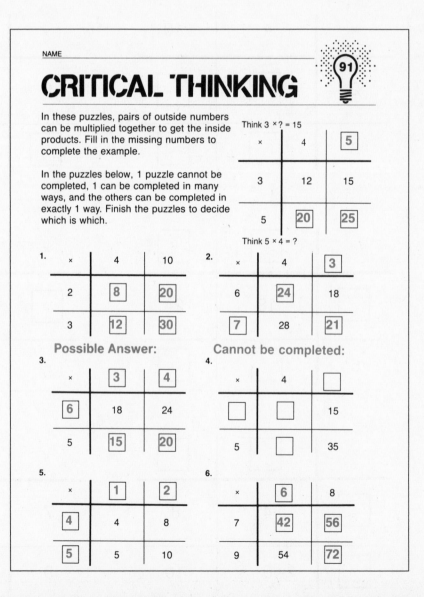

NAME _____

CRITICAL THINKING

In these puzzles, pairs of outside numbers can be multiplied together to get the inside products. Fill in the missing numbers to complete the example.

In the puzzles below, 1 puzzle cannot be completed, 1 can be completed in many ways, and the others can be completed in exactly 1 way. Finish the puzzles to decide which is which.

Think 3 × ? = 15

×	4	**5**
3	12	15
5	**20**	**25**

Think 5 × 4 = ?

1.

×	4	10
2	**8**	**20**
3	**12**	**30**

2.

×	4	**3**
6	**24**	18
7	28	**21**

Possible Answer:

3.

×	**3**	**4**
6	18	24
5	**15**	**20**

Cannot be completed:

4.

×	4	☐
☐	☐	15
5	☐	35

5.

×	**1**	**2**
4	4	8
5	5	10

6.

×	**6**	8
7	**42**	**56**
9	54	**72**

DECISION MAKING

These five children need markers.

We all need markers for art class.

We each need a red one.

Each of us has $1.00.

ANY COLOR 50¢ each

6-PACK SPECIAL $2.00
2 RED
2 BLACK
2 BLUE

MARKER MANIA

10-PACK SPECIAL $3.00
3 RED   2 BLUE
3 BLACK 2 GREEN

1. Describe some ways the children could buy markers if they spend all the money.

_____

_____

_____

_____

2. How could they buy enough markers and still have money left over?

_____

_____

3. Decide what you think the children should do. Tell why.

_____

_____

_____

Use with
Objective 92
pages 330–331

Focus
Decision Making

Overview
Students decide which combinations of markers to buy, based on certain restrictions of price and color.

Teaching Suggestions
Make sure students understand the situation.
Question: *How much money do the students have to spend?* [$5.00] Recommend that students identify their options to Problem 1 systematically. You might suggest that they make a table to keep track of their choices.

Single marker $0.50	6-pack (2 red) $2.00	10-pack (3 red) $3.00	Total cost	Number red
1	2	0	$4.50	5
0	1	1	$5.00	5

   Encourage students to list as many solutions as possible for Problem 2.
   Another possible solution to Problem 3 would be to have the students buy a ten-pack and a six-pack. Each would get a red marker, there would be no money left, and there would be several single colors from which to choose.

Alternate Approach: It may be easier for some students to divide Problem 1 into two parts. First, have them determine how many markers can be purchased for $5.00. Then have students take color into consideration. Remind them that each of the five students needs a red marker. Students will see that some of the possibilities based on cost alone may not meet the color requirements.

Extension
Have students suppose the five children had $10.00 to spend and each student needed at least four markers, including a black marker and a blue marker. They decided that they could share three green markers among them. Have students list two possible solutions to the problem. [Possible answer: Spend $7.00 on two six-packs and a single green and a single blue marker.]

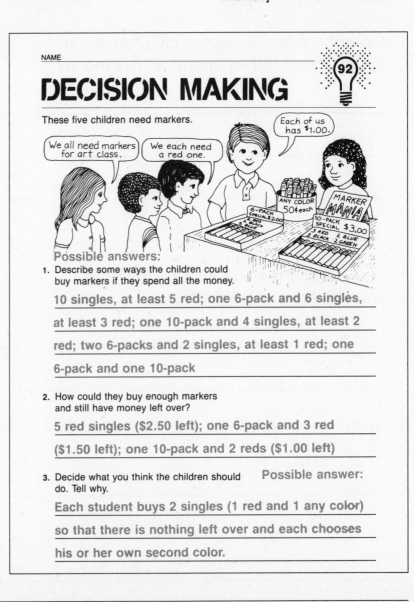

NAME _____

DECISION MAKING
92

These five children need markers.

"We all need markers for art class."
"We each need a red one."
"Each of us has $1.00."

ANY COLOR 50¢each
6-PACK SPECIAL $2.00
10-PACK SPECIAL $3.00
MARKER MANIA

Possible answers:

1. Describe some ways the children could buy markers if they spend all the money.

   10 singles, at least 5 red; one 6-pack and 6 singles, at least 3 red; one 10-pack and 4 singles, at least 2 red; two 6-packs and 2 singles, at least 1 red; one 6-pack and one 10-pack

2. How could they buy enough markers and still have money left over?

   5 red singles ($2.50 left); one 6-pack and 3 red ($1.50 left); one 10-pack and 2 reds ($1.00 left)

3. Decide what you think the children should do. Tell why.   Possible answer:

   Each student buys 2 singles (1 red and 1 any color) so that there is nothing left over and each chooses his or her own second color.

93

CRITICAL THINKING

Davy is designing a square pen for his new pet pony. The fence he needs is sold in sections. Each section is 7 feet long. First, Davy designed a small square pen.

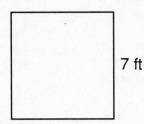

7 ft

1. How many sections of fence does he need to go around the small pen? How many feet of fence is that?

Then Davy designed a larger square pen. He thought he would need 4 times as much fence to go around the larger pen.

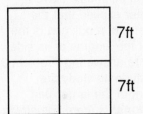

7ft

7ft

2. Why might Davy think that?

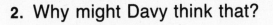

3. Do you agree? Why or why not?

4. Suppose Davy needs an even larger square pen. How many sections of fence might he need? How many feet of fence will that be?

Use after pages 332–333.

Use with

Objective 93
pages 332–333

Focus

Critical Thinking
   Using Logic
   Using Number Sense
   Explaining Reasoning/
      Justifying Answers

Overview

Students determine the perimeters of various size squares.

Teaching Suggestions

To introduce the activity, review the term *perimeter.* Have a volunteer explain that the perimeter of a polygon is the sum of the lengths of its sides.

   Before answering Problem 3, have students study the diagram of the larger pen. ***Questions:*** *Is there something in the drawing that is not needed?* [The inner sections of the fence] *How many feet of fencing does Davy need for the larger pen? How can you find this answer?* [56 feet; Add 7 eight times, or multiply 7 by 8.]

Alternate Approach: Some students may need help in solving Problem 4. Suggest that they sketch a square pen that is larger than the pen in Problem 2.

Extension

Have students suppose that Davy lives on a farm and can have many ponies. Each pony would occupy a square pen with a perimeter of 28 ft. Have students compute the least number of fence sections needed for nine ponies and sketch the arrangement of the pens. [24 fence sections which is 168 feet of fencing]

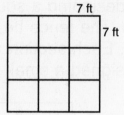

7 ft
7 ft

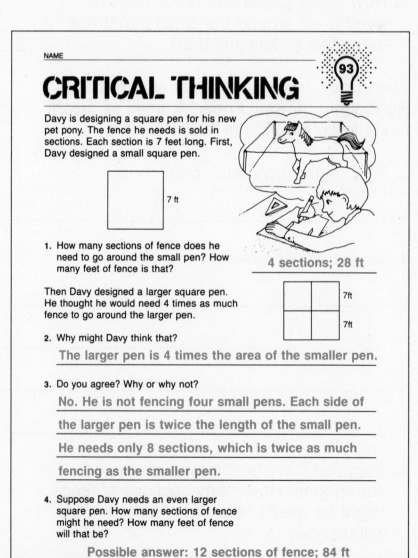

NAME _____

CRITICAL THINKING 93

Davy is designing a square pen for his new pet pony. The fence he needs is sold in sections. Each section is 7 feet long. First, Davy designed a small square pen.

7 ft

1. How many sections of fence does he need to go around the small pen? How many feet of fence is that?

4 sections; 28 ft

7 ft
7 ft

Then Davy designed a larger square pen. He thought he would need 4 times as much fence to go around the larger pen.

2. Why might Davy think that?

   The larger pen is 4 times the area of the smaller pen.

3. Do you agree? Why or why not?

   No. He is not fencing four small pens. Each side of

   the larger pen is twice the length of the small pen.

   He needs only 8 sections, which is twice as much

   fencing as the smaller pen.

4. Suppose Davy needs an even larger square pen. How many sections of fence might he need? How many feet of fence will that be?

   Possible answer: 12 sections of fence; 84 ft

PROBLEM SOLVING

Megan's science class is studying birds. On Monday, Megan put 72 oz of bird seed in the feeder. Every day she recorded how much bird seed was left.

Day	Bird Seed
Monday	72 oz
Tuesday	64 oz
Wednesday	56 oz
Thursday	48 oz

1. How much bird seed did the birds eat each day?

_____

2. If the birds continue to eat the same amount of seed each day, how much will be left on Sunday?

_____

3. On what day might Megan predict all the seed will be gone?

_____

4. Write a number sentence to answer this question: "In how many days will all the bird seed be gone?"

_____

Use with

Objective 94
pages 334–335

Focus

Problem Solving
   Write a Number Sentence
   Find a Pattern
   Make a Table

Overview

Students determine how much of a given quantity remains in a container over a number of days in order to predict how long the quantity will last.

Teaching Suggestions

Have students *find a pattern* in the table to conclude that 8 oz of seed were eaten each day.

   To solve Problem 2, students might extend the table and the pattern: Friday, 40 oz; Saturday, 32 oz; Sunday, 24 oz. Then, for Problem 3, they can continue until there is no feed left: Monday, 16 oz; Tuesday, 8 oz; Wednesday, 0 oz.

   Question: On which day might there be just less than half the original amount of seed in the feeder? [Thirty-six ounces is half of the original amount. Thus, on Saturday, just under half of the bird seed might be left.]

Alternate Approach: To solve Problems 2 and 3, students might use multiplication. From Thursday to Sunday is 3 days. In 3 days, the birds might eat 24 oz of food. 48 – 24 = 24, so 24 oz would be left on Sunday. For Problem 3, students might reason that 24 oz of food would last for 3 more days. Three days after Sunday is Wednesday.

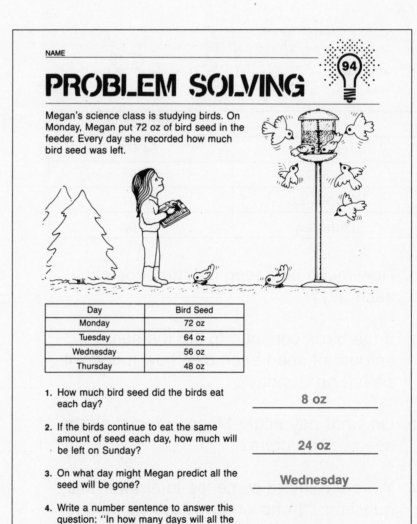

NAME _____

PROBLEM SOLVING
94

Megan's science class is studying birds. On Monday, Megan put 72 oz of bird seed in the feeder. Every day she recorded how much bird seed was left.

Day	Bird Seed
Monday	72 oz
Tuesday	64 oz
Wednesday	56 oz
Thursday	48 oz

1. How much bird seed did the birds eat each day?

   8 oz

2. If the birds continue to eat the same amount of seed each day, how much will be left on Sunday?

   24 oz

3. On what day might Megan predict all the seed will be gone?

   Wednesday

4. Write a number sentence to answer this question: "In how many days will all the bird seed be gone?"

   Possible answer: $72 \div 8 = 9$

VISUAL THINKING

Find and color all the **9**s hidden in the picture. (Hint: 63 ÷ 9 = how many you have to find.)

Use after pages 336–337.

Use with
Objective 95
pages 336–337

Focus
Visual Thinking
   Spatial Perception

Materials
Colored pencils
Visual Thinking transparency
   (optional)

Overview
Students find and color the
total number of hidden number
9s in a picture.

Teaching Suggestions
*Question: How can you find
the number of 9s hidden in the
picture?* [Solve the number
sentence at the top of the
activity.] *How many 9s are
hidden in the picture?* [7] *How
many colored pencils will you
need if you color each 9 a
different color?* [7] Some
students may find more 9s if
they count the eyes of the
players in the foreground.

   For more practice, have
students draw simple stick
figures using the numbers one
through nine.

Alternate Approach: Using the
overhead transparency, have
student volunteers try to find
and trace the 9s for the class.

Extension
Have students bring in copies
of local newspaper puzzle
pages. Hidden picture puzzles
are often found in the weekend
editions of many papers.
Photocopy the puzzles and
distribute them to students.

NAME _____

VISUAL THINKING

95

Find and color all the **9**s hidden in the
picture. (Hint: 63 ÷ 9 = how many you
have to find.)

DECISION MAKING

Shawna has 32 school pictures to put in her scrapbook. She can fit 8 pictures on each page. Sometimes Shawna likes to write something special next to a picture. These are some of the page designs Shawna has in mind for her scrapbook.

A

B

C

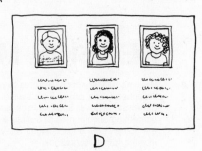

D

E

1. If Shawna wants to fill each page and have every page use the same design, which designs could she choose? Which would use the fewest pages?

   _____

   _____

2. If you were Shawna, which design or designs would you choose? Why? Tell how many pages of each design you would use.

   _____

   _____

   _____

Use with
Objective 96
pages 338–339

Focus
Decision Making

Materials
32 counters for each student

Overview
Students make decisions about space allocation and the design of scrapbook pages based on an analysis of options.

Teaching Suggestions
Tell students that they might want to use counters to solve some of these problems.

To solve Problem 1, students should identify their options. They should realize that they can put 32 pictures into equal groups of 8 (Design A), into equal groups of 4 (Design B) and into equal groups of 2 (Design E). They cannot put 32 pictures into equal groups of 6 (Design C) or equal groups of 3 (Design E).

For Problem 2, tell students that more than one design can be used. For example, Shawna might use 3 Design As for 24 pictures, 2 Design Ds for 6 pictures, and 1 Design E for the remaining 2 pictures.

Extension
For each design have students determine the number of pages Shawna would use if she used the same design for each page. They should realize that if some pictures are left over, they will need to use another page, even if it is not completely filled. [Design A, 4 pages; Design B, 8 pages; Design C, 6 pages; Design D, 11 pages; Design E, 16 pages]

NAME _____

DECISION MAKING

Shawna has 32 school pictures to put in her scrapbook. She can fit 8 pictures on each page. Sometimes Shawna likes to write something special next to a picture. These are some of the page designs Shawna has in mind for her scrapbook.

A   B

C   D   E

1. If Shawna wants to fill each page and have every page use the same design, which designs could she choose? Which would use the fewest pages?

   A, B, or E; design A uses the fewest pages

2. If you were Shawna, which design or designs would you choose? Why? Tell how many pages of each design you would use.

   Possible answer: Use a variety of designs, such as 4

   design Es for favorite friends, 4 design Ds for good

   friends, and 2 design Cs for the other classmates.

97

PROBLEM SOLVING

Mr. March's class is running two booths at the school fair.

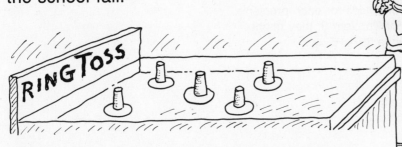

Decide how you will solve each problem. Ring A if you will add, S if you will subtract M if you will multiply, or D if you will divide. Then find the answer.

1. If you played 26 games of Ring Toss and lost 11 times, how many times did you win?

    A   S   M   D

_____

2. If you throw 3 balls each time you play Hit the Spot, how many balls do you throw in 9 games?

    A   S   M   D

_____

3. If you get 5 rings for each game of Ring Toss, how many games would you play if you tossed 35 rings?

    A   S   M   D

_____

4. In Hit the Spot, Duane hit the spot 16 times, Maria hit it 15 times, and Gary hit it 14 times. How many times did the friends hit the spot?

    A   S   M   D

_____

5. Each hour, 5 students take turns running Ring Toss. If each works the same number of minutes, how long does each run the game?

    A   S   M   D

_____

Use with
Objective 97
pages 342–343

Focus
Problem Solving
   Choose an Operation

Materials
Counters

Overview
Students choose among four mathematical operations to solve problems.

Teaching Suggestions
The answers shown on the activity page provide one method of solving each problem. Other operations, however, are possible.

   For Problem 1, students must subtract 11 from 26 to find out that 15 games were won.

   Most students will multiply to determine the number of balls thrown in Problem 2. They could, however, add 3 nine times. Similarly, most students will divide in Problem 3 instead of using repeated subtraction.

   For Problem 4, be sure students know that there are 60 minutes in one hour and that to solve the problem, they must divide 60 into 5 equal groups. Let them try to devise methods for finding the answer. If necessary, help them by suggesting, for example, that they put 60 objects into 5 equal groups. If you do not have 60 counters for each student, let them work in groups.

Alternate Approach: Have students write number sentences for each problem. For Problem 3, they might write $35 \div 5 = x$.

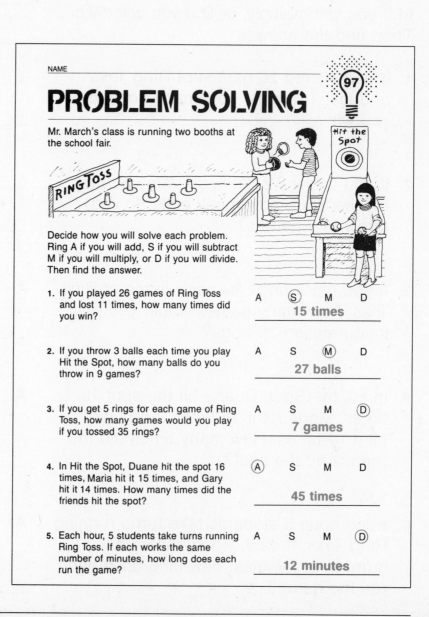

NAME

PROBLEM SOLVING 97

Mr. March's class is running two booths at the school fair.

Decide how you will solve each problem. Ring A if you will add, S if you will subtract M if you will multiply, or D if you will divide. Then find the answer.

1. If you played 26 games of Ring Toss and lost 11 times, how many times did you win?

   A (S) M D
   15 times

2. If you throw 3 balls each time you play Hit the Spot, how many balls do you throw in 9 games?

   A S (M) D
   27 balls

3. If you get 5 rings for each game of Ring Toss, how many games would you play if you tossed 35 rings?

   A S M (D)
   7 games

4. In Hit the Spot, Duane hit the spot 16 times, Maria hit it 15 times, and Gary hit it 14 times. How many times did the friends hit the spot?

   (A) S M D
   45 times

5. Each hour, 5 students take turns running Ring Toss. If each works the same number of minutes, how long does each run the game?

   A S M (D)
   12 minutes

CRITICAL THINKING

Think about the pictures as you find the missing numbers in each table.

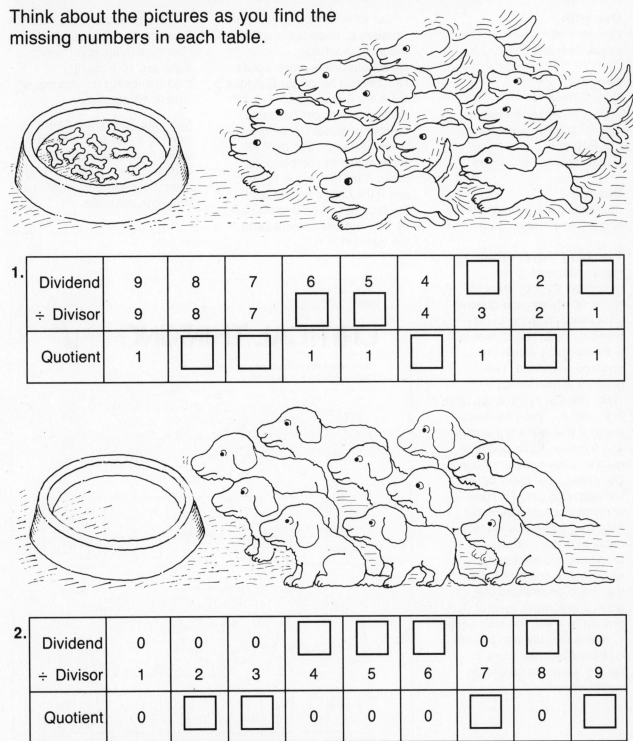

1.

Dividend	9	8	7	6	5	4	☐	2	☐
÷ Divisor	9	8	7	☐	☐	4	3	2	1
Quotient	1	☐	☐	1	1	☐	1	☐	1

2.

Dividend	0	0	0	☐	☐	☐	0	☐	0
÷ Divisor	1	2	3	4	5	6	7	8	9
Quotient	0	☐	☐	0	0	0	☐	0	☐

3. On a separate sheet of paper, write a short story about the 10 puppies. Show what you know from the tables.

Use with

Objective 98
pages 344–345

Focus

Critical Thinking
Using Number Sense
Finding/Extending/Using
Patterns
Making Generalizations

Overview

Students *make generalizations* about 0 and 1 in division.

Teaching Suggestions

Have volunteers give definitions for the terms *dividend, divisor,* and *quotient.* [The dividend is the number being divided. The divisor is the number by which the dividend is divided. The quotient is the result.]

For the first entry in the table in Problem 1, have students imagine that there are 9 dogs and 9 bones. Each dog is to get the same number of bones. *Question: How many bones will each dog get?* [1] Have students complete the table. After they have finished, you might give them other dividends and divisors for which the quotient is 1. See if they have *generalized* that when any number (except 0) is divided by itself, the quotient is 1. Stress that division by zero is impossible. Ask them if putting things into 0 groups makes sense.

Call attention to the table in Problem 2. Suppose there are 0 bones and 1 dog.
Questions: How many bones can the dog have? [0] *Suppose there are 0 bones and 2 dogs. Each dog is to get the same number of bones. How many bones will each dog get?* [0] Have students complete the table. After they have finished, see if they have *generalized* the fact that when 0 is divided by any number (except zero) the quotient is 0.

The stories students write for Problem 3 might include specific examples for which there are 10 bones (or 0 bones) being divided equally among 10 puppies.

Alternate Approach: After working a few examples in a table, have students *look for and describe a pattern*. Then have them *use the pattern* to complete the table.

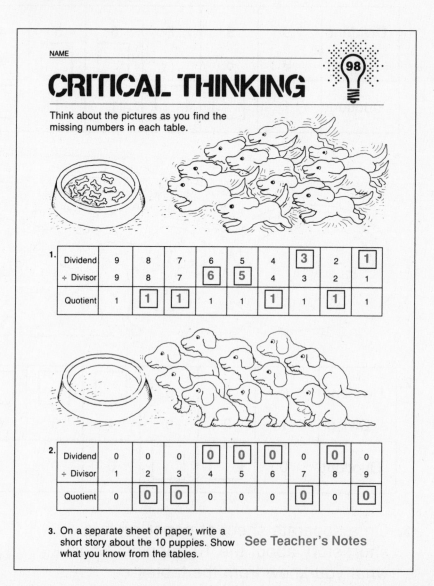

NAME _____

CRITICAL THINKING

98

Think about the pictures as you find the missing numbers in each table.

1.

Dividend	9	8	7	6	5	4	3	2	1
÷ Divisor	9	8	7	6	5	4	3	2	1
Quotient	1	1	1	1	1	1	1	1	1

2.

Dividend	0	0	0	0	0	0	0	0	0
÷ Divisor	1	2	3	4	5	6	7	8	9
Quotient	0	0	0	0	0	0	0	0	0

3. On a separate sheet of paper, write a short story about the 10 puppies. Show what you know from the tables.   See Teacher's Notes

VISUAL THINKING

Imagine that each design wheel below is turning. Finish the designs in the wheels that come next in each row.

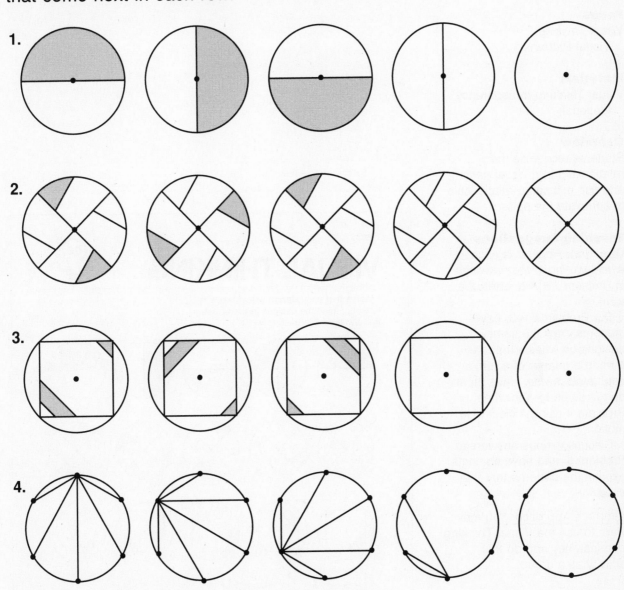

1.

2.

3.

4.

5. Make a design wheel pattern of your own.

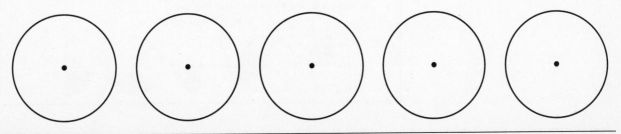

Use with
Objective 99
pages 346–347

Focus
Visual Thinking
   Visual Patterns

Materials
Visual Thinking transparency
   (optional)

Overview
Students recognize the
relationship in a *visual pattern*
and use this same relationship
to complete the pattern.

Teaching Suggestions
*Question: How far is each
wheel turning in the drawings
in Problem 1?* [A quarter of a
turn]

   For Problems 1–3, have
students draw the same
designs on wheels that are
turning a quarter of a turn
counterclockwise. Have them
do the same for the wheel in
Problem 4 using a clockwise
motion.

   Discuss various answers to
Problem 5, and have students
explain the patterns that they
used.

Alternate Approach: You may
want to use the Visual Thinking
transparency and do this
activity as a group.

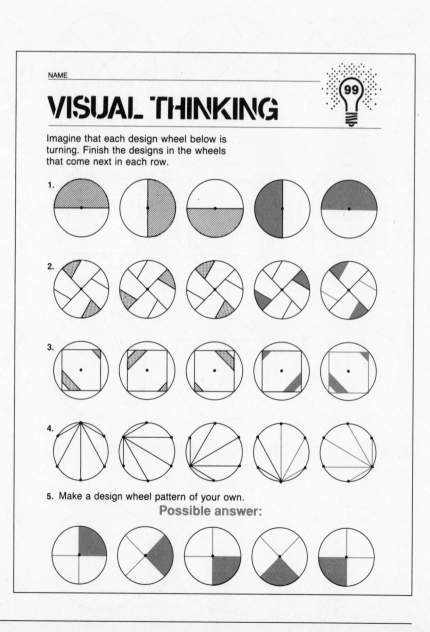

CRITICAL THINKING

Justine and Eric are packing bags of trail mix. They want to divide each kind of food equally among the bags.

30 ALMONDS

35 PEANUTS

42 RAISINS

49 WALNUTS

TRAIL MIX

Tell what will be left over if they pack

1. all 7 bags.

2. only 6 bags.

3. only 5 bags.

_____   _____   _____

_____   _____

Tell how many more of each type of food they would need so that there would be no food left over when they packed.

4. all 7 bags.

5. only 6 bags.

6. only 5 bags.

_____   _____   _____

_____   _____

Use with
Objective 100
pages 348–349

Focus
Critical Thinking
    Using Number Sense

Overview
Students use their knowledge of division to solve problems.

Teaching Suggestions
To solve Problem 1, students must divide the total number of each ingredient by the number of bags of trail mix. For example, the number of raisins, peanuts, and walnuts can be divided by 7 without a remainder. When 30 is divided by 7, there is a remainder of 2. Thus, to pack seven bags, the children will have only two almonds left over. *Questions: If seven bags of mix are packed, how many raisins are in each bag? How many walnuts? How many peanuts? How many almonds?* [42 ÷ 7 = 6 raisins; 49 ÷ 7 = 7 walnuts; 35 ÷ 7 = 5 peanuts; 30 ÷ 7 = 4 R2, 4 almonds.]

To solve Problems 4–6, students must add a number of each ingredient so that the total is a a number that can be divided by the number of bags. For Problem 6, for example, 30 and 35 can be divided by 5, so no more almonds or peanuts need to be added. However, one walnut and three raisins must be added to get 50 and 45, respectively.

Question: For Problems 4–6, rather than add more ingredients, how many of each ingredient can be removed so that no food would be left over? [Remove two almonds for seven bags; five peanuts and one walnut for six bags; two raisins and four walnuts for five bags.]

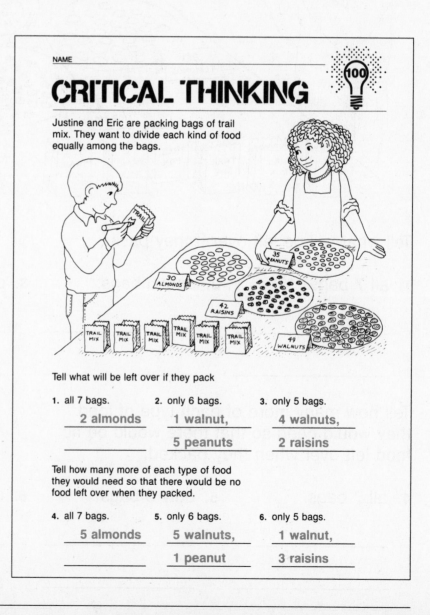

NAME _____

CRITICAL THINKING 100

Justine and Eric are packing bags of trail mix. They want to divide each kind of food equally among the bags.

Tell what will be left over if they pack

1. all 7 bags.

   2 almonds

2. only 6 bags.

   1 walnut,

   5 peanuts

3. only 5 bags.

   4 walnuts,

   2 raisins

Tell how many more of each type of food they would need so that there would be no food left over when they packed.

4. all 7 bags.

   5 almonds

5. only 6 bags.

   5 walnuts,

   1 peanut

6. only 5 bags.

   1 walnut,

   3 raisins

VISUAL THINKING

Imagine that you fold a sheet of paper in two. Then imagine that you use a hole punch to make one or more holes in the paper you have folded.

In each row, the picture at the left shows the folded paper. Ring the letter of the picture on the right that shows how it will look when you unfold it.

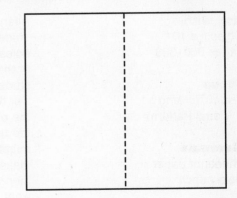

1.         

          a.   **b.**   **c.**

2. 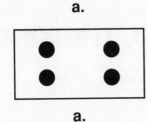   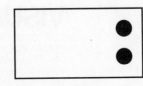   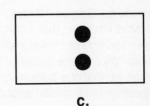

          a.   **b.**   **c.**

Now imagine that you fold a sheet of paper into three equal parts. Ring the letter of the picture on the right that shows how each sheet will look when you unfold it.

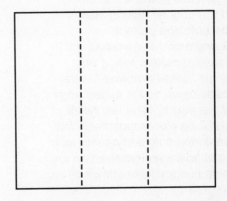

3.         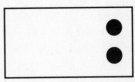

          a.   **b.**   **c.**

4. 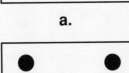   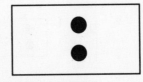   

          a.   **b.**   **c.**

Use with
Objective 101
pages 360–363

Focus
Visual Thinking
    Visual Patterns

Materials
Sheets of paper
Hole punch

Overview
Students study patterns of holes in folded paper to determine which of three patterns could be formed when the paper is unfolded.

Teaching Suggestions
Remind students that each hole is punched through all the thicknesses of the folded paper, so that the pattern must appear in each folded section.

Discuss how the placement of the original hole(s) affects the unfolded pattern.
Questions: How would the unfolded pattern look if the single hole in Problem 1 were made closer to the folded edge of the paper? [The two holes would be closer together.] *How would the unfolded pattern look if the hole were centered on the folded edge?* [Like choice **a**]

Alternate Approach: Have students fold paper and punch holes to correspond with each of the given problems. As students unfold their papers, ask them to pay attention to the placement of the holes in the unfolded paper. Students might use more folds and make their own hole patterns, then ask each other to predict what the unfolded pattern would look like before actually unfolding the paper.

Extension
Have students make hole patterns in paper that has been folded diagonally. Ask them to form a mental image and draw what the unfolded pattern would look like.

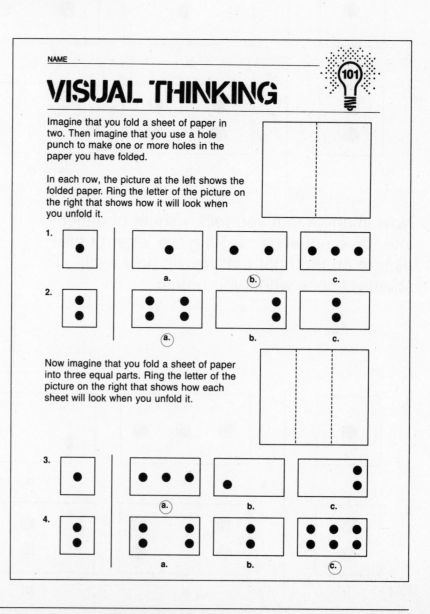

CRITICAL THINKING

Use the picture to answer the questions.

1. Devon said, "At the costume party, $\frac{3}{8}$ of us wore animal costumes, $\frac{5}{8}$ dressed as types of people, and $\frac{1}{8}$ came dressed as objects." Is Devon right or wrong?

   _____

2. Tell how someone could know the answer to Exercise 1 without knowing what the costumes were.

   _____

3. Devon wrote three correct fractions to tell how many people dressed up as animals, people, and objects. What was the denominator of each fraction? How do you know?

   _____

4. What was the sum of the three numerators? How do you know?

   _____

5. Write fractions to tell how many dressed as animals, people, and objects.

   _____

Use with
Objective 102
pages 364–365

Focus
Critical Thinking
  Drawing Conclusions

Overview
Students *draw conclusions* based on a picture and their knowledge of fractions.

Teaching Suggestions
Guide students in studying the picture. Have volunteers make a list of facts on the board. Accept all reasonable responses. [8 people, some girls, some boys, some dressed as animals, etc.] Encourage students to *draw their own conclusions* from the list of facts.

   Point out that there may not be enough information to *draw a conclusion.* **Question:** *Why can't you tell how many people in the picture are girls?* [Because of the costumes]

   Explain to students that when Devon said "3/8 of us wore animal costumes," he meant that 3 out of 8 people at the party wore animal costumes. **Questions:** *What did Devon mean when he said "5/8 dressed as types of people?"* [5 of the 8 people at the party dressed as types of people.] *What did he mean when he said, "1/8 came dressed as objects?"* [1 of the 8 people dressed as an object.]

Extension
Have students bring in pictures and use them to write a story involving fractions.

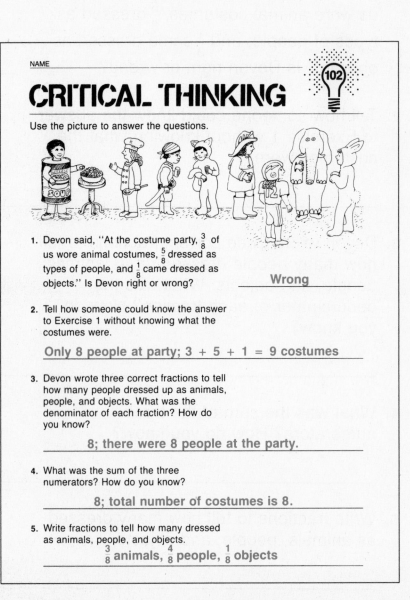

NAME _____

CRITICAL THINKING

Use the picture to answer the questions.

1. Devon said, "At the costume party, $\frac{3}{8}$ of us wore animal costumes, $\frac{5}{8}$ dressed as types of people, and $\frac{1}{8}$ came dressed as objects." Is Devon right or wrong?   **Wrong**

2. Tell how someone could know the answer to Exercise 1 without knowing what the costumes were.

   Only 8 people at party; 3 + 5 + 1 = 9 costumes

3. Devon wrote three correct fractions to tell how many people dressed up as animals, people, and objects. What was the denominator of each fraction? How do you know?

   8; there were 8 people at the party.

4. What was the sum of the three numerators? How do you know?

   8; total number of costumes is 8.

5. Write fractions to tell how many dressed as animals, people, and objects.
   $\frac{3}{8}$ animals, $\frac{4}{8}$ people, $\frac{1}{8}$ objects

VISUAL THINKING

Imagine that you are going to fold each
picture on the dashed line. Ring the number
of each picture for which the two parts
will match.

Example: The two parts match.   The two parts do not match.

1.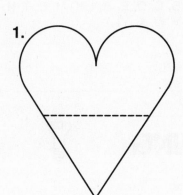

2.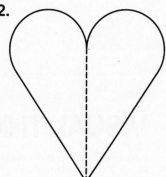

3.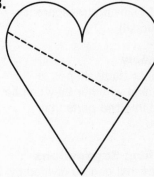

4.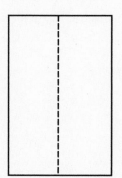

5.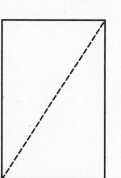

6.

7.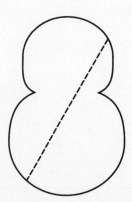

8.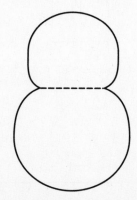

9.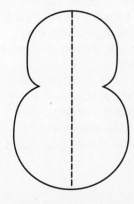

Use with
Objective 103
pages 366–367

Focus
Visual Thinking
  Spatial Perception

Materials
Tracing paper (optional)
Scissors (optional)
Hand-held rectangular mirror
  (optional)
Visual Thinking transparency
  (optional)

Overview
Students study shapes to
determine whether they can be
folded into two parts that
match.

Teaching Suggestions
Figures that can be divided by
a line into two matching parts
have a *line of symmetry*. The
two parts are (mirror)
reflections of each other.

Cut three triangles out of
construction paper, one with
three equal sides (equilateral),
one with two equal sides
(isosceles), and one with no
equal sides (scalene).
Demonstrate (by folding) that
the isosceles triangle can be
folded in one way so that the
parts match (it has one line of
symmetry). Then show that the
equilateral triangle has three
lines of symmetry (one through
each vertex), and that the
scalene triangle has no lines of
symmetry.

If you have a mirror, hold it
along the dotted line in each
figure. Ask if the part of the
figure on the paper and its
image form the original figure.

Alternate Approach: Have
students trace and cut out the
given shapes, then fold each
along the given lines to see
whether the parts match.

Extension
Give students half of a figure
(drawn on graph paper) and
have them draw the matching
half.

Have students determine
which letters of the alphabet
can be folded into matching
parts. [These capital letters can
be written so that they have a
line (or lines) of symmetry: A,
B, C, D, E, H, I, K, M, O, T, U,
V, W, X, Y]

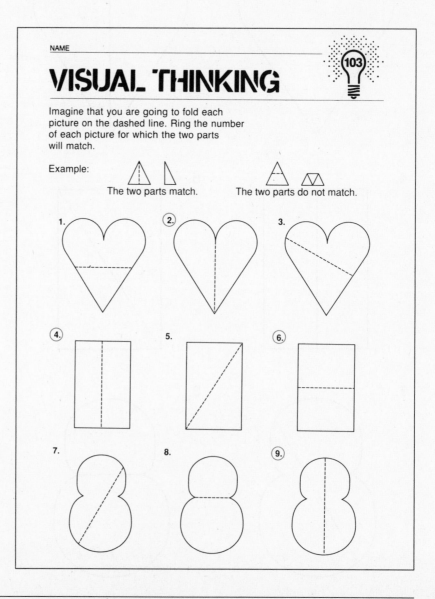

NAME

VISUAL THINKING
103

Imagine that you are going to fold each
picture on the dashed line. Ring the number
of each picture for which the two parts
will match.

Example:

The two parts match.   The two parts do not match.

1.   2.   3.

4.   5.   6.

7.   8.   9.

DECISION MAKING

Use the picture and the words to help you
make a decision.

Lynn is setting the table for 4 people. She
cannot reach all of the plates and glasses.
Here is what she can reach:

- $\frac{1}{2}$ of the flowered plates

- $\frac{1}{3}$ of the plain plates

- $\frac{1}{3}$ of the striped glasses

- $\frac{1}{2}$ of the flowered glasses

1. Can she reach 4 flowered plates?
   4 plain plates? 4 striped glasses?
   4 flowered glasses?

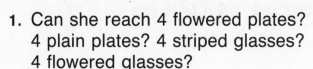

_____ _____ _____ _____

Lynn likes some combinations of plates and
glasses better than others. Here is the order
in which she likes them:

Best: plain plates with striped glasses
Second: flowered plates with flowered glasses
Third: flowered plates with striped glasses
Least: plain plates with flowered glasses

2. Which plates and glasses should Lynn
   use to set the table? Explain.

_____

_____

_____

Use with
Objective 104
pages 368–369

Focus
Decision Making

Overview
Students study a picture, analyze data, and evaluate options to make a decision.

Teaching Suggestions
Have students determine how many of each item is pictured.
Questions: How many flowered plates are there altogether? [8] *What is 1/2 of that number?* [4] Similarly, have students find the fractional parts of the other groups of items.

Elicit that the decision must be based on Lynn's preference *and* on her limitations (how high she can reach).

Discuss other alternatives.
Question: What could Lynn do so that she could use the combination she likes best? [Use a step stool; get someone to help her reach the other items.]

Extension
Ask volunteers to give examples of decisions they made where they could not have their first choice because of some limitation. Have students discuss what they might have done to overcome the limitation in order to get their first choice.

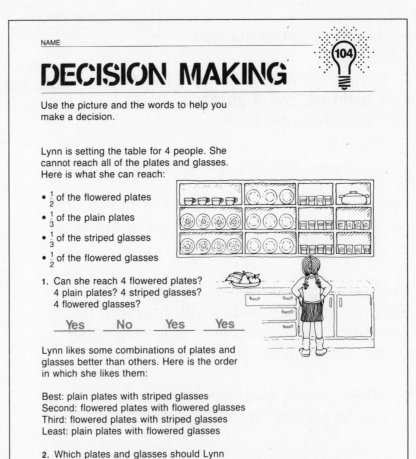

NAME _____

DECISION MAKING

(104)

Use the picture and the words to help you make a decision.

Lynn is setting the table for 4 people. She cannot reach all of the plates and glasses. Here is what she can reach:

- $\frac{1}{2}$ of the flowered plates
- $\frac{1}{3}$ of the plain plates
- $\frac{1}{3}$ of the striped glasses
- $\frac{1}{2}$ of the flowered glasses

1. Can she reach 4 flowered plates?
   4 plain plates? 4 striped glasses?
   4 flowered glasses?

   __Yes__ __No__ __Yes__ __Yes__

Lynn likes some combinations of plates and glasses better than others. Here is the order in which she likes them:

Best: plain plates with striped glasses
Second: flowered plates with flowered glasses
Third: flowered plates with striped glasses
Least: plain plates with flowered glasses

2. Which plates and glasses should Lynn use to set the table? Explain.

   __Possible answer: flowered plates, flowered glasses;__

   __this is combination she likes second best; she__

   __cannot reach enough plates for one she likes best.__

PROBLEM SOLVING

Read and solve each problem.

1. Wendy is twice as old as Joe. When Wendy is 20, Joe will be 16. How old are both Wendy and Joe now?

_____

2. Subtracting Rick's age from Ken's age leaves 4. The sum of their ages is 18. How old are Ken and Rick?

_____

3. The sum of Jerry's age and Eve's age is 24. Jerry is 6 years younger than Eve. How old are Jerry and Eve?

_____

4. When Mrs. Perez's age is divided by her son's, the quotient is 5. Mrs. Perez is 28 years older than her son. How old are they?

_____

Use after pages 370–371.

Teacher Notes

Use with
Objective 105
pages 370–371

Focus
Problem Solving
  Try and Check

Overview
Students *try and check* different pairs of numbers to solve age problems.

Teaching Suggestions
In this activity, students guess pairs of numbers then *try and check* to see if the numbers satisfy the given conditions. If students guess incorrectly, have them decide if the next guess should be higher or lower. If necessary, guide students in making their guesses. **Question:** *Why isn't 15 a good starting guess for Joe's age in Problem 1?* [If Joe were 15, Wendy would be 2 × 15, or 30, but the problem states that she is not yet 20.]

Help students identify and/or calculate the difference between the two people's ages. **Question:** *What is the difference between Wendy's age and Joe's age?* [20 – 16 = 4] Point out that the difference between the ages remains the same regardless of how old the people are, and regardless of how else the ages are otherwise related. Thus the students should pick pairs of numbers to *try and check* what numbers have a difference of 4. The answer is the pair for which one number is twice the other.

For Problem 2, students should *try and check* pairs of numbers that have a difference of 4 until they find a pair that also has a sum of 18. For Problem 3, they should *try and check* numbers that have a sum of 24 until they find a pair that also has a difference of 6.

In Problem 4, a good starting guess for Mrs. Perez's age is 30, the first number greater than 28 that can be divided evenly by 5.

Alternate Approach: Have students *make a table,* such as the one below, listing possibilities. Then circle the pair of numbers that checks.

Wendy	Joe	Difference
2	1	1
4	2	2
6	3	3
8	4	4 ✓

NAME

PROBLEM SOLVING

Read and solve each problem.

1. Wendy is twice as old as Joe. When Wendy is 20, Joe will be 16. How old are both Wendy and Joe now?

   Wendy: 8, Joe: 4

2. Subtracting Rick's age from Ken's age leaves 4. The sum of their ages is 18. How old are Ken and Rick?

   Ken: 11, Rick: 7

3. The sum of Jerry's age and Eve's age is 24. Jerry is 6 years younger than Eve. How old are Jerry and Eve?

   Jerry: 9, Eve: 15

4. When Mrs. Perez's age is divided by her son's, the quotient is 5. Mrs. Perez is 28 years older than her son. How old are they?

   Mrs. Perez: 35, son: 7

CRITICAL THINKING

Use the pictures to answer the questions.

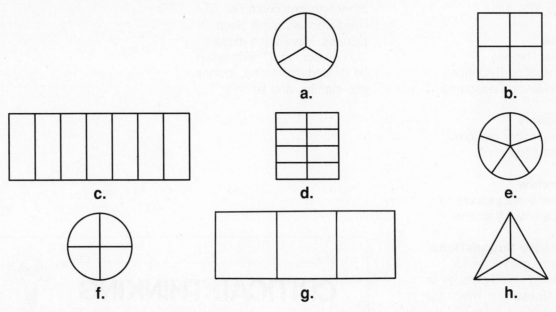

a.

b.

c.

d.

e.

f.

g.

h.

1. Jason says that $\frac{4}{5}$ is greater than $\frac{2}{3}$. Robbie does not agree. Which pictures can they use to decide? Who is right?

_____ _____

2. Jill says that $\frac{1}{3}$ is greater than $\frac{4}{7}$. Juan does not agree. Which pictures can they use to decide? Who is right?

_____ _____

3. Nancy says that $\frac{1}{4}$ is less than $\frac{2}{8}$. Gina does not agree. Which pictures can they use to decide? Who is right?

_____ _____

Explain your answer.

_____ _____

4. Glenn sees that none of the pictures shows tenths. He says that he can use one picture to show that $\frac{1}{5}$ is less than $\frac{3}{10}$. Which picture can he use? How can he use it?

_____

_____

_____

Use with
Objective 106
pages 372–373

Focus
Critical Thinking
Evaluating Evidence
Explaining Reasoning

Materials
Tracing paper (optional)
Scissors (optional)

Overview
Students use pictures to compare two fractions.

Teaching Suggestions
Develop guidelines for choosing which pictures to use. **Questions:** *Which part of each fraction helps you decide which picture to use?* [Denominator] *What does it tell you?* [The number of equal parts the figure is divided into] Point out that some pictures are divided into the same number of parts as others. For example, **a, g,** and **h** are all divided into thirds. **Question:** *How do you know which picture to use for Problem 1?* [Use the picture that is the same size and shape as the picture that is divided into fifths.] You might suggest that students shade the fractional parts of the pictures they select.

Alternate Approach: Have students trace each picture and shade the parts that represent each fraction. Then have students compare the shaded parts to see how they are related. To compare the fractions, students might superimpose their tracings over one another.

Extension
Have students decide what other fractions could be compared using the given pictures. Have them explain their reasoning. [Thirds could be divided into sixths, fourths into eighths, and so on.]

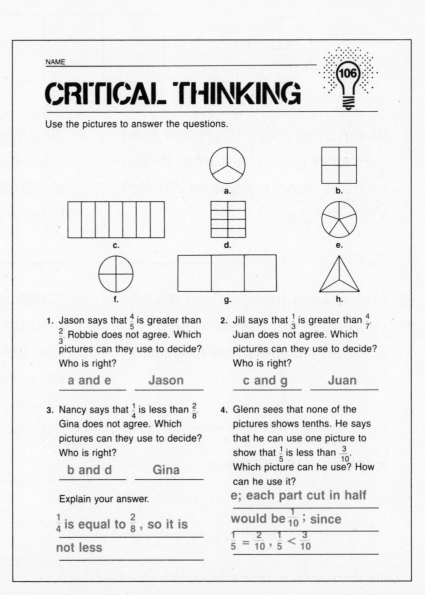

NAME

CRITICAL THINKING 106

Use the pictures to answer the questions.

a. b.

c. d. e.

f. g. h.

1. Jason says that $\frac{4}{5}$ is greater than $\frac{2}{3}$. Robbie does not agree. Which pictures can they use to decide? Who is right?

  a and e   Jason

2. Jill says that $\frac{1}{3}$ is greater than $\frac{4}{7}$. Juan does not agree. Which pictures can they use to decide? Who is right?

  c and g   Juan

3. Nancy says that $\frac{1}{4}$ is less than $\frac{2}{8}$. Gina does not agree. Which pictures can they use to decide? Who is right?

  b and d   Gina

Explain your answer.

$\frac{1}{4}$ is equal to $\frac{2}{8}$, so it is

not less

4. Glenn sees that none of the pictures shows tenths. He says that he can use one picture to show that $\frac{1}{5}$ is less than $\frac{3}{10}$. Which picture can he use? How can he use it?

e; each part cut in half

would be $\frac{1}{10}$; since

$\frac{1}{5} = \frac{2}{10}$, $\frac{1}{5} < \frac{3}{10}$

CRITICAL THINKING

Write fractions on the bars at the bottom of the page to name each part. Then trace and cut out the bars and paste each in the correct space at the top of the page. Then answer the questions.

$\frac{1}{2}$ $\frac{1}{2}$

$\frac{1}{3}$ $\frac{1}{3}$ $\frac{1}{3}$

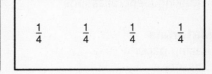

$\frac{1}{4}$ $\frac{1}{4}$ $\frac{1}{4}$ $\frac{1}{4}$

$\frac{1}{5}$ $\frac{1}{5}$ $\frac{1}{5}$ $\frac{1}{5}$ $\frac{1}{5}$

$\frac{1}{6}$ $\frac{1}{6}$ $\frac{1}{6}$ $\frac{1}{6}$ $\frac{1}{6}$ $\frac{1}{6}$

$\frac{1}{7}$ $\frac{1}{7}$ $\frac{1}{7}$ $\frac{1}{7}$ $\frac{1}{7}$ $\frac{1}{7}$ $\frac{1}{7}$

1. How did the denominators change as you put the bars in order? _____

2. All of the bars are the same length. How did the size of the parts change as you put the bars in order? _____

3. Explain the changes you described in Exercises 1 and 2.

_____

_____

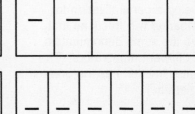

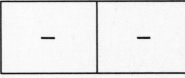

Use with
Objective 107
pages 374–377

Focus
Critical Thinking
    Ordering and Sequencing
    Making Generalizations

Materials
Tracing paper
Scissors
Paste

Overview
Students use fraction bars to *order* and compare fractions and to *make generalizations* about the numerators and denominators of these fractions.

Teaching Suggestions
Have students use the pasted-in fraction bars to compare several fractions. *Questions: Which is larger: 1/2 or 1/3?* [1/2] *1/3 or 1/5?* [1/3] *1/5 or 1/7?* [1/5] Also include fractions with numerators greater than 1. *Question: Which is larger, 2/5 or 2/3?* [2/3] Lead students to generalize that when two fractions have the same numerators but different denominators, the greater fraction has the lesser denominator.

    Use the fraction bars to develop a generalization for comparing two fractions that have the same denominators but different numerators. [The greater fraction has the greater numerator.]

Extension
Have students make fraction bars for eighths, ninths, tenths, and twelfths. Ask them to develop a way to compare two fractions, such as 2/3 and 3/4, that have different numerators and different denominators.

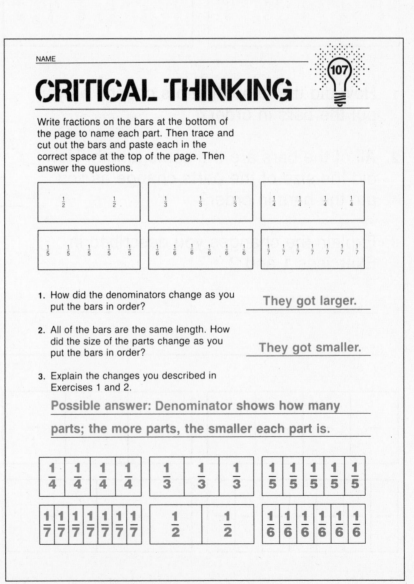

NAME

CRITICAL THINKING 107

Write fractions on the bars at the bottom of the page to name each part. Then trace and cut out the bars and paste each in the correct space at the top of the page. Then answer the questions.

| $\frac{1}{2}$ | $\frac{1}{2}$ | | $\frac{1}{3}$ | $\frac{1}{3}$ | $\frac{1}{3}$ | | $\frac{1}{4}$ | $\frac{1}{4}$ | $\frac{1}{4}$ | $\frac{1}{4}$ |

| $\frac{1}{5}$ | $\frac{1}{5}$ | $\frac{1}{5}$ | $\frac{1}{5}$ | $\frac{1}{5}$ | | $\frac{1}{6}$ | $\frac{1}{6}$ | $\frac{1}{6}$ | $\frac{1}{6}$ | $\frac{1}{6}$ | $\frac{1}{6}$ | | $\frac{1}{7}$ | $\frac{1}{7}$ | $\frac{1}{7}$ | $\frac{1}{7}$ | $\frac{1}{7}$ | $\frac{1}{7}$ | $\frac{1}{7}$ |

1. How did the denominators change as you put the bars in order?   They got larger.

2. All of the bars are the same length. How did the size of the parts change as you put the bars in order?   They got smaller.

3. Explain the changes you described in Exercises 1 and 2.

    Possible answer: Denominator shows how many parts; the more parts, the smaller each part is.

| $\frac{1}{4}$ | $\frac{1}{4}$ | $\frac{1}{4}$ | $\frac{1}{4}$ | $\frac{1}{3}$ | $\frac{1}{3}$ | $\frac{1}{3}$ | $\frac{1}{5}$ | $\frac{1}{5}$ | $\frac{1}{5}$ | $\frac{1}{5}$ | $\frac{1}{5}$ |

| $\frac{1}{7}$ | $\frac{1}{7}$ | $\frac{1}{7}$ | $\frac{1}{7}$ | $\frac{1}{7}$ | $\frac{1}{7}$ | $\frac{1}{7}$ | $\frac{1}{2}$ | $\frac{1}{2}$ | $\frac{1}{6}$ | $\frac{1}{6}$ | $\frac{1}{6}$ | $\frac{1}{6}$ | $\frac{1}{6}$ | $\frac{1}{6}$ |

PROBLEM SOLVING

Read and solve each problem. Use the
squares at the right to help you.

1. Dori skated $\frac{8}{10}$ mi. She stopped for a
   drink. Then she skated $\frac{5}{10}$ mi more. Write
   a decimal and a fraction to show how far
   she skated in all.

   _____

2. Sean skated 1.4 mi before he took a rest.
   After that, he skated 1.2 mi more. Write a
   decimal and a fraction to show how far he
   skated in all.

   _____

3. Jorge stopped for a snack after skating $\frac{7}{10}$
   mi. He skated another $\frac{8}{10}$ mi and stopped
   for another snack. Then he skated $\frac{9}{10}$ mi
   more. Write a decimal and a fraction to
   show how far he skated in all.

   _____

4. Who skated the greatest distance? _____

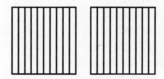
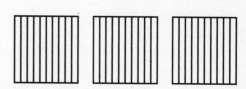

Use with
Objective 108
pages 380–381

Focus
Problem Solving
   Draw a Picture

Overview
Students shade fractional parts to add like fractions and solve problems involving mixed numbers and decimals.

Teaching Suggestions
Explain to students that they can *draw pictures* to solve these problems. Have a volunteer read Problem 1. Point out that the squares at the right are each divided into tenths. ***Questions:*** *How many tenths will you shade to show the distance Dori skated before she stopped for a drink?* [8] *After she stopped?* [5] Have students shade 8 tenths and then 5 tenths. ***Questions:*** *How many tenths are shaded?* [13] *How many whole miles did Dori skate?* [1] *How much more did she skate?* [0.3 mi] *How far did she skate in all?* [1.3 mi] Have students write this number as a decimal and as a fraction.

   Suggest that the students do Problems 2–4 independently. Problem 4 can be solved by comparing the shaded regions.

Alternate Approach: Give students a number line from 0 to 4 marked in tenths. Have them use different colored pencils to show each skater's distance.

Extension
Give students squares marked in eighths and have them use them to find sums such as 1-3/8 + 1-2/3, 7/8 + 7/8, 1-1/8 + 3/8 + 5/8.

NAME

PROBLEM SOLVING

Read and solve each problem. Use the squares at the right to help you.

SKATE–A–THON TODAY

1. Dori skated $\frac{8}{10}$ mi. She stopped for a drink. Then she skated $\frac{5}{10}$ mi more. Write a decimal and a fraction to show how far she skated in all.

   1.3 mi, $1\frac{3}{10}$ mi

2. Sean skated 1.4 mi before he took a rest. After that, he skated 1.2 mi more. Write a decimal and a fraction to show how far he skated in all.

   2.6 mi, $2\frac{6}{10}$ mi

3. Jorge stopped for a snack after skating $\frac{7}{10}$ mi. He skated another $\frac{8}{10}$ mi and stopped for another snack. Then he skated $\frac{9}{10}$ mi more. Write a decimal and a fraction to show how far he skated in all.

   2.4 mi, $2\frac{4}{10}$ mi

4. Who skated the greatest distance?

   Sean

DECISION MAKING

Use the words and pictures to help you make a decision.

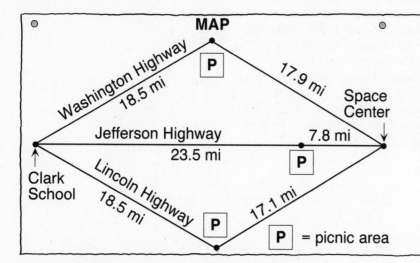

MAP

Washington Highway 18.5 mi
17.9 mi
Space Center
Jefferson Highway 23.5 mi
7.8 mi
Clark School
Lincoln Highway 18.5 mi
17.1 mi

P = picnic area

NEEDS FOR TRIP

✱ Most Important!
Stop for picnic about halfway.

Also Important:
Keep trip short.

VISIT SPACE CENTER BROCHURES

The third graders at Clark School are planning a trip to the Space Center.

1. Compare the three different routes they can take. Write the names of the three highways below.

   Longest: _____

   Second longest: _____

   Shortest: _____

2. Which highways meet the most important needs for the trip?

   _____

3. Which route should the students choose? Give a reason for your answer.

   _____

Use with
Objective 109
pages 382–383

Focus
Decision Making

Overview
Students study a map, consider other factors, and evaluate options to make a decision.

Teaching Suggestions
Help students interpret the map. **Questions:** *How do you know where the picnic areas are?* [Look for **P** inside a square.] *How can you tell which is the shortest route?* [Add distances and compare them.]

Discuss how the needs for the trip influence the decision. **Questions:** *If the most important need was to take the shortest route, how would it affect the answer to Problem 2?* [Jefferson Highway would be selected.]

Extension
Have students plan a trip along several routes to a local museum, park, or other attraction. Ask them to develop a list of needs for the trip, including method of transportation, lunch stop, etc. Have students put the needs in order of importance, and make a decision about the route they would choose.

NAME _____

DECISION MAKING
(109)

Use the words and pictures to help you make a decision.

MAP

Washington Highway 18.5 mi
P
17.9 mi
Space Center
Jefferson Highway 23.5 mi
7.8 mi
P
Clark School
Lincoln Highway 18.5 mi
P
17.1 mi
P = picnic area

NEEDS FOR TRIP
✳ Most Important!
Stop for picnic about halfway.

Also Important:
Keep trip short.

VISIT SPACE CENTER BROCHURES

The third graders at Clark School are planning a trip to the Space Center.

1. Compare the three different routes they can take. Write the names of the three highways below.

   Longest: **Washington Highway**

   Second longest: **Lincoln Highway**

   Shortest: **Jefferson Highway**

2. Which highways meet the most important needs for the trip?

   Washington Highway, Lincoln Highway

3. Which route should the students choose? Give a reason for your answer.

   Possible answer: Lincoln Highway meets most

   important needs

VISUAL THINKING

In each row, see how much of the square is shaded. Ring the letter of the circle in that row that has about an equal part shaded.

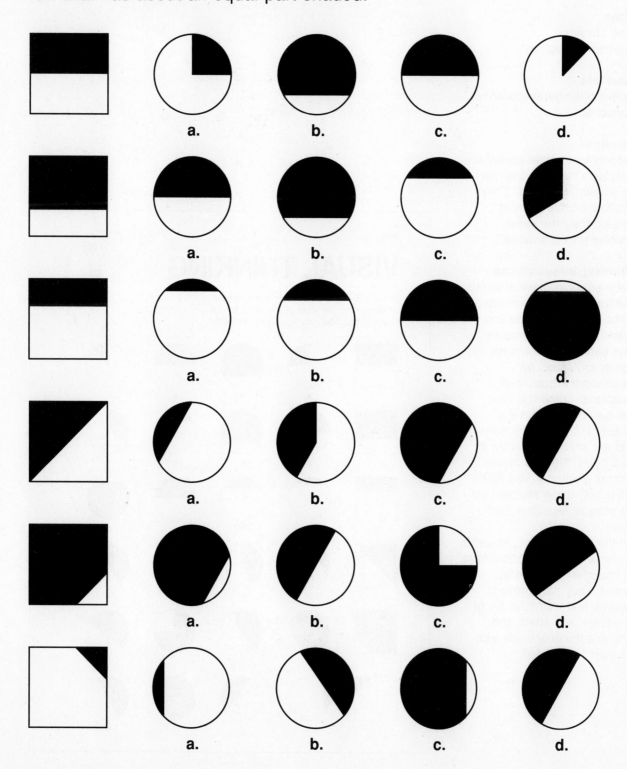

a.   b.   c.   d.

a.   b.   c.   d.

a.   b.   c.   d.

a.   b.   c.   d.

a.   b.   c.   d.

a.   b.   c.   d.

Use with

Objective 110
pages 384–387

Focus

Visual Thinking
Spatial Perception

Materials

Visual Thinking transparency
(optional)

Overview

Students use *spatial perception* to decide what fractional part of a square is shaded. They then find a circle for which approximately the same fractional part is shaded.

Teaching Suggestions

Where possible, have students write fractions for the shaded portions of the squares and circles. Help them eliminate some choices as being too large or too small, by comparing the fractions.
Questions: In the first row, what part of the square is shaded? [1/2] *What fractional parts are shaded in circles **a** and **d**?* [1/4, 1/8] *Are these fractions greater or less than 1/2?* [Less] *Is the shaded part of **b** more or less than 1/2?* [More]

In the last two rows, students may have difficulty determining the fractional part that is shaded. They may reason, however, that less than 1/4 of the square is shaded, and circle **a** is the only circle with less than 1/4 shaded.

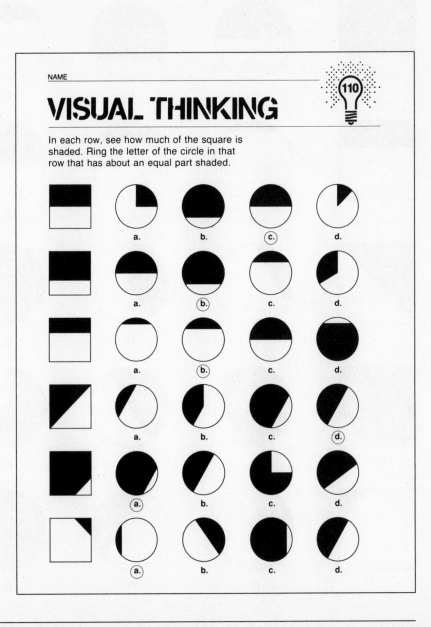

NAME

VISUAL THINKING

In each row, see how much of the square is shaded. Ring the letter of the circle in that row that has about an equal part shaded.

DECISION MAKING

Nita and Danny are writing songs. They plan to enter their best song in a contest. Use the picture to help them make a decision.

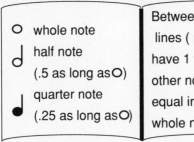

○   whole note

♩   half note
(.5 as long as ○)

♪   quarter note
(.25 as long as ○)

Between each pair of lines (| |) you can have 1 whole note or other notes that are equal in length to a whole note.

Contest Rules
1. All parts must have the correct number of notes.
2. Use whole notes, half notes, and quarter notes.

Here are parts of three songs that Nita and Danny wrote.

Happy Song   **Glad Song**   **Smile Song**

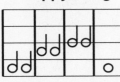      

1. Which songs have the correct numbers of notes?

_____

2. Which songs use all three kinds of notes?

_____

3. Which song should Nita and Danny enter in the contest? Why?

_____

_____

Teacher Notes

Use with
Objective 111
pages 388–389

Focus
Decision Making

Overview
Students study pictures, consider other factors, and evaluate options to make a decision.

Teaching Suggestions
Have a student volunteer who is familiar with reading music explain the relationship among whole, quarter, and half notes. [Two half notes = one whole note; four quarter notes = one whole note.]

List the combinations that are equal in length to a whole note on the chalkboard. Tell students to use this list to solve the problems.

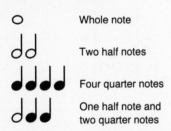

○   Whole note

    Two half notes

    Four quarter notes

    One half note and two quarter notes

If necessary, help students interpret the information in the pictures showing the songs. For each group of notes (measures) in each song, ask if there are notes that equal one whole note. In the "Smile Song," students should notice that in the first measure the half note and two of the quarter notes make a whole note, so there is more than a whole note. Similarly, in the last measure, two of the three half notes make a whole note.

For Problem 2, students should notice that the "Happy Song" uses only half notes and a whole note.

Extension
Have students write their own songs that meet the contest rules. Perhaps some students can play their songs in class.

NAME _____

DECISION MAKING

111

Nita and Danny are writing songs. They plan to enter their best song in a contest. Use the picture to help them make a decision.

○   whole note

  half note
(.5 as long as ○)

  quarter note
(.25 as long as ○)

Between each pair of lines (| |) you can have 1 whole note or other notes that are equal in length to a whole note.

Contest Rules
1. All parts must have the correct number of notes.
2. Use whole notes, half notes, and quarter notes.

Here are parts of three songs that Nita and Danny wrote.

Happy Song   **Glad Song**   **Smile Song**

1. Which songs have the correct numbers of notes?

    Happy Song, Glad Song

2. Which songs use all three kinds of notes?

    Glad Song, Smile Song

3. Which song should Nita and Danny enter in the contest? Why?

    Possible answer: Glad Song; it is the only one that

    follows both rules.

T111

NAME _____

PROBLEM SOLVING

Read each problem. Name two strategies that you could use to solve it. Then use the first strategy to solve the problem. Write your answer. Solve the problem again by using the other strategy and write your answer.

1. A freight train has a total of 18 tanker cars and boxcars. There are $\frac{1}{2}$ as many tanker cars as there are boxcars. How many are there of each kind?

   Strategy 1: _____   Strategy 2: _____

   Answer: _____   Answer: _____

2. Did both strategies give you the same answer to the problem?   _____

3. When the freight train began its trip on Tuesday it had 24 cars in all. It added 1 car on Wednesday, 2 cars on Thursday, 3 cars on Friday, and so on. On what day did the number of cars pass 40?

   Strategy 1: _____   Strategy 2: _____

   Answer: _____   Answer: _____

4. Did both strategies give you the same answer to the problem?   _____

Problem Solving and Critical Thinking/**EXPLORING MATHEMATICS** © Scott, Foresman and Company/3   Use after pages 390–391.

Use with
Objective 112
pages 390–391

Focus
Problem Solving
　Try and Check
　Draw a Picture
　Find a Pattern
　Make a Table

Overview
Students try two different ways to solve each of two problems.

Teaching Suggestions
Discuss how to use each strategy and help students decide which strategy is most useful for certain types of problems.

In *try and check,* students guess numbers and check to see if their guess satisfies the given conditions. **Question: How can an incorrect guess help you?** [Determines whether the next guess should be higher or lower.]

By *drawing a picture,* students can see how numbers in a problem are related to each other. A picture may also give clues about the solution of the problem.

When a sequence of numbers seems to change by the same amount each time, students can try to *find a pattern.* This strategy is also useful when a sequence seems to repeat. **Question: When would you make a table to solve a problem?** [When a problem has many related steps over a period of time; to see if there is a pattern; to help keep track of the numbers used to *try and check*]

In Problem 1, students are to find two numbers such that one number is twice the other and their sum is 18. They might solve the problem by *trying and checking* pairs of numbers. They might list pairs of numbers in a table until they find a pair that satisfies the conditions. Or they might *draw a picture* of 18 boxes and mark off two boxcars for every tanker. Accept any strategies the students can justify.

A table for Problem 3 might look like this:

Day	Cars added	Total
Tues.	0	24
Wed.	1	25
Thur.	2	27
Fri.	3	30
Sat.	4	34
Sun.	5	39
Mon.	6	45

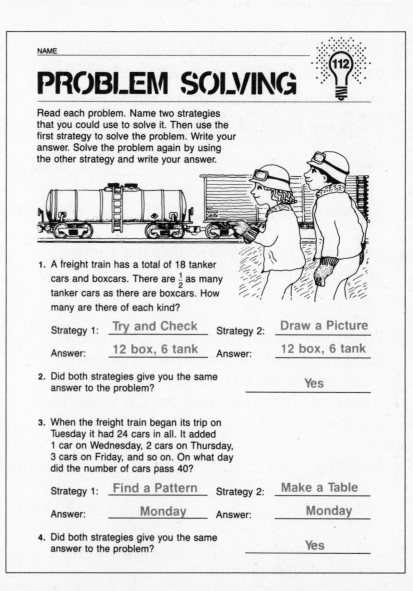

NAME

PROBLEM SOLVING 112

Read each problem. Name two strategies that you could use to solve it. Then use the first strategy to solve the problem. Write your answer. Solve the problem again by using the other strategy and write your answer.

1. A freight train has a total of 18 tanker cars and boxcars. There are $\frac{1}{2}$ as many tanker cars as there are boxcars. How many are there of each kind?

　Strategy 1: __Try and Check__　Strategy 2: __Draw a Picture__

　Answer: __12 box, 6 tank__　Answer: __12 box, 6 tank__

2. Did both strategies give you the same answer to the problem?　__Yes__

3. When the freight train began its trip on Tuesday it had 24 cars in all. It added 1 car on Wednesday, 2 cars on Thursday, 3 cars on Friday, and so on. On what day did the number of cars pass 40?

　Strategy 1: __Find a Pattern__　Strategy 2: __Make a Table__

　Answer: __Monday__　Answer: __Monday__

4. Did both strategies give you the same answer to the problem?　__Yes__

CRITICAL THINKING

Sometimes you can estimate by using a whole number instead of a decimal. Sometimes it is important to use the decimal number.

1. How much paint does each can shown at right hold?

   Large: _____   Small: _____

2. Now write estimates of the amount of paint in the two cans.

   Large: _____   Small: _____

3. Which measurement would you use to determine about how much more paint the large can holds? Why?

   _____

   _____

4. How wide is the piece of wallpaper shown at right?

   _____

5. Now write an estimate of the width of wallpaper being measured.

   _____

6. Which measurement for the width of the wallpaper would you use, 30 cm, 32 cm, or 32.2 cm? Why?

   _____

   _____

    Use after pages 392–393.

Use with
Objective 113
pages 392–393

Focus
Critical Thinking
   Explaining Reasoning/
   Justifying Answers

Overview
Students decide when it is
appropriate to use an estimate
and explain their reasoning.

Teaching Suggestions
Estimation is used to get an
approximate answer quickly. It
can also be used to tell if a
final answer is reasonable.

   If students have trouble
estimating in Problems 2 and
4, tell them to think about
which whole number is closest
to the decimal.

   Discuss situations related to
those in the activity where an
estimate is or is not
appropriate. *Question: When
might you need to use more
than an estimate of an amount
of paint?* [Possible answer:
When mixing paints to get a
specific color] *Question: When
would an estimate of the width
of the wallpaper be used?*
[Possible answer: When
deciding how many rolls to buy
to cover a given area]

Extension
Have students plan a project,
such as making a flower box or
planting seeds. Ask them to
make a list of the materials
they would need. Have them
decide when they can estimate
amounts and when they should
not estimate.

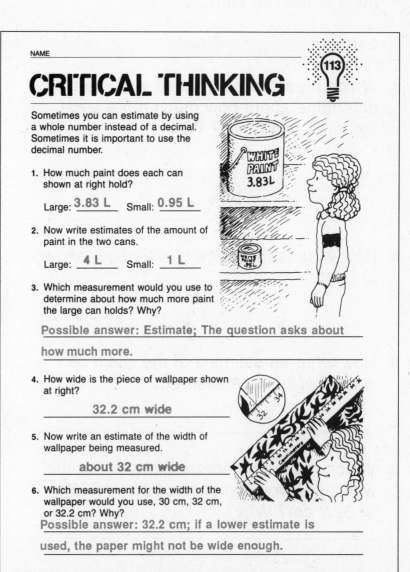

NAME

CRITICAL THINKING   113

Sometimes you can estimate by using
a whole number instead of a decimal.
Sometimes it is important to use the
decimal number.

1. How much paint does each can
   shown at right hold?

   Large: __3.83 L__   Small: __0.95 L__

2. Now write estimates of the amount of
   paint in the two cans.

   Large: __4 L__   Small: __1 L__

3. Which measurement would you use to
   determine about how much more paint
   the large can holds? Why?

   Possible answer: Estimate; The question asks about

   how much more.

4. How wide is the piece of wallpaper shown
   at right?

   __32.2 cm wide__

5. Now write an estimate of the width of
   wallpaper being measured.

   __about 32 cm wide__

6. Which measurement for the width of the
   wallpaper would you use, 30 cm, 32 cm,
   or 32.2 cm? Why?

   Possible answer: 32.2 cm; if a lower estimate is

   used, the paper might not be wide enough.

CRITICAL THINKING

Use the pictures to help you answer questions about a game that Peter and Foumi are playing.

They turn the number cards facedown. Peter takes three cards.

He uses the three cards to show these times.

$2 : 5\ 8$ $8 : 2\ 5$ $8 : 5\ 2$ $5 : 2\ 8$

Then Foumi shows each time on the clock.
Write the time that each clock shows.

1. 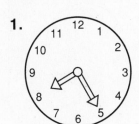 $\boxed{} : \boxed{}\boxed{}$

2. 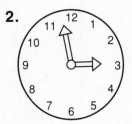 $\boxed{} : \boxed{}\boxed{}$

3. If Peter and Foumi take three cards each time, are there any times that Peter and Foumi will not be able to show? Explain your answer.

_____

_____

4. Will Peter and Foumi always be able to show a time with three of the number cards? Explain you answer.

_____

_____

Use with
Objective 114
pages 408–411

Focus
Critical Thinking
    Explaining Reasoning/
        Justifying Answers

Materials
Cardboard (optional)
Brass fasteners (optional)

Overview
Students use numbered cards and clocks to answer questions about a hypothetical game about time.

Teaching Suggestions
Make sure students understand the game by asking the following questions. *Questions: How many hours are shown on the face of a clock?* [12] *How many minutes are in one hour?* [60] This should help students realize the limited number of possibilities with the numbered cards.

Before answering Problem 3, students must realize that since the boys draw only three cards at a time, any time with four digits cannot be shown. Students should also realize that any time with the same digit cannot be shown. Ask students to *explain the reasoning* used to solve this problem.

Another solution to Problem 4 is not being able to show a time if the cards numbered 6, 7, and 8 are drawn.

Alternate Approach: Have pairs of students make and play the game. Cards, a clock, and two hands can be made from lightweight cardboard. Attach the hands with a brass fastener.

Extension
Have students imagine that the boys showed these "times": 3:82, 5:90, 9:78, and 12:84.

Have them convert them to show less than 60 minutes. The first time, 3:82, can be converted to 4:22 by rewriting 82 min as 1 h and 22 min.

$$3:82 = 3 \text{ h} + 82 \text{ min}$$
$$= 3 \text{ h} + 60 \text{ min} + 22 \text{ min}$$
$$= 3 \text{ h} + 1 \text{ h} + 22 \text{ min}$$
$$= 4 \text{ h} + 22 \text{ min}$$
$$= 4:22$$

Similarly, 5:90 becomes 6:30, 9:78 becomes 10:18, and 12:84 becomes 1:24.

NAME

CRITICAL THINKING

(114)

Use the pictures to help you answer questions about a game that Peter and Foumi are playing.

| 0 | 1 | 2 | 3 | 4 | 5 | 6 | 7 | 8 | 9 |

They turn the number cards facedown. Peter takes three cards.   2   8   5

He uses the three cards to show these times.

2 : 5 8   8 : 2 5   8 : 5 2   5 : 2 8

Then Foumi shows each time on the clock. Write the time that each clock shows.

1.   8 : 2 5

2.   2 : 5 8

3. If Peter and Foumi take three cards each time, are there any times that Peter and Foumi will not be able to show? Explain your answer.

Possible answer: Yes; they will not be able to show

times such as 10:48 or 1:33.

4. Will Peter and Foumi always be able to show a time with three of the number cards? Explain you answer.

Possible answer: No, they cannot show a time with

the number cards 7, 8, and 9.

DECISION MAKING

Use the calendar and the list to help you make a decision.

The Minnows have swim practices every Monday and Thursday. They have swim meets planned for every Saturday in April.

Coach Lane wants to hold two extra practices in April. He is busy every Sunday. He asked the swimmers to write down the days that they are busy.

APRIL

Sun.	Mon.	Tues.	Wed.	Thurs.	Fri.	Sat.
	1	2	3	4	5	6
7	8	9	10	11	12	13
14	15	16	17	18	19	20
21	22	23	24	25	26	27
28	29	30				

Swimmer	Busy Days
1. Luis	Tuesdays-Scout Meeting
2. Roger	Fridays-Violin Lessons
3. Jenny	Tuesdays-Computer Club
4. Jackie	Wednesdays-Dance Class
5. Emily	April 17-Dentist
6. Mark	Tuesdays-Scouts

1. Is there any day of the week that Coach Lane and all the swimmers have free? _____

2. Coach Lane thinks that Jackie needs the least practice. Roger and Emily are new, so they need the most. Which dates are best for extra practice: April 5 and 17, April 9 and 30, or April 10 and 24? _____

3. Why are these the best days?

_____

_____

Use with
Objective 115
pages 412–413

Focus
Decision Making

Overview
Students analyze various options to make a swim team schedule.

Teaching Suggestions
Have volunteers read the introductory paragraph and the "Busy Days" chart. Then have them define the problem. [The coach must find days when most of the students are free.] Have students cross off the busy days from the calendar to facilitate their solving the first problem.

Have students explain why they did not choose certain days in Problem 2 to help eliminate guessing. You may want to pose questions like the following. *Questions: Why are April 5th and 17th not good days for extra practice?* [Roger and Emily, who need practice, are busy on the 5th and the 17th.] *Why are the 9th and the 30th also not good days?* [Luis, Jenny, and Mark are busy.]

Extension
Have students pick a day for an after-school party by determining which day the majority of the students could come.

NAME

DECISION MAKING

(115)

Use the calendar and the list to help you make a decision.

The Minnows have swim practices every Monday and Thursday. They have swim meets planned for every Saturday in April.

Coach Lane wants to hold two extra practices in April. He is busy every Sunday. He asked the swimmers to write down the days that they are busy.

APRIL

Sun.	Mon.	Tues.	Wed.	Thurs.	Fri.	Sat.
	1	2	3	4	5	6
7	8	9	10	11	12	13
14	15	16	17	18	19	20
21	22	23	24	25	26	27
28	29	30				

Swimmer	Busy Days
1. Luis	Tuesdays - Scout Meeting
2. Roger	Fridays - Violin Lessons
3. Jenny	Tuesdays - Computer Club
4. Jackie	Wednesdays - Dance Class
5. Emily	April 17 - Dentist
6. Mark	Tuesdays - Scouts

1. Is there any day of the week that Coach Lane and all the swimmers have free? **No**

2. Coach Lane thinks that Jackie needs the least practice. Roger and Emily are new, so they need the most. Which dates are best for extra practice: April 5 and 17, April 9 and 30, or April 10 and 24? **April 10 and 24**

3. Why are these the best days?

   Possible answer: The only swimmer who can't be there is Jackie, who needs the least practice.

PROBLEM SOLVING

Read and solve each problem.

1. Kurt got on the Hills of Thrills at 2:55 P.M. The car made 4 trips around the track. Each trip took 2 minutes. What time was it when Kurt's ride ended?

2. Each car on the Hills of Thrills can hold 6 people. There are 8 cars in all. How many people are on the ride when half of the cars are full?

3. On the carousel, you can ride on a horse, a tiger, or a swan. There are 10 fewer swans than there are tigers, and 10 fewer tigers than horses. If there are 26 horses, how many carousel animals are there in all?

4. The park will close at 5:00 P.M. A Ferris wheel ride lasts 3 minutes, and a carousel ride takes 2 minutes. There is a 2 minute walk between the rides. It is 4:52 P.M. Can Mia ride both before closing time?

Use with

Objective 116
pages 414–415

Focus

Problem Solving
Choose an Operation
Work Backward

Overview

Students *choose operations* to use to solve simple word problems.

Teaching Suggestions

To compute Kurt's time on the ride in Problem 1, students must multiply the number of trips by the time per trip. Kurt spent 8 minutes on the roller coaster. This time must then be added to the time he got on the ride.

To solve Problem 2, students must divide the total number of cars by 2 to get half of the cars, which is 4. 4 × 6 = 24 people. **Question: *How many people are aboard the Hills of Thrills when all the cars are full?* [48]**

To solve Problem 3, students *work backward* starting with the number of horses. There are 10 fewer tigers than horses: 26 – 10 = 16 tigers. There are 10 fewer swans than tigers: 16 – 10 = 6 swans. The total number of animals is 26 + 16 + 6, or 48.

In Problem 4, 3 + 2 + 2 = 7 minutes and 4:52 + 7 min = 4:59. If Mia can get off one ride, walk to the other and get on immediately, she will finish the second ride one minute before the park closes.

Alternate Approach: Have students *write number sentences* to help them solve the problems.

Extension

Have students suppose that half of the horses, a quarter of the tigers, and a third of the swans on the carousel go up and down. Have them compute the number of moving animals. [Thirteen horses, four tigers, and two swans, or a total of 19 animals, move.]

NAME _____

PROBLEM SOLVING

Read and solve each problem.

1. Kurt got on the Hills of Thrills at 2:55 P.M. The car made 4 trips around the track. Each trip took 2 minutes. What time was it when Kurt's ride ended?

   3:03 P.M.

2. Each car on the Hills of Thrills can hold 6 people. There are 8 cars in all. How many people are on the ride when half of the cars are full?

   24 people

3. On the carousel, you can ride on a horse, a tiger, or a swan. There are 10 fewer swans than there are tigers, and 10 fewer tigers than horses. If there are 26 horses, how many carousel animals are there in all?

   48 animals

4. The park will close at 5:00 P.M. A Ferris wheel ride lasts 3 minutes, and a carousel ride takes 2 minutes. There is a 2 minute walk between the rides. It is 4:52 P.M. Can Mia ride both before closing time?

   Yes, if she doesn't have

   to wait.

VISUAL THINKING

See the pattern in each row. Then draw the
picture that comes next in that row.

1.

2.

3.

4.

5.

6.

Use after pages 416-417.

Use with
Objective 117
pages 416–417

Focus
Visual Thinking
   Visual Patterns

Materials
Visual Thinking transparency
   (optional)

Overview
Students recognize the relationship in a *visual pattern* and use this relationship to complete the pattern.

Teaching Suggestions
For Problems 1 and 2, most students will realize that every other figure is the same. Problem 3 may be difficult for some students. Guide those students through the problem.
Questions: How is the second figure different from the first? [The first circle has a vertical line and the second circle has the same vertical line and a horizontal line.] *How are the second and third circles related to the first two circles?* [Now there are two horizontal lines and two vertical lines.] *What pattern do you see?* [In each pair of circles, the number of horizontal and vertical lines increases by 1.]

For Problems 4 through 6, you might have students verbalize the patterns shown. In Problem 4, it appears that every third square has an **X** through it. For Problem 5, the triangular shape alternates between the outside and inside of the circle and the circle rotates clockwise. In Problem 6, the circle inside the square rotates in a clockwise direction.

Alternate Approach: You may want to use the optional transparency and do this activity as a group.

Extension
Have students draw four more pictures in each pattern. For Problems 5 and 6, have them tell how many pictures there are in the pattern before the original figure appears again. [Problem 5, in the 9th picture; Problem 6, in the 9th picture]

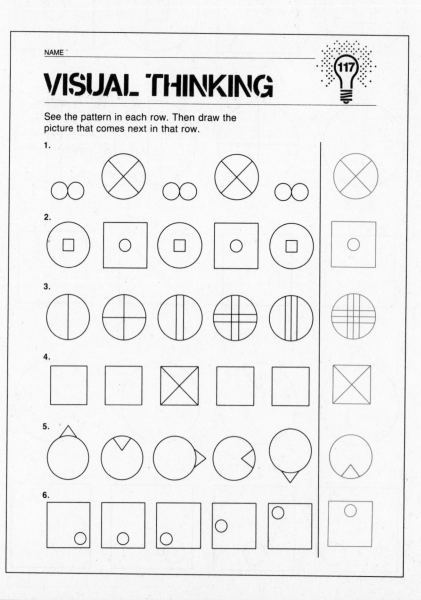

NAME

VISUAL THINKING 117

See the pattern in each row. Then draw the picture that comes next in that row.

1.
2.
3.
4.
5.
6.

DECISION MAKING

Use the words and pictures to help you
make a decision.

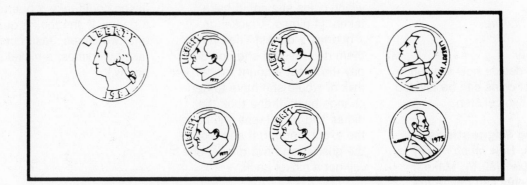

- Michelle needs $0.40 for milk.
- Jason needs $0.26 for an apple.
- Both want to take the exact amount.

1. Write two ways that Michelle can take the
   exact amount she needs from the coins
   on the table.

   First way: _____

   Second way: _____

2. Write two ways that Jason can take the exact amount he needs from
   the coins on the table.

   First way: _____

   Second way: _____

3. Which coins should Michelle take? Tell why.

   _____

   _____

   _____

Use with
Objective 118
pages 420–421

Focus
Decision Making

Overview
Students decide how a given number of coins can be divided between two children.

Teaching Suggestions
Question: How much money is on the table? [$0.71] Make sure students can define the problem. From the coins shown, they want to take 40¢ and 26¢. For Problems 1 and 2, they identify the options for taking 40¢ and for taking 26¢. Then in Problem 3, they decide which combination of options will solve the problem.

Questions: If Michelle took 1 quarter, 1 dime, and 1 nickel, could Jason take 26¢ from the coins left? Why or why not? [No. He needs either a nickel or a quarter, both of which are gone.] *Is there another way Michelle could take 40¢?* [Yes. She could take 4 dimes.] *Now can Jason take 26¢?* [Yes. He can take a quarter and a penny.]

Alternate Approach: Show the 7 coins using play money or slips of paper. Have students act out the problem.

Extension
Have students suppose Michelle made a mistake and took $0.45. Have them explain which coins she could have taken. [4 dimes, 1 nickel or 1 quarter, 2 dimes] Then have them determine if she could pay the exact amount for her milk or would she have to get change back. If she took the dimes and nickel, she will have the exact amount. If she took the quarter and two dimes, she will get a nickel back.

Ask if there is any way Michelle could take 45¢ and still leave 26¢ for Jason. [If she took four dimes and a nickel, Jason could take a quarter and a penny. If she took a quarter and two dimes, Jason could take two dimes, a nickel and a penny.]

NAME

DECISION MAKING

Use the words and pictures to help you make a decision.

- Michelle needs $0.40 for milk.
- Jason needs $0.26 for an apple.
- Both want to take the exact amount.

1. Write two ways that Michelle can take the exact amount she needs from the coins on the table.

   First way: _____ 1 quarter, 1 dime, 1 nickel _____

   Second way: _____ 4 dimes _____

2. Write two ways that Jason can take the exact amount he needs from the coins on the table.

   First way: _____ 1 quarter, 1 penny _____

   Second way: _____ 2 dimes, 1 nickel, 1 penny _____

3. Which coins should Michelle take? Tell why.

   Possible answer: 4 dimes. Then Jason can take a
   quarter and a penny. If she takes the other coins, he
   won't be able to take the exact amount.

PROBLEM SOLVING

The students at Morgan School are raising money to buy a new flagpole for the school.

Read and solve each problem.

1. Ms. Bee's class made 250 small paper flags so they could give one to each person who donated. At the end of the first day, they had 212 flags left. How many people had donated?

_____

2. The students raised $43.75 the first week and $51.30 the next week. How much did they have then?

_____

3. Josh donated to the flagpole fund every week. He gave $0.25 the first week and $0.85 the second week. How much did he give in two weeks?

_____

4. Rosa brought $1.65 to school on Tuesday. She spent $1.25 for lunch and gave the rest to the flagpole fund. How much did she give?

_____

Use after pages 422-423.

Use with
Objective 119
pages 422–423

Focus
Problem Solving
  Choose an Operation

Overview
Students *choose an operation* to solve word problems.

Teaching Suggestions
To compute the number of people who donated to the flagpole fund, students must subtract the remaining flags, 212, from the number of original flags, 250, to find out that 38 people donated to the fund.

  Students must add the two sums of money in Problem 2 to find out that the group raised $95.05 by the second week.

  After solving Problem 3, ask students the following.
Question: How much more did Josh give the second week? [$0.60]

  To calculate Rosa's contribution, students must subtract the cost of her lunch from the money she brought that day to find that she contributed $0.40. *Question: How much did Josh and Rosa contribute to the fund?* [$0.25 + $0.85 + $0.40 = $1.50]

NAME _____

PROBLEM SOLVING

The students at Morgan School are raising money to buy a new flagpole for the school.

Read and solve each problem.

1. Ms. Bee's class made 250 small paper flags so they could give one to each person who donated. At the end of the first day, they had 212 flags left. How many people had donated?

   38 people

2. The students raised $43.75 the first week and $51.30 the next week. How much did they have then?

   $95.05

3. Josh donated to the flagpole fund every week. He gave $0.25 the first week and $0.85 the second week. How much did he give in two weeks?

   $1.10

4. Rosa brought $1.65 to school on Tuesday. She spent $1.25 for lunch and gave the rest to the flagpole fund. How much did she give?

   $0.40

VISUAL THINKING

Look at the two pictures at the left of each row. Ring the letter of the picture on the right that is made by putting those two pictures together. The pictures may be turned or flipped, but they cannot overlap, and there cannot be gaps.

1.

 a.　　 b.　　 c.　　d.

2.

a.　　b.　　 c.　　d.

3.

 a.　　 b.　　 c.　　 d.

4.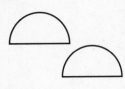

a.　　b.　　c.　　 d.

5.

a.　　b.　　c.　　d.

6.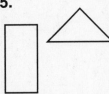

 a.　　 b.　　 c.　　 d.

  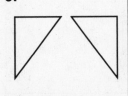

Use with
Objective 120
pages 424–425

Focus
Visual Thinking
Spatial Perception

Materials
Visual Thinking transparency
  (optional)
Tracing paper (optional)
Scissors (optional)

Overview
Students study shapes to
determine what figure is made
when two shapes are put
together.

Teaching Suggestions
To discourage guessing, you
may want to have students
explain why they did not
choose the other figures shown
in each group.

Alternate Approach: Allow
students having difficulties with
this activity to trace the shapes
in the first row onto tracing
paper. Let them cut out the
shapes and manipulate them
to solve the problems. You can
also use the Visual Thinking
transparency and do this
activity as a group.

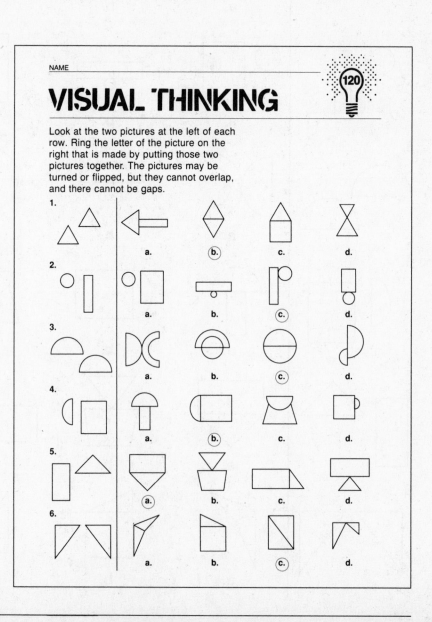

NAME _____

VISUAL THINKING

Look at the two pictures at the left of each
row. Ring the letter of the picture on the
right that is made by putting those two
pictures together. The pictures may be
turned or flipped, but they cannot overlap,
and there cannot be gaps.

PROBLEM SOLVING

Read and solve each problem.

1. Karen and Steve were going to buy a birthday present for Dad. Karen had saved some money. Steve had saved $6.50. Mom gave them $1.00. When they put it all together, they had $12.00. How much had Karen saved?

_____

2. To get to the mall, they took the bus from Jay Street to New Street. They changed buses and rode 5 blocks east and 3 blocks north to the mall. They rode 17 blocks in all. How far is it from Jay Street to New Street?

_____

3. At the mall, Karen and Steve bought a birthday card for Dad. Then they spent $8.95 for a gift and $1.75 for wrapping paper and a bow. They got $0.05 change from their $12.00. How much did the card cost?

_____

4. After shopping, they waited for the bus for 5 minutes, and the ride took 35 minutes. It took 5 minutes to walk home after the bus dropped them off. Karen and Steve got home just in time for dinner at 6:00 P.M. What time did they finish shopping?

_____

Use after pages 426-427.

Use with
Objective 121
pages 426–427

Focus
Problem Solving
  Write a Number Sentence
  Work Backward

Overview
Students solve word problems by *writing number sentences* and *working backward.*

Teaching Suggestions
To solve these problems, students might choose to *work backward.*

  In Problem 1, they should begin with the total of $12.00, subtract the $1.00 given to them, and subtract the $6.50 Steve contributed. [$12.00 – $1.00 – $6.50 = $4.50.] In Problem 2, they should *work backward* from the 17 blocks the children rode in all and subtract 3 blocks and 5 blocks. In Problem 3, they should start with $12.00 and subtract $0.05, $1.75, and $8.95. Finally, in Problem 4, they should begin at 6:00 P.M. and count back 5 minutes, 35 minutes, and 5 minutes.

Alternate Approach: Have students *write number sentences* to solve Problems 1 through 3.

NAME

PROBLEM SOLVING

Read and solve each problem.

1. Karen and Steve were going to buy a birthday present for Dad. Karen had saved some money. Steve had saved $6.50. Mom gave them $1.00. When they put it all together, they had $12.00. How much had Karen saved?

    $4.50

2. To get to the mall, they took the bus from Jay Street to New Street. They changed buses and rode 5 blocks east and 3 blocks north to the mall. They rode 17 blocks in all. How far is it from Jay Street to New Street?

    9 blocks

3. At the mall, Karen and Steve bought a birthday card for Dad. Then they spent $8.95 for a gift and $1.75 for wrapping paper and a bow. They got $0.05 change from their $12.00. How much did the card cost?

    $1.25

4. After shopping, they waited for the bus for 5 minutes, and the ride took 35 minutes. It took 5 minutes to walk home after the bus dropped them off. Karen and Steve got home just in time for dinner at 6:00 P.M. What time did they finish shopping?

    5:15 P.M.

CRITICAL THINKING

Use the picture to answer the questions.

Alison estimated the cost of the party supplies at $11.00. Rodney added the prices on a calculator. His total was $12.06.

1. Write an estimate that you think Alison used for each item to make a total of $11.00.

   paper plates   _____

   paper cups   _____

   paper napkins   _____

   paper tablecloth   _____

   plastic forks   _____

   plastic spoons   _____
                       _____
   TOTAL   _____

2. Write an estimate for each item that would have given a better total estimate.

   paper plates   _____

   paper cups   _____

   paper napkins   _____

   paper tablecloth   _____

   plastic forks   _____

   plastic spoons   _____
                       _____
   TOTAL   _____

3. Explain how Alison could have made a better estimate.

_____

_____

Teacher Notes

Use with
Objective 122
pages 428–429

Focus
Critical Thinking
   Using Number Sense
   Explaining Reasoning/
      Justifying Answers

Overview
Students round prices up or down to estimate the total cost of party supplies.

Teaching Suggestions
Review rounding of numbers with the following examples. Have students round 11, 29, 34, 56, and 77 to the nearest ten. [10, 30, 30, 60, and 80] Now have them round 101, 238, 456, 590, and 876 to the nearest hundred. [100, 200, 500, 600, and 900] Make sure they remember that 5s are rounded up.

Some students may make fairly accurate estimates for Problem 1 and thus may have difficulties answering Problem 2. Explain that the answers may be very similar or even the same.

Alternate Approach: Have students convert the prices into cents. The paper plates cost 279¢, the forks 149¢, and so on. Then have them construct number lines from 100 to 300. Let them place each price, in cents, on the line to help them round the prices.

Extension
Have students solve this problem: Suppose Greta rounded the number of books she has to the nearest ten. She said she had about 20 story books about animals, about 30 books about people, and about 50 science books. Have students compute the least number and most number of each kind of book. [Greta has at least 15 to 24 animal books; 25 to 34 people books; and 45 to 54 science books.]

NAME _____

CRITICAL THINKING

Use the picture to answer the questions.

Alison estimated the cost of the party supplies at $11.00. Rodney added the prices on a calculator. His total was $12.06.

Possible answers are given.

1. Write an estimate that you think Alison used for each item to make a total of $11.00.

paper plates	$ 3.00
paper cups	$ 2.00
paper napkins	$ 2.00
paper tablecloth	$ 2.00
plastic forks	$ 1.00
plastic spoons	$ 1.00
TOTAL	$11.00

2. Write an estimate for each item that would have given a better total estimate.

paper plates	$ 3.00
paper cups	$ 2.00
paper napkins	$ 2.00
paper tablecloth	$ 2.50
plastic forks	$ 1.50
plastic spoons	$ 1.50
TOTAL	$12.50

3. Explain how Alison could have made a better estimate.

   She could have estimated each price to the nearest half-dollar.

VISUAL THINKING

See how the pair of pictures on the left of each row are alike. Ring the letter of the pair of pictures on the right that are alike in the same way.

1.

    a.   b.   c.

2.

    a.   b.   c.

3.

    a.   b.   c.

4.

    a.   b.   c.

5.

    a.   b.   c.

6.

    a.   b.   c.

Use after pages 440-441.

Use with
Objective 123
pages 440–441

Focus
Visual Thinking
  Visual Patterns

Materials
Visual Thinking transparency
  (optional)

Overview
Students choose a pair of
pictures that show a pattern
similar to that in a given pair of
pictures.

Teaching Suggestions
Have students choose their
answers by visual means and
then check their answers by
describing the relationship
between the two figures on the
left. *Questions: What is the
relationship between the two
figures on the left in Problem 1?*
[The left square is smaller than
the right square.] *What must be
the relationship of the two
circles in the correct answer?*
[The left circle must be smaller
than the right circle.] Have
students check their answers
in this way.

Extension
Have students draw another
pair of pictures for each
problem that follows the given
pattern.

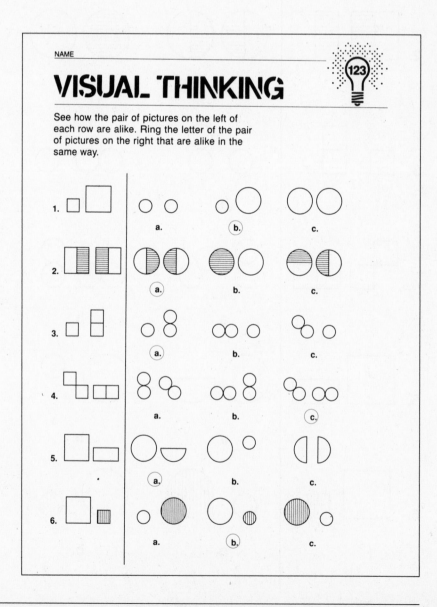

CRITICAL THINKING

There are 6 Little League teams in Exton. Each team has 20 players. How many players are there in Little League?

Teri thinks:

Each team has 20 players.
$$20 = 2 \text{ tens}$$

There are 6 teams, so there are 6 groups of 2 tens.

She draws this picture.

10	10		10	10		10	10
10	10		10	10		10	10

She counts by tens to get the answer.

Greg thinks:

If each team had 10 players, there would be 6 tens.

Each team has 20 players, so there are 2 groups of 6 tens.

He draws this picture.

10	10	10	10	10	10
10	10	10	10	10	10

He counts by tens to get the answer.

1. How many players does Teri count? How many players does Greg count? _____

2. How are their pictures different? How are their pictures the same?

_____

_____

3. Mark the statement below that you think Teri and Greg showed was true.

_____ There is more than one right answer.

_____ There is one right answer and one right way to find it.

_____ There is one right answer but more than one way to find it.

Use with
Objective 124
pages 442–443

Focus
Critical Thinking
   Using Number Sense
   Using Logic

Materials
12 base-10 rods for each pair
   of students

Overview
Students compare two ways of
performing an arithmetic
operation.

Teaching Suggestions
Group students into pairs and
distribute the rods. Tell
students that each rod
represents 10 players. Have
students group the rods in a
number of different ways.
*Question: Which grouping do
you find easiest to count?*
[Answers will vary.]
   Have students complete
Problems 1 and 2 on their own.
   For each choice in Problem
3, have students explain why it
is incorrect or correct.

Extension
Have students set up groups
for 6 teams with 25 players on
a team.

NAME _____

CRITICAL THINKING

There are 6 Little League teams in Exton. Each team has 20 players.
How many players are there in Little League?

Teri thinks:

Each team has 20 players.
         20 = 2 tens

There are 6 teams, so there are
6 groups of 2 tens.

She draws this picture.

| 10 | 10 | | 10 | 10 | | 10 | 10 |
| 10 | 10 | | 10 | 10 | | 10 | 10 |

She counts by tens to get the
answer.

Greg thinks:

If each team had 10 players, there
would be 6 tens.

Each team has 20 players, so there
are 2 groups of 6 tens.

He draws this picture.

| 10 | 10 | 10 | 10 | 10 | 10 |
| 10 | 10 | 10 | 10 | 10 | 10 |

He counts by tens to get the
answer.

1. How many players does Teri count? How
   many players does Greg count?   120; 120

2. How are their pictures different? How are
   their pictures the same?
   Possible answers: Different groups of tens; Both
   show 12 tens.

3. Mark the statement below that you think
   Teri and Greg showed was true.

   _____ There is more than one right answer.

   _____ There is one right answer and one
         right way to find it.

   __X__ There is one right answer but more
         than one way to find it.

PROBLEM SOLVING

125

Use the picture to help you solve the problems.

WE MUST HAVE PICKED A THOUSAND BERRIES.

WE PUT 31 BERRIES IN EACH BASKET.

THERE ARE 6 BASKETS ON EACH TRAY.

1. Estimate the number of berries on each tray. _____

2. Estimate the number of berries in all. _____

3. Complete the table to find the number of berries on each tray.

Number of baskets	1	2	3	4	5	6
Number of berries	31	62	93			

4. Now complete this table to find the number of berries in all. Use your answer to Exercise 3.

THERE ARE 6 TRAYS.

Number of trays	1	2	3	4	5	6
Number of berries						

5. Was your estimate more or fewer than the actual number of berries? How many more or fewer? _____

Use with
Objective 125
pages 444–445

Focus
Problem Solving
  Make a Table

Overview
Students estimate a total number from given information and then they *make a table* to find the actual number.

Teaching Suggestions
Question: Why is it sometimes useful to estimate? [Answers will vary. Students should understand that there are times when precise calculations are not necessary or convenient.] For Problems 1 and 2 explain that rounding numbers is one way to estimate. *Question: With 31 berries in each basket and 6 baskets on each tray, what is a good way to estimate the number of berries on each tray?* [30 × 6] Have students solve Problem 1. Make sure students notice, from the lower picture, that there are 6 trays in all. Estimates may vary. You might want to ask these guiding questions. *Questions: What can 180 be rounded to?* [200] *6 trays of approximately 200 berries equals how many berries?* [1,200] Have students solve Problem 2.

Explain that in Problems 3 and 4, students are going from estimation to calculating exact amounts. Then have them complete the tables independently. They should notice that they can complete the table for Problem 3 by adding 31 to the previous number of berries. Then they can complete Problem 4 by adding 186 to the previous number of berries.

Have students solve Problem 5 and then figure out approximately how many baskets of berries are represented by the difference between the estimate and the exact number. Have students discuss whether the difference is significant. If the students estimated 1,200 berries in Problem 2 and computed 1,116 in Problem 4, the difference is 84, or almost 3 baskets.

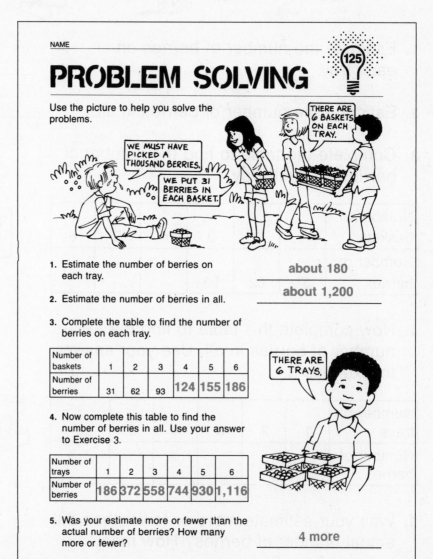

VISUAL THINKING

Find and color all the circles in the picture.
(Hint: The number of circles is equal to
3 groups of 13.)

KIKI The JUGGLER AND BOBO The DOG

Teacher Notes

Use with
Objective 126
pages 446–449

Focus
Visual Thinking
  Spatial Perception

Materials
Crayons
Visual Thinking transparency
  (optional)

Overview
Students find all the circles
shown in a picture.

Teaching Suggestions
Distribute crayons. **Question:
How many are 13 groups of 3?**
[39] Have students do the
activity on their own and then
have a partner count the
circles they colored.

Alternate Approach: Using the
optional transparency, have
student volunteers color the
circles using overhead
markers.

Extension
Have students find shapes in
the picture that approximate
other geometric figures such
as rectangles and triangles.

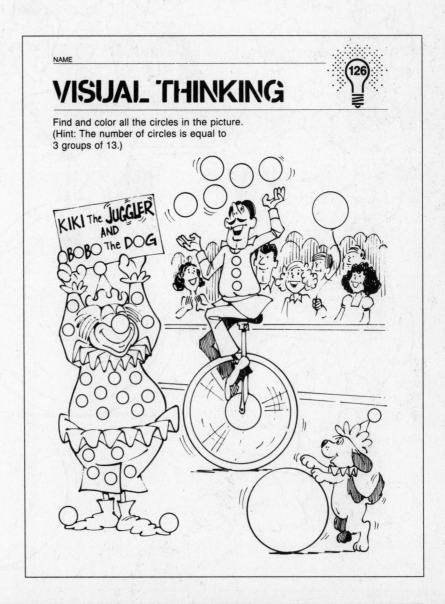

NAME _____

VISUAL THINKING

126

Find and color all the circles in the picture.
(Hint: The number of circles is equal to
3 groups of 13.)

KIKI The JUGGLER AND BOBO The DOG

DECISION MAKING

Use the picture to help you make a decision.

18 Red Yo-Yos	Sunshine Yo-Yos
18 Blue Yo-Yos	
18 Yellow Yo-Yos	

16 Green Yo-Yos	Rainbow Yo-Yos
16 Blue Yo-Yos	
16 Red Yo-Yos	
16 Yellow Yo-Yos	

12 Red Yo-Yos	Yoohoo Yo-Yos
12 Blue Yo-Yos	
12 Yellow Yo-Yos	
12 Green Yo-Yos	
12 Red Yo-Yos	

Mr. Young is buying yo-yos to sell in his toy store. Here are his needs:

• He wants to buy boxes that are all the same size.
• He wants to buy at least 55 yo-yos.
• He wants to buy at least 18 red yo-yos.

1. How many Sunshine Yo-Yos can Mr. Young buy? How many red yo-yos would he have?

_____

2. How many Rainbow Yo-Yos can Mr. Young buy? How many red yo-yos would he have?

_____

3. How many Yoohoo Yo-Yos can Mr. Young buy? How many red yo-yos would he have?

_____

4. What brand of yo-yos should Mr. Young buy? Explain why.

_____

_____

Use with
Objective 127
pages 450–451

Focus
Decision Making

Overview
Students analyze options and make a decision for buying yo-yos.

Teaching Suggestions
Tell students that the boxes of each brand of yo-yos are sold as a unit. Boxes cannot be sold individually. Then have students analyze Mr. Young's needs so that they know exactly what he wants.
Questions: Can he buy boxes of different brands? [No, all boxes must be of the same size.] *Does the number of green yo-yos enter into his decision?* [No]

Have students complete Problems 1–3.

Introduce Problem 4 by asking which brand gives Mr. Young 55 or more yo-yos in all *and* at least 18 red yo-yos.

Alternate Approach: Have students use the process of elimination to find which brands have 55 or more yo-yos. [Rainbow and Yoohoo] Then have them find which of these has 18 or more red yo-yos. [Yoohoo Yo-Yos]

Extension
Ask students what factors a store owner would consider that are not mentioned among Mr. Young's needs. [Possible answers: price, quality, popularity, and so on.]

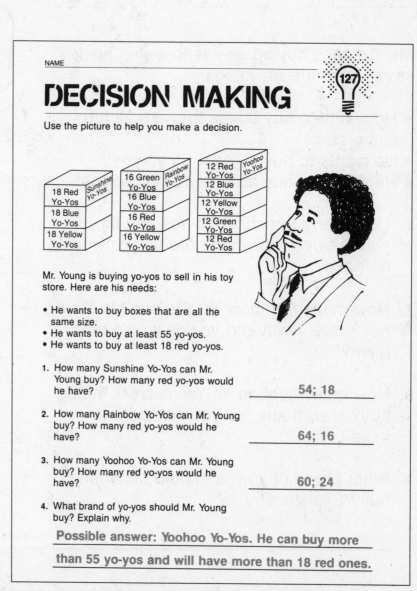

NAME _____

DECISION MAKING 127

Use the picture to help you make a decision.

18 Red Yo-Yos / 18 Blue Yo-Yos / 18 Yellow Yo-Yos — Sunshine Yo-Yos

16 Green Yo-Yos / 16 Blue Yo-Yos / 16 Red Yo-Yos / 16 Yellow Yo-Yos — Rainbow Yo-Yos

12 Red Yo-Yos / 12 Blue Yo-Yos / 12 Yellow Yo-Yos / 12 Green Yo-Yos / 12 Red Yo-Yos — Yoohoo Yo-Yos

Mr. Young is buying yo-yos to sell in his toy store. Here are his needs:

• He wants to buy boxes that are all the same size.
• He wants to buy at least 55 yo-yos.
• He wants to buy at least 18 red yo-yos.

1. How many Sunshine Yo-Yos can Mr. Young buy? How many red yo-yos would he have? **54; 18**

2. How many Rainbow Yo-Yos can Mr. Young buy? How many red yo-yos would he have? **64; 16**

3. How many Yoohoo Yo-Yos can Mr. Young buy? How many red yo-yos would he have? **60; 24**

4. What brand of yo-yos should Mr. Young buy? Explain why.

Possible answer: Yoohoo Yo-Yos. He can buy more than 55 yo-yos and will have more than 18 red ones.

CRITICAL THINKING

Solve each problem. Underline any information in the problem that you did not need.

ARBOR ARMS APARTMENT

1. The Arbor Arms has 12 floors. There are 6 apartments on each floor. Rico lives on Floor 3. How many apartments are there in the Arbor Arms?

_____

2. Each elevator in the Arbor Arms can hold 24 people. There are 4 elevators. How many people can ride the elevators at one time?

_____

3. Mr. Dunn gets exercise by climbing the stairs. He has lost 11 pounds so far. Mr. Dunn walks up 5 flights. There are 15 steps in each flight. How many steps does Mr. Dunn climb?

_____

4. A window washer washed the windows in 14 apartments. Each apartment has 7 windows. The window washer used a total of 10 buckets of water. How many windows did he wash?

_____

Use with
Objective 128
pages 454–455

Focus
Critical Thinking
Evaluating Evidence and
Conclusions

Overview
Students identify unnecessary
information in problems. Then
they solve the problems.

Teaching Suggestions
For each problem have
students ask themselves,
"What information do I need to
solve the problem?" Go over
Problem 1 with the class. The
problem asks for the number of
apartments in the building.
*Questions: What information
do you need to answer the
question?* [The number of
floors and the number of
apartments on each floor] *Is
there information that did not
help you answer the question?*
[Yes; Rico lives on Floor 3.]
    Have students complete the
remaining problems on their
own.

Extension
Have students create problems
in which the underlined
information *is* essential.

NAME

CRITICAL THINKING

Solve each problem. Underline any
information in the problem that you did
not need.

ARBOR ARMS
APARTMENT

1. The Arbor Arms has 12 floors.
   There are 6 apartments on each
   floor. ~~Rico lives on Floor 3.~~ How
   many apartments are there in
   the Arbor Arms?
   72 apartments

2. Each elevator in the Arbor Arms
   can hold 24 people. There are 4
   elevators. How many people can
   ride the elevators at one time?
   96 people

3. Mr. Dunn gets exercise by
   climbing the stairs. ~~He has lost
   11 pounds so far.~~ Mr. Dunn
   walks up 5 flights. There are 15
   steps in each flight. How many
   steps does Mr. Dunn climb?
   75 steps

4. A window washer washed the
   windows in 14 apartments. Each
   apartment has 7 windows. ~~The
   window washer used a total of
   10 buckets of water.~~ How many
   windows did he wash?
   98 windows

CRITICAL THINKING

129

Use the picture to help you answer
the questions.

1. Cheryl drew a crooked line on her math
   paper. The exercises to the left of the line
   are different from the exercises to the
   right of the line. How are they different?

   _____

   _____

   _____

2. Cheryl did not have to complete the
   exercises to know where to draw the line.
   She just looked at the numbers in the
   ones place to tell whether an exercise
   should be on the left side or the right side
   of the line. Explain how she did it.

   _____

   _____

   _____

   _____

   _____

Teacher Notes

Use with
Objective 129
pages 456–457

Focus
Critical Thinking
   Classifying and Sorting
   Using Number Sense
   Making Generalizations

Overview
Students determine a strategy for separating multiplication problems into two groups.

Teaching Suggestions
Have students identify the pattern of numbers in the chart. They should see that each column contains numbers in increasing order from 22–25. The numbers in the first column are multiplied by 2, the numbers in the second column are multiplied by 3, and so on. This means that the product increases as one moves down and to the right. Then have students answer Problems 1 and 2.

Alternate Approach: Have students write in all the products before attempting Problems 1 and 2.

Extension
If a similar chart were made in which the numbers 12, 13, 14, and 15 are each multiplied by 2, 3, and 4, would the line have to be drawn differently? [No, since only the ones place is significant.]

NAME _____

CRITICAL THINKING

Use the picture to help you answer the questions.

22 ×2	22 ×3	22 ×4
23 ×2	23 ×3	23 ×4
24 ×2	24 ×3	24 ×4
25 ×2	25 ×3	25 ×4

1. Cheryl drew a crooked line on her math paper. The exercises to the left of the line are different from the exercises to the right of the line. How are they different?

   Possible answer: Do not have to rename the ones in the exercises to the left; do have to rename the ones in the exercises to the right.

2. Cheryl did not have to complete the exercises to know where to draw the line. She just looked at the numbers in the ones place to tell whether an exercise should be on the left side or the right side of the line. Explain how she did it.

   Possible answer: She multiplied the numbers in the ones place mentally. If the product was less than 10, she knew she would not have to rename. If the product was 10 or greater, she knew she would have to rename.

PROBLEM SOLVING

Tell whether you will add, subtract, multiply, or divide to solve the problem. Then solve the problem.

1. There are 32 signs to read as you walk along the nature trail. Of these signs, 9 identify different kinds of trees. How many signs do not identify trees?

   What you will do: _____ Answer: _____

2. Students are allowed to come in groups of 3 to peek at some baby birds in a nest. There are 27 students in this class. How many groups will look at the baby birds?

   What you will do: _____ Answer: _____

3. Each of the 27 students received 6 information sheets about the nature trail. How many sheets were given out?

   What you will do: _____ Answer: _____

4. The students saw 7 squirrel nests, 12 bird nests, and 2 wasp nests along the trail. How many nests did they see?

   What you will do: _____ Answer: _____

Teacher Notes

Use with
Objective 130
pages 458–459

Focus
Problem Solving
   Choose an Operation

Materials
Counters (optional)

Overview
Students choose which operations are needed to solve problems.

Teaching Suggestions
You may want to discuss the four operations in relation to kinds of problems. For each, ask students to "ask" a question that might be in a problem for that operation. For example:

Addition: How many are there after groups of things are put together?

Subtraction: How many are there after a number of things are taken away from a larger group?

Multiplication: How many are there in all when groups containing the same number of things are put together?

Division: How many groups are there when a larger number of things are separated into smaller groups of the same size?

Alternate Approach: Have students work in small groups and act out each problem using counters.

Extension
Have students write their own explanations for when to use the different operations.

NAME

PROBLEM SOLVING 130

Tell whether you will add, subtract, multiply, or divide to solve the problem. Then solve the problem.

1. There are 32 signs to read as you walk along the nature trail. Of these signs, 9 identify different kinds of trees. How many signs do not identify trees?

   What you will do: __Subtract__   Answer: __23 signs__

2. Students are allowed to come in groups of 3 to peek at some baby birds in a nest. There are 27 students in this class. How many groups will look at the baby birds?

   What you will do: __Divide__   Answer: __9 groups__

3. Each of the 27 students received 6 information sheets about the nature trail. How many sheets were given out?

   What you will do: __Multiply__   Answer: __162 sheets__

4. The students saw 7 squirrel nests, 12 bird nests, and 2 wasp nests along the trail. How many nests did they see?

   What you will do: __Add__   Answer: __21 nests__

CRITICAL THINKING

Use the picture to help you answer
the questions.

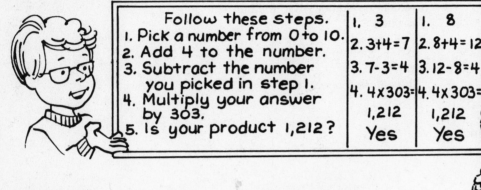

Follow these steps.
1. Pick a number from 0 to 10.
2. Add 4 to the number.
3. Subtract the number you picked in step 1.
4. Multiply your answer by 303.
5. Is your product 1,212?

1. 3	1. 8
2. 3+4=7	2. 8+4=12
3. 7-3=4	3. 12-8=4
4. 4×303= 1,212 Yes	4. 4×303= 1,212 Yes

Mike is playing a math trick on his friends.
They followed the steps that Mike gave them.

1. What two numbers did Mike's
   friends pick?   _____

2. Did both friends get the same product?   _____

3. Try the trick with another number.

   Number you picked: _____   Product you got: _____

4. The answer you get when you subtract in
   Step 3 is always multiplied by 303. The
   product is always 1,212. What answer
   must you get every time you subtract in
   Step 3?   _____

5. Look at Steps 1, 2, and 3. Why will you
   always get the same answer in Step 3, no
   matter what number you pick?

   _____

   _____

   _____

Use with

Objective 131
pages 460–461

Focus

Critical Thinking
  Using Number Sense
  Explaining Reasoning/
    Justifying Answers

Overview

Students analyze a math trick
to determine how it works.

Teaching Suggestions

Have students answer
Problems 1–3 on their own.
Then have several student
volunteers come to the board
and write the 5 steps of the
trick for the numbers they
chose in Problem 3. *Question:
What is the same about step 3
for each student?* [The answer
is 4.] Have students answer
Problems 4 and 5.

  *Questions: Will the trick
work if the number you pick in
Step 1 is greater than 10?* [Yes]
*What would happen if the
number in Step 2 was 7, rather
than 4?* [The final answer,
regardless of the number
picked in Step 1, would be
7 × 303, or 2,121.]

Extension

Have students create other
tricks which yield the same
results no matter what number
is used.

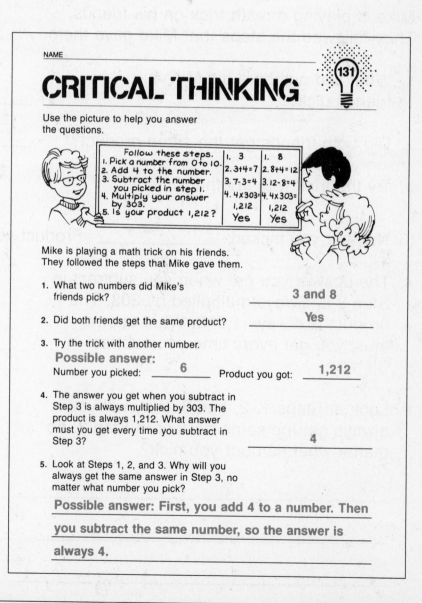

NAME _____

CRITICAL THINKING ⟨131⟩

Use the picture to help you answer
the questions.

> Follow these steps.
> 1. Pick a number from 0 to 10.
> 2. Add 4 to the number.
> 3. Subtract the number
>   you picked in step 1.
> 4. Multiply your answer
>   by 303.
> 5. Is your product 1,212?

	I. 3	I. 8
2.	3+4=7	2. 8+4=12
3.	7-3=4	3. 12-8=4
4.	4×303=	4. 4×303=
	1,212	1,212
	Yes	Yes

Mike is playing a math trick on his friends.
They followed the steps that Mike gave them.

1. What two numbers did Mike's
   friends pick?   **3 and 8**

2. Did both friends get the same product?   **Yes**

3. Try the trick with another number.
   Possible answer:
   Number you picked: ____**6**____   Product you got: ____**1,212**

4. The answer you get when you subtract in
   Step 3 is always multiplied by 303. The
   product is always 1,212. What answer
   must you get every time you subtract in
   Step 3?   **4**

5. Look at Steps 1, 2, and 3. Why will you
   always get the same answer in Step 3, no
   matter what number you pick?

   Possible answer: First, you add 4 to a number. Then

   you subtract the same number, so the answer is

   always 4.

PROBLEM SOLVING

Read and solve each problem.

1. Elena collected data and found that
   17 people wanted a new playground, but
   14 people did not want one. How many
   people did Elena ask? _____

2. Donald asked 43 people if they would
   be willing to help plant flowers in his
   neighborhood. If 29 people said they
   would help, how many people said they
   would not? _____

3. When Melissa collected data, she spoke
   to 12 people each day. She spent 4 days
   collecting the data. How many people did
   she speak to? _____

4. Brad and Kathy asked the same question
   when they collected data, but they spoke
   to different people. Brad asked 18 people,
   and Kathy asked twice as many as Brad
   did. How many people did they ask in all? _____

Use with
Objective 132
pages 472–473

Focus
Problem Solving
   Choose an Operation

Overview
Students use information concerning data collection to *choose an operation* to solve problems.

Teaching Suggestions
Have students discuss the type of data collected when they ask or answer questions. *Questions: Suppose two classmates asked different friends whether or not they had any pets. How would you decide how many friends in all had answered?* [Find out how many each had asked and add the numbers together.] *How would you decide how many more of these people had pets than did not have pets?* [Subtract, if possible.] *Would you know how many pets the people had? Explain.* [No; they asked if people had pets and not how many each had.] *If everyone in the class asked exactly the same number of friends, what would be a quick way to find out how many responses there were?* [Multiply the number of students by the number of friends each asked.]

If students have difficulty with the questions suggested in the preceding paragraph, include numbers with the questions.

Have students complete the activity. Then, for each problem, have a volunteer read the problem and identify the operation or operations needed to solve it. Have another volunteer write a number sentence for the problem. A third may give the answer in a complete sentence and decide if it is reasonable.

Extension
For Problems 1 and 2, have students make up a different problem using the given data. For Problems 3 and 4, have students find alternate methods to solve each problem.

NAME _____

PROBLEM SOLVING (132)

Read and solve each problem.

1. Elena collected data and found that 17 people wanted a new playground, but 14 people did not want one. How many people did Elena ask?

   _____ 31 people

2. Donald asked 43 people if they would be willing to help plant flowers in his neighborhood. If 29 people said they would help, how many people said they would not?

   _____ 14 people

3. When Melissa collected data, she spoke to 12 people each day. She spent 4 days collecting the data. How many people did she speak to?

   _____ 48 people

4. Brad and Kathy asked the same question when they collected data, but they spoke to different people. Brad asked 18 people, and Kathy asked twice as many as Brad did. How many people did they ask in all?

   _____ 54 people

133

DECISION MAKING

Use the tally chart and other information to help you make a decision.

The third grade made a tally chart to show their favorite playground activities. Complete the chart.

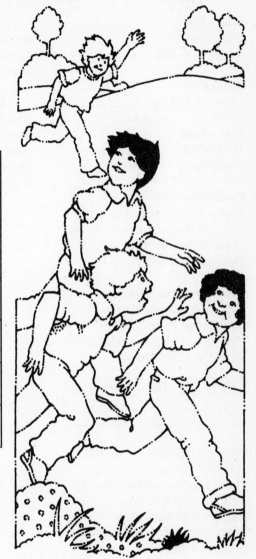

Our Favorite Playground Activities		
Activity	Tally	Number
chair tag		5
shadow tag	~~IIII~~ III	8
follow the leader	III	
kickball	II	7
relay races		4

1. It is a cloudy day, but it is not raining. The students are using their tally chart to help them choose an activity for the playground. What do you think they should choose?

_____

2. Was there more than one thing that helped you make your decision? Explain your answer.

_____

_____

_____

Use with
Objective 133
pages 474–475

Focus
Decision Making

Materials
15 to 20 chips or unit cubes in each of 4 or more colors

Overview
Students complete a tally chart and use the information in the chart to decide which activity a class might most enjoy.

Teaching Suggestions
Display a pile of chips in the front of the room. On the chalkboard, make a chart and fill in the color names.

Color	Tally	Number

Ask one volunteer to be the recorder at the chalkboard. Have another student take a handful of chips. One-by-one, have this student name the color and place each chip in a different pile or bag. The recorder should tally each color as it is reported. Repeat with other students until all the chips have been counted and categorized. Ask students to summarize the procedure, tell some things they know about the chips, and discuss why it is useful to group using tallies.

Have students read and discuss the situation on the activity page. **Question:** *How many students named a favorite activity? Explain how you know.* [27; Add the number of tallies.] After students complete the activity and make their decisions, have them share their ideas and justify their decisions.

Extension
Have each student list three playground activities that he or she likes. Each then surveys classmates with Yes or No questions to see if classmates also like each activity and then makes a chart of the results. Students may discuss or write a short paragraph comparing their chart to the chart on the activity page.

NAME _____

DECISION MAKING

Use the tally chart and other information to help you make a decision.

The third grade made a tally chart to show their favorite playground activities. Complete the chart.

Our Favorite Playground Activities		
Activity	Tally	Number
chair tag	ЖⅠ	5
shadow tag	ЖⅠ ⅠⅠⅠ	8
follow the leader	ⅠⅠⅠ	3
kickball	ⅠⅠ ЖⅠ	7
relay races	ⅠⅠⅠⅠ	4

1. It is a cloudy day, but it is not raining. The students are using their tally chart to help them choose an activity for the playground. What do you think they should choose?

   Possible answer: Kickball

2. Was there more than one thing that helped you make your decision? Explain your answer.

   Possible answer: Yes. Tally chart shows shadow tag

   as favorite, but day is cloudy. Used that fact and tally

   chart to decide on kickball.

CRITICAL THINKING

134

The tally chart below shows data collected from 20 students.

Favorite Vegetable	Tally
carrots	|||| |||
spinach	||
corn	||||
peas	||||	

1. Draw a pictograph below to show this data. Write a title in the space above the graph, and choose a picture to stand for a certain number of people.

_____

carrots	
spinach	
corn	
peas	

Each _____ stands for _____ people.

2. Which vegetable was the favorite of most of the students?

_____

Use with

Objective 134
pages 476–479

Focus

Critical Thinking
  Reasoning with Graphs and
  Charts

Overview

Students use data from a tally chart to label, design, and interpret a pictograph.

Teaching Suggestions

On the chalkboard, draw a chart like the one below.

	Bottom	Top
solid color		
striped		
plaid		
print		
other		

Have students one-by-one mark a tally in the chart to describe the outfit they are wearing (for a dress, consider the top and skirt separately). Students who are seated should check that every "fifth" student in a category correctly groups the tallies. As a class, discuss the chart and the totals. Talk about how they are the same and why they are easy to calculate. *Questions: Suppose we made a pictograph for the chart. What do we have to decide?* [What the picture will be and how many people it stands for.] *If you use a circle for every 2 people, how would you show 3 people?* [1-1/2 circles]

If you used a circle for every 3 people, how would you show 4 people? [1-1/3 circles] *Which do you think would be a better choice? Why?* [Possible answer: A circle for every 2 people, because a half-circle is easier to draw than a third of a circle.] *Would 5 be a good amount for a picture? Why or why not?* [Yes, because there would be as many pictures as groups of 5 tally marks, but it might be difficult to draw the leftovers.]

Have students complete the activity and then share their results. *Questions: How did you decide how many pictures you needed?* [Find the total number of tallies in each row and divide by the number each picture stands for.] *How might graphs be different?* [Use different pictures or have pictures stand for other amounts.]

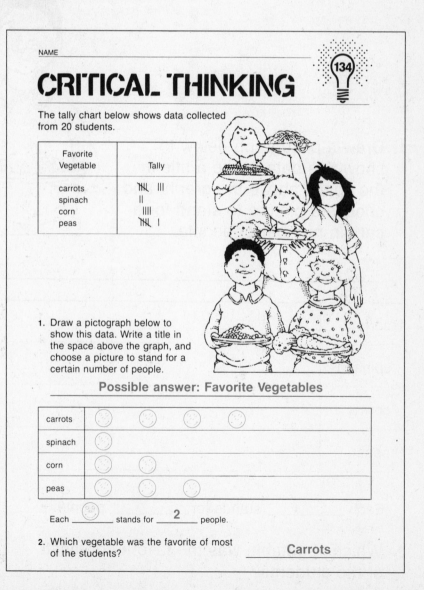

NAME _____

CRITICAL THINKING (134)

The tally chart below shows data collected from 20 students.

Favorite Vegetable	Tally
carrots	𝗜𝗜𝗜𝗜 𝗜𝗜𝗜
spinach	𝗜𝗜
corn	𝗜𝗜𝗜𝗜
peas	𝗜𝗜𝗜𝗜 𝗜

1. Draw a pictograph below to show this data. Write a title in the space above the graph, and choose a picture to stand for a certain number of people.

Possible answer: **Favorite Vegetables**

carrots	◯ ◯ ◯ ◯
spinach	◯
corn	◯ ◯
peas	◯ ◯ ◯

Each _____ stands for ___2___ people.

2. Which vegetable was the favorite of most of the students?

Carrots

VISUAL THINKING

The bar on the left was made by putting two parts together. Ring the letter of the picture on the right that shows the two parts.

1.

a.   **b.**   **c.**

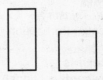

2.

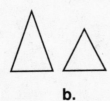

a.   **b.**   **c.**

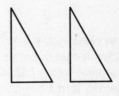

3.

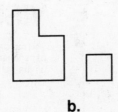

a.   **b.**   **c.**

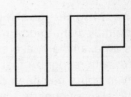

4.

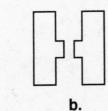

a.   **b.**   **c.**

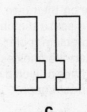

5.

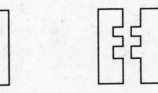

a.   **b.**   **c.**

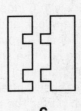

6.

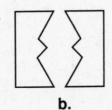

a.   **b.**   **c.**

Teacher Notes

Use with
Objective 135
pages 480–483

Focus
Visual Thinking
  Spatial Perception

Materials
Index cards (optional)
Scissors (optional)
Visual Thinking transparency
  (optional)

Overview
Students study shapes to
determine which pair, when put
together, forms the given
shape.

Teaching Suggestions
You may want to do Problem 1
as an example. Make sure
students recognize that the
given figure has been divided
into two equal parts.

Have students complete the
activity on their own. As a
class, discuss the choices for
each problem, pointing out why
the alternate choices would not
fit together or would not make
the correct shape.

Alternate Approach: Provide
partners with 6 index cards.
Have them look at the pictures
in Problems 1 through 6 and
describe how the shapes are
alike and different. [Each
problem shows a rectangle cut
into two parts. The parts may
or may not be the same size or
shape.]

Have one student cut an
index card in two parts to
match a given figure. Then
have the other put the pieces
together to form the rectangle.
Together they should check the
pieces with the choices and
agree upon an answer. Have
partners change roles and
repeat for the other problems.

Extension
Provide students with index
cards and have them cut the
cards into four or more pieces
to make a jigsaw puzzle.
Students may then trade
puzzle pieces with a classmate
and try to put together the
other's puzzle.

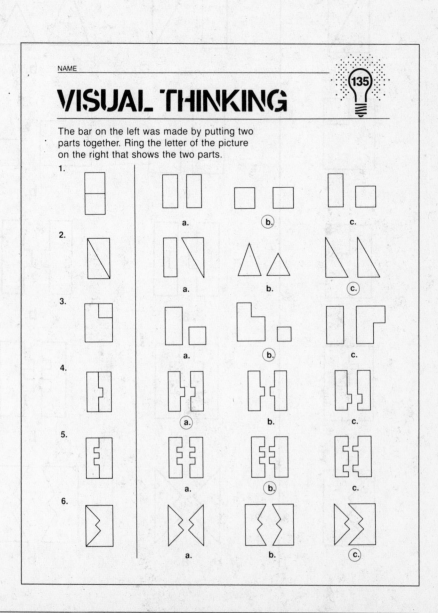

NAME _____

VISUAL THINKING
135

The bar on the left was made by putting two
parts together. Ring the letter of the picture
on the right that shows the two parts.

CRITICAL THINKING

136

Use the table to help you solve the problem.

How Fast Animals Run					
Animal	zebra	deer	lion	elephant	rabbit
Speed (miles per hour)	40	30	50	25	35

Abby wants to share some facts she learned about how fast different animals can run. She would like to make it easy for other students to compare the different speeds.

1. In making a bar graph, should Abby count by 2s, by 5s, or by 10s? Why?

_____

_____

2. Draw bars to show the information from the table on the graph below.

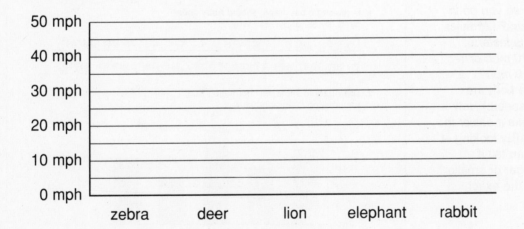

3. Which animal can run the fastest? _____

4. Which animal runs the slowest? _____

Use with
Objective 136
pages 486–487

Focus
Critical Thinking
    Reasoning with Graphs and
    Charts

Overview
Students use data from a table to complete a bar graph and interpret the information to solve problems.

Teaching Suggestions
Ask students how fast they think they travel on a bicycle, in a car, and in an airplane. [Students may estimate bicycling at 10 to 20 miles per hour, cars at 50 to 60 miles per hour, and airplanes at hundreds of miles per hour.] Discuss the meaning of speed, miles per hour, and the abbreviation mph. *Questions: What does it mean if you ride your bike at a speed of 10 mph?* [In one hour, you will travel a distance of 10 miles.] *At a speed of 10 miles per hour, how far would you go in 2 hours? In 3 hours?* [20 miles; 30 miles] *Which is faster: driving a car at 10 mph or riding a bike at 10 mph?* [Neither, because both are going the same speed.] *How does a graph make it easier to compare things?* [By looking at the graph, you can tell if something is bigger or smaller without knowing the exact number values.]

Why would you make a bar graph rather than a pictograph? [Possible answers: It is hard to think of a picture to represent miles per hour; you do not have to worry about parts of pictures; it is easier to make bars; it is easier to compare lengths of bars.] *In Problem 2, some lines are not labeled. What do they represent?* [Speeds half way between the speeds shown: 5, 15, 25, 35, and 45 mph]

Extension
Explain that over short distances, a human can run almost 28 mph and a black mamba snake can slither 10 mph. Have students include this information and make another bar graph which shows the seven animals in order from fastest to slowest. [The order should be lion, zebra, rabbit, deer, human, elephant, snake.]

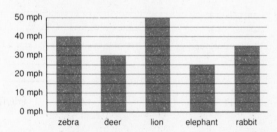

NAME _____

CRITICAL THINKING

Use the table to help you solve the problem.

How Fast Animals Run					
Animal	zebra	deer	lion	elephant	rabbit
Speed (miles per hour)	40	30	50	25	35

Abby wants to share some facts she learned about how fast different animals can run. She would like to make it easy for other students to compare the different speeds.

1. In making a bar graph, should Abby count by 2s, by 5s, or by 10s? Why?

   By 5s. The numbers in the table can all be shown easily that way because they are all divisible by 5.

2. Draw bars to show the information from the table on the graph below.

3. Which animal can run the fastest? _____ Lion

4. Which animal runs the slowest? _____ Elephant

PROBLEM SOLVING

Paul used a grid to make a map of his patio and then gave it to his grandchildren. He said, "My mailbox is at letter A (0, 0), and the orange tree is at letter R (2, 1). I hid a surprise at another point."

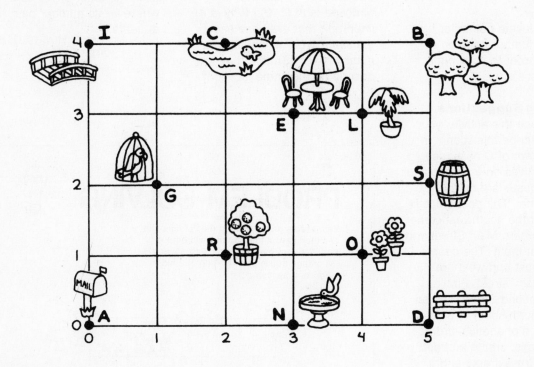

1. Which letter has the number pair (2, 4)? _____

2. What is the number pair for letter B? _____

3. On the map, find the letters for the following number pairs. Write the letters for the number pairs in order. You will spell out the surprise and its location.

___ ___ ___ ___ ___ ___ ___ ___ ___
(1, 2) (4, 1) (4, 3) (5, 0) (2, 4) (4, 1) (0, 4) (3, 0) (5, 2)

___ ___ ___ ___ ___ ___ ___ ___ ___ ___
(0, 4) (3, 0) (5, 4) (0, 4) (2, 1) (5, 0) (2, 4) (0, 0) (1, 2) (3, 3)

Use with
Objective 137
pages 488–489

Focus
Problem Solving
   Make a Graph

Overview
Students locate points for different number pairs on a graph in order to spell out a secret message.

Teaching Suggestions
To introduce this activity, you might describe this scene: In the tiny town of Crossstreets, everyone lives on a corner, and no two houses are on the same corner. The post office is located at the southwest corner of town, where Main Street and Ash Street meet. The streets running east and west are named Main Street, First Street, Second Street, and so on. The north-south streets are named in alphabetical order.

   As a class, create a street map for Crossstreets and locate at least six families. *Questions: What is the most number of families that could live in Crossstreets?* [Multiply the number of north-south streets by the number of east-west streets.] *Suppose the postman goes from the post office to each of the six houses and he always goes first east and then north. How would he reach each family?* [Name the number of blocks along Main Street and then the number of blocks up the alphabetical street.]

Have students read the story for the activity. *Questions: Is the number pair (2, 1) the same as (1, 2)?* [No; (2, 1) means 2 over and 1 up; (1, 2) means 1 over and 2 up.] *What is at each location?* [The orange tree is at (2, 1) and the birdcage is at (1, 2).] *Why is it important that everyone uses the same order when giving a number pair?* [So that they are describing the same location]

Alternate Approach: Review how items are located. Have students select a patio item and identify its letter and number pair. Then have them search through the number pairs listed in Problem 3 and fill in the letter of the item wherever its number pair appears.

NAME _____

PROBLEM SOLVING

Paul used a grid to make a map of his patio and then gave it to his grandchildren. He said, "My mailbox is at letter *A* (0, 0), and the orange tree is at letter *R* (2, 1). I hid a surprise at another point."

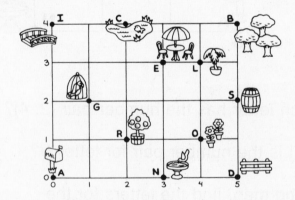

1. Which letter has the number pair (2, 4)? _____ *C*

2. What is the number pair for letter *B*? _____ (5, 4)

3. On the map, find the letters for the following number pairs. Write the letters for the number pairs in order. You will spell out the surprise and its location.

G	O	L	D	C	O	I	N	S
(1, 2)	(4, 1)	(4, 3)	(5, 0)	(2, 4)	(4, 1)	(0, 4)	(3, 0)	(5, 2)

I	N	B	I	R	D	C	A	G	E
(0, 4)	(3, 0)	(5, 4)	(0, 4)	(2, 1)	(5, 0)	(2, 4)	(0, 0)	(1, 2)	(3, 3)

VISUAL THINKING

Each line begins at a letter on the left and ends at a letter on the right. Follow each line with your eyes. Do not jump to a different line. Write *certain, possible,* or *impossible* for each statement.

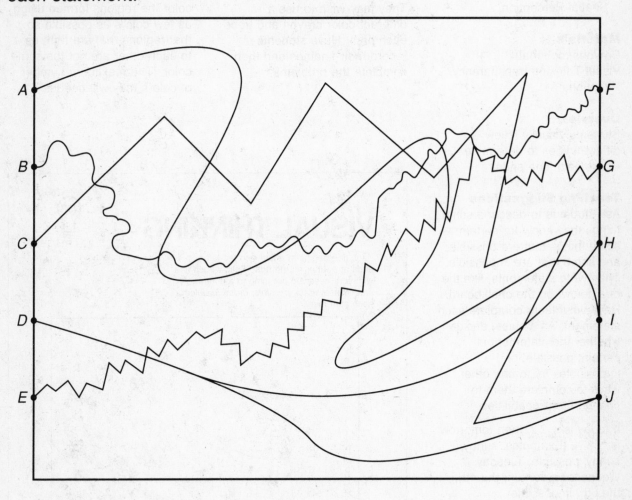

1. The line that begins at *A* ends at *I*. _____

2. The line that begins at *D* ends at *J*. _____

3. The line that begins at *B* ends at *H*. _____

4. The line that begins at *C* ends at *J*. _____

5. The line that begins at *E* ends at *F*. _____

Use with
Objective 138
pages 490–491

Focus
Visual Thinking
  Spatial Perception

Materials
Crayons (optional)
Visual Thinking transparency
  (optional)

Overview
Students visually follow
different lines to determine
where each line ends.

Teaching Suggestions
Ask students to describe some
things they know for certain,
some things that are possible,
and some that are impossible.
Then write statements, like the
one below, on the chalkboard.
Have volunteers complete each
statement. As a class, decide
whether the statement is
certain, possible, or
impossible. Try to find other
ways to complete them to
change the probabilities.

If today is __?__ then tomorrow
is __?__ . [Examples: sunny,
sunny, possible; Tuesday,
Wednesday, certain; the 4th,
the 6th, impossible]

  Have students read the
instructions on the page. Be
sure they understand what is
meant by not jumping to a
different line. When they finish
the problems, discuss their
results and their methods for
deciding.

Alternate Approach: Have
students put a finger on the
line that begins at each point
on the left and follow the line
with their finger until it reaches
a letter or letters on the right.
They may wish to use a
different color crayon and trace
each path. Have students
record their findings and then
complete the problems.

Extension
Have students make three
paths (like the ones on the
activity page) from the left side
to the right side of an unlined
sheet of paper. Ask them to
color the regions formed using
as few colors as possible so
that regions that are right next
to each other are not the same
color. [The maximum number
of colors they will need is 4.]

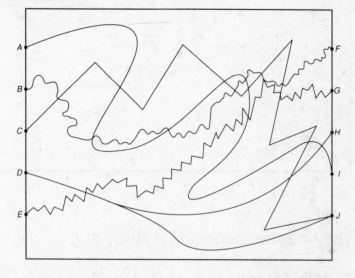

NAME _____

VISUAL THINKING

Each line begins at a letter on the left and
ends at a letter on the right. Follow each line
with your eyes. Do not jump to a different
line. Write *certain*, *possible*, or *impossible* for
each statement.

1. The line that begins at *A* ends at *I*.   ____certain____

2. The line that begins at *D* ends at *J*.   ____possible____

3. The line that begins at *B* ends at *H*.   ___impossible___

4. The line that begins at *C* ends at *J*.   ____certain____

5. The line that begins at *E* ends at *F*.   ___impossible___

NAME _____

PROBLEM SOLVING

Use the list to help you solve the problems.

TOYS	How Many I Have
Planes	4
Robots	7
Fire Engines	5
Pandas	2
Whistles	6

Jeremy makes grab bags for parties.

1. Suppose that Jeremy makes a grab bag for 10 children. The first child is equally likely to get each of the 5 kinds of toys. How many of each toy did Jeremy put in the bag?

   _____

2. Suppose that Jeremy makes a grab bag for 12 children. The first child is equally likely to get a whistle, a fire engine, or a plane. How many of each toy did Jeremy put in the bag?

   _____

3. Suppose that Jeremy makes a grab bag for 12 children. He uses all he has of 3 different kinds of toys. Which 3 toys does he use?

   _____

4. Suppose that Jeremy makes a grab bag that contains only fire engines and whistles. The first child is more likely to get a fire engine. If Jeremy puts all the fire engines he has in the bag, what is the greatest number of toys he can use?

   _____

Use with
Objective 139
pages 492–493

Focus
Problem Solving
Use Logical Reasoning

Materials
Colored chips (optional)
Paper bags (optional)

Overview
Students use information in a list to determine the number of items they must have in order to create certain probabilities.

Teaching Suggestions
Have students discuss what it means for events to be "equally likely." Ask a volunteer to read and describe the situation in his or her own words. *Questions: In Problem 1, what does the second sentence tell you?* [There are the same number of each kind of toy.] *If there are 10 toys and 5 kinds of toys, how many of each kind are there? Why?* [2; because 2 × 5 = 10]

In Problem 2, there must be an equal number of each of the 3 toys in the bag for a total of 12 toys. Therefore, there are 4 of each kind. *Questions: Could Jeremy use robots instead of whistles in Problem 2?* [Yes] *Could he use pandas?* [No; he only has 2 pandas.]

In Problem 3, students should look for 3 toys for which the total number is 12. There is only one such combination.

Ask students to explain their reasoning in Problem 4. Since Jeremy is using 5 fire engines and the first child is more likely to get a fire engine, there must be fewer than 5 whistles. Therefore, the maximum number of toys is 5 fire engines and 4 whistles.

Extension
Partners assign colored chips to certain toys: whistles worth 5¢, pandas worth 10¢, and robots worth 25¢. Partners decide how many of each color chip to put in a bag so that a person who chooses a chip is as likely to get a toy worth more than 20¢ as he or she is to get one worth less than 20¢. Have them keep tallies and decide if the results were as expected.

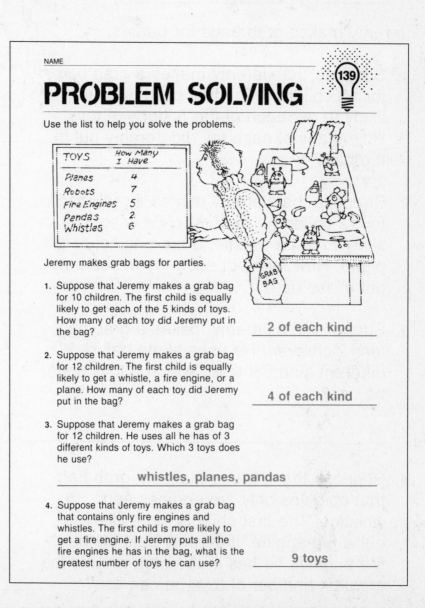

NAME

PROBLEM SOLVING 139

Use the list to help you solve the problems.

TOYS	How Many I Have
Planes	4
Robots	7
Fire Engines	5
Pandas	2
Whistles	8

Jeremy makes grab bags for parties.

1. Suppose that Jeremy makes a grab bag for 10 children. The first child is equally likely to get each of the 5 kinds of toys. How many of each toy did Jeremy put in the bag?

   2 of each kind

2. Suppose that Jeremy makes a grab bag for 12 children. The first child is equally likely to get a whistle, a fire engine, or a plane. How many of each toy did Jeremy put in the bag?

   4 of each kind

3. Suppose that Jeremy makes a grab bag for 12 children. He uses all he has of 3 different kinds of toys. Which 3 toys does he use?

   whistles, planes, pandas

4. Suppose that Jeremy makes a grab bag that contains only fire engines and whistles. The first child is more likely to get a fire engine. If Jeremy puts all the fire engines he has in the bag, what is the greatest number of toys he can use?

   9 toys

CRITICAL THINKING

Use spinners A, B, and C below to answer the questions.

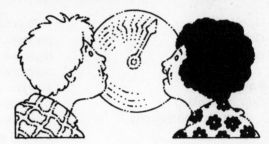

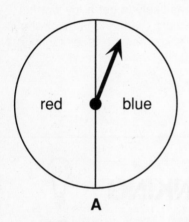

A

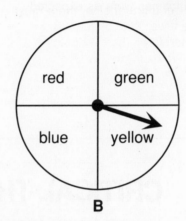

B

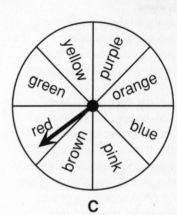

C

1. Doreen and Scott together spin a spinner 100 times. For 25 of the spins, the outcome is red. Which spinner do you think they used? Can you be sure?

_____ _____

2. They spin a spinner 100 times. It lands on purple 15 times. Which spinner do you think they used? Can you be sure?

_____ _____

3. They spin a spinner 100 times. For 10 of the spins, the outcome is blue. Which spinner do you think they used? Can you be sure?

_____ _____

4. They spin a spinner 100 times. It lands on blue 54 times. Which spinner do you think they used? Can you be sure?

_____ _____

5. They spin a spinner 100 times. It lands on green 11 times. Which spinner do you think they used? Can you be sure?

_____ _____

Use with
Objective 140
pages 494–495

Focus
Critical Thinking
  Drawing Conclusions

Overview
Students analyze color and section sizes of circular spinners to decide which given outcomes may have occurred.

Teaching Suggestions
Discuss how each spinner is divided. Have volunteers identify the number of equal parts and the fraction of each spinner that is each color. Then do the problems as a group activity or let the students proceed individually. In either case, have students explain their answers.

Extension
Have students work with a partner. Assign each pair of students a letter, A, B, or C. Have the A students use a spinner marked in two colors, spin it 100 times and record the results. Have the B students use a spinner marked in four different colors and have the C group use a spinner marked in 8 different colors. If spinners are not available, students can make them by drawing circles on a piece of cardboard and using a large paper clip attached at the center as a spinner. Discuss the results.

To continue the activity, have partners design a spinner they think will have more red outcomes than white outcomes and just as many white outcomes as blue outcomes. Have partners test their spinner and see if the outcomes were as expected.

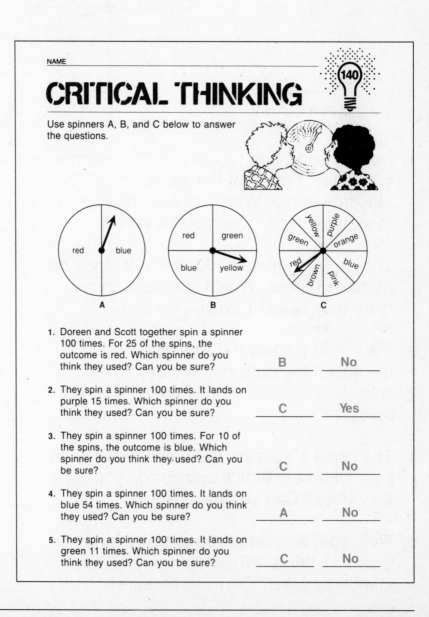

NAME _____

CRITICAL THINKING

Use spinners A, B, and C below to answer the questions.

A | B | C

1. Doreen and Scott together spin a spinner 100 times. For 25 of the spins, the outcome is red. Which spinner do you think they used? Can you be sure? ___B___ ___No___

2. They spin a spinner 100 times. It lands on purple 15 times. Which spinner do you think they used? Can you be sure? ___C___ ___Yes___

3. They spin a spinner 100 times. For 10 of the spins, the outcome is blue. Which spinner do you think they used? Can you be sure? ___C___ ___No___

4. They spin a spinner 100 times. It lands on blue 54 times. Which spinner do you think they used? Can you be sure? ___A___ ___No___

5. They spin a spinner 100 times. It lands on green 11 times. Which spinner do you think they used? Can you be sure? ___C___ ___No___

VISUAL THINKING

141

One picture in each row is divided into parts
that are all equal in size. Ring the letter of
that picture.

1.

a.

b.

c.

d.

2.

a.

b.

c.

d.

3.

a.

b.

c.

d.

4.

a.

b.

c.

d.

5.

a.

b.

c.

d.

6.
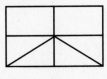
a.
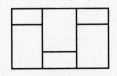
b.
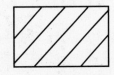
c.
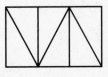
d.

Use after pages 506–507.

Use with
Objective 141
pages 506–507

Focus
Visual Thinking
   Spatial Perception

Materials
Tracing paper (optional)
Visual Thinking transparency
   (optional)

Overview
Students decide which of four
figures in a group are divided
into equal parts.

Teaching Suggestions
You might have students briefly
explain their choices by writing
a sentence or two on the back
of the activity page.

   You might also have
students name as many
shapes as they can in each
figure. For example, Figure **1b**
contains a triangle; **4a** is made
of two rectangles; **6a** is made
of four triangles and two
rectangles, and so on.

*Question: How many different
triangles can you find in Figure
6d?* [Most students will find six
right triangles. Some may even
see the two equilateral
triangles in the center of the
figure, which would make a
total of eight triangles.]

Alternate Approach: Allow
students who are having
difficulties with this activity to
use tracing paper to solve the
first two problems. Have them
trace one portion of each figure
and compare the tracing to
other parts of the figure.
Encourage them to solve the
remaining problems visually.

Extension
Have students decide which
figures show symmetry and
have them explain how the
figure would have to be folded
to show this symmetry. For
example, **1a** and **1c** have a
vertical line of symmetry, **1c**
and **1d** have a horizontal line
of symmetry, and **1b** has a
diagonal line of symmetry.

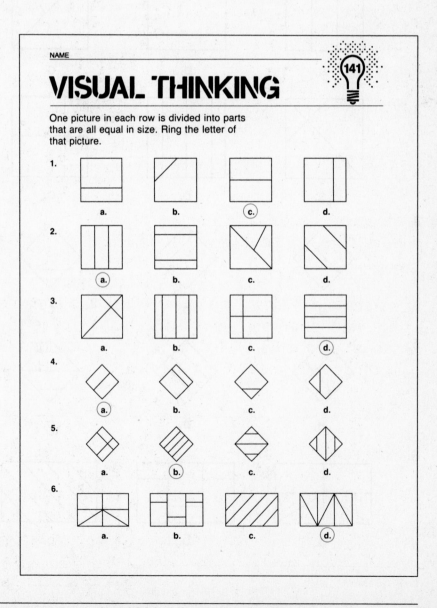

NAME

VISUAL THINKING

One picture in each row is divided into parts
that are all equal in size. Ring the letter of
that picture.

PROBLEM SOLVING

Use the picture to help you solve the problems below.

A group of baseball players lost their jerseys. They found them at the Lost and Found booth.

1. Jared said, "When you multiply the number on my jersey by 5, the product is 85." What number is on Jared's jersey?

_____

2. Hannah said, "The number on my jersey is the quotient of 156 divided by 6." What number is on Hannah's jersey?

_____

3. Ray said, "The number on my jersey is the missing factor that is multiplied by 9 to equal 126." What number is on his jersey?

_____

4. Vicki said, "When you take half the number on Ray's jersey and multiply it by the number on my jersey, the product is 231." What number is on Vicki's jersey?

_____

Teacher Notes

Use with
Objective 142
pages 508–509

Focus
Problem Solving
  Choose an Operation
  Write a Number Sentence
  Try and Check

Overview
Students use their knowledge of multiplication and division to solve simple word problems.

Teaching Suggestions
Make sure students realize that the numbers they will be working with are those shown on the jerseys.

Have students show their work by having them *write the number sentences* they used to solve the problems.

Students can solve Problem 1 by writing a number sentence: $n \times 5 = 85$. Then they can *try and check* all the numbers shown on the shirts.

Before students begin Problem 2, ask the following.
Questions: What is a quotient? [The result, or answer, of a division problem] *What is the 6 in Problem 2?* [The divisor] *What number sentence would you write for this problem?* [Possible answer: $156 \div 6 = n$]

Ask students what number sentence they would write to solve Problem 3 and how they would solve it. [Possible answer: $9 \times n = 126$; Divide 126 by 9]

For Problem 4, students must divide 14, the answer to Problem 3, by 2 and divide the result into 231 to get the number on Vicki's jersey. Number sentences they might write are $14 \div 2 = n$, $n = 7$; $7 \times x = 231$, $x = 33$.

Extension
Have each student pretend the remaining jersey, number 57, is his or hers. Have them then write problems similar to the ones given. Check the problems as a class to make sure each answer is 57.

NAME

PROBLEM SOLVING ·142·

Use the picture to help you solve the problems below.

LOST AND FOUND

A group of baseball players lost their jerseys. They found them at the Lost and Found booth.

1. Jared said, "When you multiply the number on my jersey by 5, the product is 85." What number is on Jared's jersey?

    _____17_____

2. Hannah said, "The number on my jersey is the quotient of 156 divided by 6." What number is on Hannah's jersey?

    _____26_____

3. Ray said, "The number on my jersey is the missing factor that is multiplied by 9 to equal 126." What number is on his jersey?

    _____14_____

4. Vicki said, "When you take half the number on Ray's jersey and multiply it by the number on my jersey, the product is 231." What number is on Vicki's jersey?

    _____33_____

VISUAL THINKING

Look at the shapes on the left in each row.
All of the shapes but one are put together to
make the picture on the right. Ring the letter
of the shape on the left that is not used.

1.   a.   b.   c.   d.

2.   a.   b.   c.   d.   e.

3.   a.   b.   c.   d.   e.

4.   a.   b.   c.   d.   e.

5.   a.   b.   c.   d.   e.

6.   a.   b.   c.   d.   e.   f.

Use with
Objective 143
pages 510–513

Focus
Visual Thinking
  Spatial Perception

Materials
Visual Thinking transparency
  (optional)

Overview
Students study shapes to
determine which, when put
together, form a given shape.

Teaching Suggestions
Make sure students realize that
none of the shapes overlap.

  After students finish this
activity, have them describe
what the finished shapes
resemble.

Alternate Approach: Have
students trace the shapes at
the left, cut them out, and use
as many of them as necessary
to make the figure at the right.

Extension
Have students use squares,
rectangles, triangles, and
circles cut from colored paper
to make the following objects:
a snowperson, a tree, a
person's face, a rabbit, or
some other animal. Display the
''art'' around the classroom.

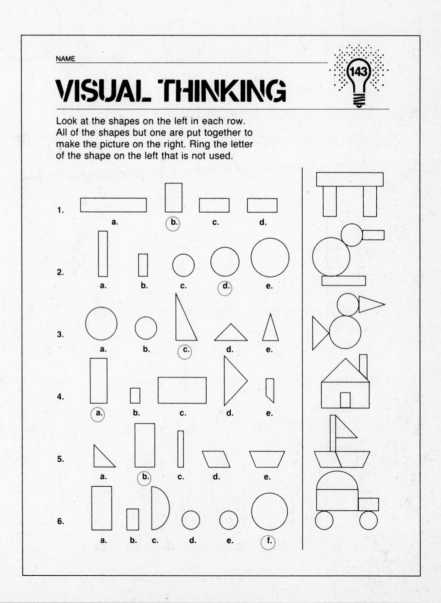

NAME

VISUAL THINKING

Look at the shapes on the left in each row.
All of the shapes but one are put together to
make the picture on the right. Ring the letter
of the shape on the left that is not used.

DECISION MAKING

Dennis has 8 goats to feed. Each should get an equal amount of each type of food. The goats want as much food as possible. To Dennis, it is even more important not to waste food.

A
81 cabbage leaves
52 carrots
16 apples

B
95 cabbage leaves
77 carrots
21 apples

C
75 cabbage leaves
72 carrots
18 apples

1. Complete the table for Basket A.

Kind of food	Number per goat	How many left over
cabbage		
carrots		
apples		
TOTAL		

2. Complete the table for Basket B.

Kind of food	Number per goat	How many left over
cabbage		
carrots		
apples		
TOTAL		

3. Complete the table for Basket C.

Kind of food	Number per goat	How many left over
cabbage		
carrots		
apples		
TOTAL		

4. Which basket should Dennis choose? Explain your answer.

_____

_____

_____

_____

Use with
Objective 144
pages 514–515

Focus
Decision Making

Materials
Calculators (optional)

Overview
Students identify and analyze various options regarding what and how much to feed eight goats.

Teaching Suggestions
To complete the tables for each basket, students must divide the number of each kind of food by eight, the number of goats. They are to then add their results to get the total pieces of food for each goat and the number of left over foods. For example, in Basket A there are 81 cabbage leaves, 52 carrots, and 16 apples. Dividing each of these numbers by eight gives the answers for Problem 1.

For Problem 4, some students may feel that using Basket B is the logical choice because the goats will get the most amount of food, even though there is a lot leftover.

Alternate Approach: Some students may find it helpful to write a number sentence for each kind of food in each basket. You might have some students use a calculator to check their divisions. To do this, tell them to multiply the quotient and divisor and add the remainder. The result should be the dividend.

Extension
Have students make a basket with the leftovers. This basket would contain 11 pieces of cabbage, 9 carrots, and 7 apples. Have students add just enough of each food so that each goat gets the same amount and no food is left over. Thus, the basket should contain five more cabbage leaves, seven more carrots, and one more apple.

NAME _____

DECISION MAKING

Dennis has 8 goats to feed. Each should get an equal amount of each type of food. The goats want as much food as possible. To Dennis, it is even more important not to waste food.

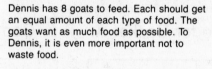

81 cabbage leaves
52 carrots
16 apples
A

95 cabbage leaves
77 carrots
21 apples
B

75 cabbage leaves
72 carrots
18 apples
C

1. Complete the table for Basket A.

Kind of food	Number per goat	How many left over
cabbage	10	1
carrots	6	4
apples	2	0
TOTAL	18	5

2. Complete the table for Basket B.

Kind of food	Number per goat	How many left over
cabbage	11	7
carrots	9	5
apples	2	5
TOTAL	22	17

3. Complete the table for Basket C.

Kind of food	Number per goat	How many left over
cabbage	9	3
carrots	9	0
apples	2	2
TOTAL	20	5

4. Which basket should Dennis choose? Explain your answer.

Possible answer: C;

Goats get more food

than from A, and less is

wasted than from B.

CRITICAL THINKING

Gabe has 19 red tickets. Chris has 16 red tickets, and Amy has 26 red tickets. Gabe says, "We can get more gold tickets if we put all of our red ones together before we trade them in." Amy says, "We still have the same number of red tickets, so we will still get the same number of gold tickets."

Tic-Tac-Toe Tournament Today
The winner of each game gets a red ticket.
Turn in 10 red tickets for 1 gold ticket.

1. If they trade in their red tickets separately, how many gold tickets will each person get?

_____

2. How many gold tickets is that in all? _____

3. If they put all of their red tickets together and trade them in, how many gold tickets will they get? _____

4. Who was right, Gabe or Amy? Explain what happened.

_____

_____

_____

Use with
Objective 145
pages 518–521

Focus
Critical Thinking
    Using Number Sense
    Evaluating Evidence
        and Conclusions

Overview
Students solve problems and
use their results to *draw
conclusions*.

Teaching Suggestions
To solve Problem 1, students
must divide the number of
tickets held by each person by
ten, the number needed for
one gold ticket.

To compute the number of
gold tickets the students will
get if they combine their red
tickets, they must find the total
number of red tickets, 19 +
16 + 26, or 61, and divide this
number by 10. **Question:** *How
many gold tickets can the
students get if they need only
5 red tickets for each gold?*
[Individually, Gabe and Chris
can each get three, and Amy
can get five. As a group, they
can get 12 gold tickets.]

Students must *evaluate the
evidence* from Problems 1–3
and the information given at
the top of the activity page to
draw conclusions in Problem 4.

Alternate Approach: After
students have answered
Problem 1, ask them how
many red tickets are left over.
[9 + 6 + 6 = 21] Then ask
how many gold tickets students
could get for 21 red tickets. [2]
Notice that this is the same
answer as combining all of the
red tickets and dividing this
total by 10.

NAME

CRITICAL THINKING

Gabe has 19 red tickets. Chris has 16 red
tickets, and Amy has 26 red tickets. Gabe
says, "We can get more gold tickets if we
put all of our red ones together before we
trade them in." Amy says, "We still have the
same number of red tickets, so we will still
get the same number of gold tickets."

Tic-Tac-Toe Tournament Today

The winner of each game gets a red ticket.
Turn in 10 red tickets for 1 gold ticket.

1. If they trade in their red tickets separately,
how many gold tickets will each person get?

          Gabe: 1, Chris: 1, Amy: 2

2. How many gold tickets is that in all?   4

3. If they put all of their red tickets together
and trade them in, how many gold tickets
will they get?   6

4. Who was right, Gabe or Amy? Explain
what happened.

Gabe; When they traded their own tickets, each had

red tickets left over. Putting their extra tickets

together, they were able to get 2 more gold ones.

PROBLEM SOLVING

Ring the letter A if you will add to solve each problem. Ring S if you will subtract, M if you will multiply, or D if you will divide. Then solve the problem.

1. A group of 5 friends bought a tape player for $75.00. They shared the cost equally. How much did each one pay?

    A S M D   _____

2. The same 5 friends also bought a pair of headphones. Each gave $3.00. How much did the headphones cost?

    A S M D   _____

3. A set of 10 blank tapes costs $12.00. If 3 of the friends share the cost, how much will each pay for the tapes?

    A S M D   _____

4. Cindy shared in the cost of the tape player, the headphones, and the tapes. How much did she spend?

    A S M D   _____

5. Cindy had $25.00 before the friends went shopping. How much did she have afterwards?

    A S M D   _____

6. The 5 friends want to share the cost of a keyboard equally. The keyboard will cost $95.00. How much will each friend pay?

    A S M D   _____

Use with
Objective 146
pages 522–523

Focus
Problem Solving
Choose an Operation

Overview
Students *choose an operation* to solve a word problem and use the result to answer successive problems.

Teaching Suggestions
For some problems, operations other than those shown can be justified.

You may want to have students *write the number sentences* they used to solve each problem.

You might also discuss alternate ways to solve the problems. For example, ask the following. **Question:** *Rather than multiplying in Problem 2, how else might you solve this problem?* [Adding $3.00 to itself five times will also give the cost of the headphones.]

In Problem 4, to compute Cindy's cost, students must add $15.00, $3.00, and $4.00 to find that she spent $22.00. In Problem 5, subtracting this amount from Cindy's original $25.00 leaves her with $3.00.

To solve Problem 5, students must divide $95.00 by 5 to see that each of the friends will pay $19.00 for the keyboard.

NAME

PROBLEM SOLVING

Ring the letter A if you will add to solve each problem. Ring S if you will subtract, M if you will multiply, or D if you will divide. Then solve the problem.

1. A group of 5 friends bought a tape player for $75.00. They shared the cost equally. How much did each one pay?

   A S M Ⓓ $15

2. The same 5 friends also bought a pair of headphones. Each gave $3.00. How much did the headphones cost?

   A S Ⓜ D $15

3. A set of 10 blank tapes costs $12.00. If 3 of the friends share the cost, how much will each pay for the tapes?

   A S M Ⓓ $4

4. Cindy shared in the cost of the tape player, the headphones, and the tapes. How much did she spend?

   Ⓐ S M D $22

5. Cindy had $25.00 before the friends went shopping. How much did she have afterwards?

   A Ⓢ M D $3

6. The 5 friends want to share the cost of a keyboard equally. The keyboard will cost $95.00. How much will each friend pay?

   A S M Ⓓ $19